# Nostalgia for the Future

D1600262

# Nostalgia for the Future

## West Africa after the Cold War

CHARLES PIOT

The University of Chicago Press
Chicago and London

**Charles Piot** is associate professor of cultural anthropology, and African and African American studies at Duke University. He is the author of *Remotely Global*.

The University of Chicago Press, Chicago 60637
The University of Chicago Press, Ltd., London
© 2010 by The University of Chicago
All rights reserved. Published 2010
Printed in the United States of America
19  18  17  16  15  14  13  12  11  10      1  2  3  4  5

ISBN-13: 978-0-226-66964-9 (cloth)
ISBN-13: 978-0-226-66965-6 (paper)
ISBN-10: 0-226-66964-5 (cloth)
ISBN-10: 0-226-66965-3 (paper)

Library of Congress Cataloging-in-Publication Data
Piot, Charles.
  Nostalgia for the future : West Africa after the Cold War / Charles Piot.
    p. cm.
  Includes bibliographical references and index.
  ISBN-13: 978-0-226-66964-9 (cloth : alk. paper)
  ISBN-13: 978-0-226-66965-6 (pbk. : alk. paper)
  ISBN-10: 0-226-66964-5 (cloth : alk. paper)
  ISBN-10: 0-226-66965-3 (pbk. : alk. paper)  1. Postcolonialism—Africa,
West.  2. Postcolonialism—Togo.  3. Africa, West—History—1960–
4. Togo—History—20th century.  5. Togo—History—21st century.   I. Title.
DT476.5 .P56 2010
966.03'3—dc22
                                                            2009045175

♾ The paper used in this publication meets the minimum requirements of the
American National Standard for Information Sciences—Permanence of Paper
for Printed Library Materials, ANSI Z39.48-1992.

*For Anne*

CONTENTS

ACKNOWLEDGMENTS

Book projects are collaborative in the fullest sense. At Duke, I am fortunate
to have not only smart but also inordinately generous intellectual colleagues
from across the disciplines. My work has benefited enormously from their
critical energy and broad-ranging interest in contemporary theory. Special
thanks to Srinivas Aravamudan, Ian Baucom, Michael Hardt, Ranji Khanna,
Wahneema Lubiano, Achille Mbembe, and Ken Wissoker. My colleagues in
Cultural Anthropology—Anne Allison, Lee Baker, Kathy Ewing, Ralph Litz-
inger, Anne-Maria Makhulu, Louise Meintjes, Mack O'Barr, Irene Silverblatt,
Orin Starn, Rebecca Stein, and former colleagues John Jackson and Deborah
Thomas—have provided the most supportive of academic environments.
Faculty in African and African American Studies—Michaeline Crichlow,
Sandy Darity, Thavolia Glymph, Karla Holloway, Bayo Holsey, Wahneema
Lubiano, Mark Anthony Neal, Rick Powell, Stephen Smith, and Maurice
Wallace—have similarly challenged and invigorated my work.

I am also fortunate to have students in the Cultural Anthropology gradu-
ate program who have prodded and challenged me on issues at the heart of
this project—about futures, hope, sovereignties, religiosities, utopias, politics. Brian Goldstone, Lia Haro, Danny Hoffman, and Louisa Lombard have
been particularly important and special interlocutors. I am also thankful to
Attiya Ahmad, Arianne Dorval, Jatin Dua, Mara Kauffman, Tami Navarro,
Senay Ozden, Juyung Shim, Yektan Turkyilmaz, and Netta van Vliet for the
ways in which I have been enriched by their theoretical-political-ethnographic
engagements with today's troubled world.

I was privileged to have the manuscript selected for a Duke Franklin
Humanities Institute book workshop. Its participants; outside interlocutors
Jean Comaroff and Jim Ferguson; and in-house scholars Srinivas Aravamu-
dan, Ian Baucom, Brian Goldstone, Michael Hardt, Lia Haro, Bayo Holsey,

Ranji Khanna, Ralph Litzinger, Anne-Maria Makhulu, Achille Mbembe, Peter Redfield, Stephen Smith, Wole Soyinka, Orin Starn, and Ken Wissoker gave incisive commentary on a penultimate draft, commentary which led to a substantial round of revisions. Chris Chia organized the workshop with her usual flair and efficiency.

Beyond Duke, I received insightful commentary on individual chapters from Peter Geschiere, Tabea Haeberlein, Charles Heller, Jim Kelly, Fred Klaits, Birgit Meyer, Joel Robbins, and Marc Schloss.

David Brent at the University of Chicago Press was superbly support-ive, and copyeditor Richard Allen made the manuscript's language and argumentation both cleaner and more elegant. Peter Geschiere and a sec-ond anonymous reviewer wrote smart, engaged, and terrifically insightful reviews.

In Togo, my debts run deep. Nicolas Batema, and especially Fidèle Ebia, were constant sources of information and critique—and of warm friend-ship. Kouwènam Basséliki, as always, translated brilliantly and provided incisive commentary on the northern communities. Henri Bamaze, Kokou Kansoukou, Celestin Katchawatou and his son Patrick, and Clover and Kodjo Afokpa prodded me throughout and offered insight into the baroque world of Togolese politics. Farendé's canton chief Karara generously pro-vided support and long hours of conversation. In Ghana, Aseye Ame-Bruce introduced me to Accra's lively church scene and escorted me to multiple sites of charismatic worship.

My daughter Kalina has always been a source of supreme joy. Part insider, for she has made many trips to the north of Togo, she has also been an astute reader of my work. Orin Starn has been a special friend and im-portant critic throughout. My partner Anne Allison not only read multiple drafts but also provided inspired insights into the text. She is a gifted reader and consummate companion. This book is dedicated to her.

May 2005. The Air France flight from Paris to Lomé was eerily empty, the cavernous jumbo jet filled with no more than two dozen people. A subdued and anxious atmosphere replaced the usually boisterous buzz of Togolese returning home. The results of the April election to replace Gnassingbé Eyadéma, the dictator of four decades who had died suddenly in February, had ignited violence when one of his sons was announced victor. Now, two weeks later, after a fierce battle with stone-throwing youth had been suppressed by government troops, a fragile calm reigned. But no one knew, least those who had been away, what prospects the future held.

I sat next to a large man reading the Bible—a Togolese pastor, I imagined, working in Lomé's burgeoning charismatic church scene. Two hours into the flight, he leaned over and, pointing to the book I was reading, *Le Togo de l'esclavage au libéralisme mafieux* (Labarthe 2005), a scathing portrait of the dead dictator's reign, whispered that I should be careful with my reading material. "Three of Eyadéma's sons are on board, and that book doesn't show the regime in a good light. You should conceal it better—and make sure to bury it in your luggage before we land."

Thanking him, I covered the book with a magazine and asked what his business was and why he had been in Paris. He told me he ran an Internet company in Lomé and had fled before the election—"in case things got hot." He added that he was actually able to save money by going to Paris because it enabled him to avoid the heavy campaign expenditures incurred by Togolese business leaders, who were expected to accompany the ruling party's candidate up and down the country.

I said that, when I saw his Bible, I assumed he must be a pastor, and I mentioned that I'd become interested in the thriving charismatic-Pentecostal church scene when I was in Lomé the previous summer. "No I'm not a pastor," he said. "But I may be one day. My whole life has turned around in the past year, thanks to Jesus. Last December, my business was at an all-time low. I was in Paris at the time, and, after a business deal went bad, I tried to commit suicide. Somehow I survived the overdose, and the doctor who saw me at the hospital said I would not have made it without God's intervention. A few days later I ran into a friend who also said my survival was a sign from God. Then my father died and I returned to Lomé for the funeral. I went to church as soon as I arrived and the next day my company was awarded a large contract. The signs from God have continued, and to-day my company is doing very, very well. I now dedicate my entire life to Jesus Christ."

I switched the conversation to politics, asking about the recent election and Togo's prospects after the dictatorship. He lowered his voice, saying that he was skeptical anything would change. "Even if 'le jeune' ['the young one,' as Togolese referred to Eyadéma's then thirty-eight-year-old son, who had just been elected to succeed his father] wants to change—and he well might, for he was educated in France and the United States and knows that the era of dictatorships in Africa is over—the political class that has been in power won't allow it. Many, even those in the ruling party, are ready for a change, but they don't trust the opposition. They think that [opposition leader] Gilchrist [Olympio] is only in politics to avenge the death of his fa-ther [who was killed by Eyadéma in 1963]. It's all so complicated. Togolese are very complicated. I don't know about our country's future anymore. Only God knows whether we have one or not."

As the plane landed, we exchanged business cards and he disappeared into Lomé's thick night air. Uncannily, this midair encounter embodied much that I have come to associate with Togo during the post-Cold War moment: an empty plane, a Bible, a success story deemed miraculous, a life of desperation turned hopeful, the long shadow of the dictator, an anxious citizenry, an uncertain future.[1]

## After the Cold War

The end of the Cold War affected this small nation as much as any other in West Africa. Surrounded throughout the early independence period (c. 1960–90) by three countries with Soviet leanings, and occupying (during the early 1980s) an at-large seat on the United Nations Security Council, Togo was of more than passing strategic interest to France and the United States. Not only were Togolese state coffers, and the pockets of the politi-cal elite, lined with money but also the international community turned a blind eye to General Eyadéma's repressive state apparatus. With the collapse of the Soviet Union and the end of the Cold War, however, much of the money disappeared and Eyadéma's regime came under attack from below as well as above. Street protests in the early 1990s were accompanied by the cutting of United States and European Union aid to Togo, and the foreign embassies supported the political opposition in calling for Eyadéma's departure. While Eyadéma remained in power throughout this time through a mix of cunning, ruthlessness, and election fraud, the Togolese state nevertheless became a shadow of its former self. It was (and remains) a state that, to cite Achille Mbembe (1992a, 2001), has been little more than a "simulacral regime" (see also de Boeck 1996), subsisting on "performance" (Comaroff and Comaroff 2006a, 2006b) and the staging of dramatic events—false coup attempts, hyperbolic celebrations of national holidays—as much as anything substantial. It is also a state that responded to its increasing evacuation with paranoia and surveillance.

Adding privation to privation, France devalued the CFA (Communauté Financière Africaine) franc in 1994 by 50 percent, and the IMF and World Bank imposed ever more stringent austerity and privatizing measures. In response to currency devaluation, the markets and the informal sector, on which most Togolese subsist, experienced a period of volatility and dramatic uncertainty. Market uncertainties were compounded by the influx of new, often cheaper, products—from East Asia, from Nigeria, and from new post-Fordist sites of production around the globe—products that often proved flawed and less durable but sold anyway because of peoples' limited means. The disarray in value registers that characterized this period was manifest in rumors in both urban and rural markets that producers were now using illicit means to manufacture their products, products that were often considered "empty" or useless when consumed. As elsewhere in Africa, this was a time of burgeoning occult economies (Comaroff and Comaroff 1999, 2000), of the proliferation of magical means of capturing value and producing wealth.

Togolese responded to the post-Cold War crisis in diverse ways. While a moment of extreme privation, it was also "productive" in the Foucaultian ([1978] 1990) sense, spawning a new round of extraordinarily inventive bricolage—of cycling and recycling, of dividing the seemingly indivisible, of surviving on nothing—and raised the art of the scam (the invention of false identities, the manufacture of papers and visas) to a new level (cf. Hibou 1999). The current moment has also produced a culture and imaginary of exile—and, indeed, one might say, an entire nation in exile. Witness the northern town of Sokodé. This sprawling settlement of rusted tin roofs—the sleepy seat of bygone colonial power in Togo's hinterland—has in the last ten years undergone a dramatic makeover. Today phone booths dot virtually every street corner and new Western Union stations go up every few months—conduits for information and money from the tens of thousands of Kotokoli who fled the country for Germany (and received political asylum there) after opposing Eyadéma during the early 1990s. It is said of Kotokoli that no Togolese group has as pure a collective fantasy as they, a dream that they will one day all live in Germany.

But fantasies of exile are by no means the provenance of the Kotokoli alone. One could say the same of residents of Lomé, where cybercafés sprout like mushrooms, filled night and day with people connecting to various elsewheres, and where playing the US State Department's green card lottery has become a national pastime. It would not be exaggerating too much to say that everyone in Togo is trying to leave—by playing the lottery, by trying to get into European or American universities, by arranging fictitious marriages with foreigners, by joining churches that might take them abroad, by hoping to be signed by a European soccer team, by joining the fan club that accompanies the national soccer team overseas. A friend whose "wife" (a female friend he married expressly to obtain a visa) was selected in the green card lottery but failed the embassy interview—after he had spent the better part of a year and all his resources preparing her for the interview—emailed me a week later to see whether I could help him get a medical visa to come to the States to get a prosthetic arm to replace an arm that had been deformed since childhood. An acquaintance had received a visa for a hip replacement, and my friend imagined a parallel line of argument might work for him as well—a suggestion I found intriguing not only for the alacrity with which he developed a new exit strategy but also for his willingness to deploy his disability in pursuit of exile. But while many, like this friend, fail in their attempts to leave (while nevertheless spending all their time trying, thus enacting a sort of virtual exile), many others have succeeded. Thus, whereas ten years ago expatriate remittances constituted only 10–20 percent of the Togolese GNP, today they are at least double that, with some estimates as high as 50 percent.

If Togo in the 1990s was characterized by the crisis of the state and its effects on imaginaries of exile, it also saw the emergence of a set of powerful new nonstate actors. Despite the fact that Eyadéma and his entourage—Togo's "neoliberal mafia," as the book I was reading on the plane referred to them—nominally held onto power, he capitulated to international pressures to liberalize Togo's economic and public spheres, opening the floodgates to a host of novel agents and agencies, most importantly NGOs and

Pentecostal churches. NGOs were now given free rein to bypass the state and operate on their own, effectively disengaging the developmental apparatus from the state apparatus. So, too, was the religious sphere liberalized for the first time—during the Cold War years, only Roman Catholics and Presbyterians, churches with deep colonial roots in this area of West Africa, were permitted to evangelize in the country—and a host of new charismatic-Pentecostal churches emerged on the scene. Within only a few years, these churches—Assemblies of God, Church of the Pentecost, Winner's Chapel, Action Faith Ministries, and hundreds more—became wildly popular and are today found in virtually every neighborhood and village throughout the country, preaching strict codes of conduct, promising this-worldly success, and promoting End Times eschatology.

This book explores changes in the cultural-political terrain of Togo since the end of the Cold War—a time in which the money has dried up, the state has pulled back from social and developmental fields, and NGOs and churches have stepped into the void and begun to reorganize the everyday lives and imaginations of those in city and village. It is a time of extreme privation, of wild invention, of dramatic transformation—a moment whose effects are felt to be more far-reaching than any in living memory. It is also a moment whose outcome is still unknown.

## After Colonialism, After Theory, After Politics

Nationalist histories portray the end of colonialism in Africa in the 1960s as a—even *the*—watershed in the continent's history, and indeed independence from colonial rule was undeniably a towering achievement for African nations. It is also true, however, that the continuities between the two periods were considerable and that the disappointments of the independence period, for all but those in power, were due in no small measure to the fact that colonial systems of dominance that had been in place for nearly a century—of an authoritarian state backed by metropolitan financial and military support, ruling its rural villages through a system of chieftaincy—remained virtually unchanged. Indeed, it was not until the end of the Cold War that a real break from the colonial system of governance took place.

The colonial regimes in Africa famously ruled their rural subjects "indirectly"—through local proxies, chiefs, they selected and in some cases created. Chiefs raised taxes and recruited labor in return for wealth and access to the means of coercion, and collaborated with local gerontocracies in instituting "customary" law and investing in "tradition." This system of managing colonial subjects, which Mamdani (1996) has referred to as "decentralized despotism," divided rural populations along ethnic or "tribal" lines and split rural from urban populations. The latter—"citizens" rather than "subjects"—had "rights" and were governed by a regime of "direct" rule and civil law. An entire system of binarisms thus came to structure and inform the colonial project: urban and rural were contrasted as European and African, nonnative and native, citizen and subject, modern and customary/ traditional. This system was most fully developed in South Africa but was present in one form or another throughout the continent (Mamdani 1996:27–32).

Ironically, perhaps, the colonial state structure reemerges as the form of the state after colonialism. Thus, the strong state apparatus of the colonial period was replaced by a dictatorial state with ongoing ties to the metropole—one form of authoritarian Europe-tethered rule by another—and the colonial state's means of managing subjects in the villages through indirect rule was reproduced by the postcolonial state's support of chiefships and its investment in "traditional" culture.

In Togo, following a volatile coup-punctuated 1960s, the dictatorial state settled into two decades of extravagant and sometimes brutal patrimonial rule. Supported and financed by his Western allies, Eyadéma ruled in classic big-man style, enriching himself and his entourage at the expense of an impoverished subject population and a silenced political opposition. He promoted a personalized cult-of-the-dictator nationalism and celebrated Togo's independence from France, even nationalizing French industry, while nevertheless making sure that European money and support never abandoned him.

While taxes on rural populations were abolished at independence, and while compulsory labor was no longer part of the state project, the indirect system of rule through strong chiefs representing state interest at the local level remained the order of the day. Thus, chiefs in the 1970s and 1980s, all approved by Eyadéma, collaborated in the state's modernization project—overseeing development initiatives and getting children to go to school—and recruited youth to perform for visiting dignitaries. In return for supporting the state-nationalist project—and as reward for loyalty to Eyadéma—chiefs received stipends and special privileges.

Taking its cue from Zaire's Mobutu (Schatzberg 1988), Eyadéma's postcolonial state also celebrated "tradition" in the villages. Government proclamations supported local ceremonies, and Eyadéma himself returned to his home village in the north each year to participate in its ceremonies and consult with village chiefs and elders. Of course, one of the principal aims of state support for local tradition was to ensure local support for the state.

It is this system of indirect rule, of decentralized despotism—and the dictatorship complex that nurtured it—that came undone in the 1990s. By the end of that decade, the state was a whisper of its former self and had withdrawn from the development field, the chiefships and the gerontocracies that long ruled the villages were in decline, the vast rural ceremonial apparatus that authorized chiefs and elders was being jettisoned and replaced by charismatic Christianity, and "democracy" and the "rights of man" were on everyone's lips, even in remote villages.

In that much of this cultural and political-economic revolution seems little more than a West African version of the global neoliberal reformation of the 1980s and 1990s that sought to scale back government, liberalize markets, and eliminate the "cultural" barriers to entrepreneurial activity—paving the way, critics insist, for the next round of capitalist accumulation (Harvey 2005, 2007; Ong 2006)—it is easy to be cynical about this moment. While not entirely unfounded, such a reading nevertheless fails to acknowledge that the rejection of the dictatorial state was driven by popular protest as much as by the World Bank and the embassies, and that the turning away from village tradition has also tapped into subaltern sentiment. Moreover, in that both refusals target pillars of the authority structure put in place by the colonial regimes, this rejection of old systems of dominance might also be read as attending to the unfinished business of national liberation and the end of colonialism—finally doing away with colonialism's system of governance and mode of domination and offering hope after the disappointments and tyrannies of the independence period.

---

If this book is about a moment in history, it is also about a mode of theorizing.

My earlier work (Piot 1999, 2001, 2002) on the villages of Eyadéma's homeland was situated within a Cold War context and drew heavily on postcolonial theory. It sought not only to theorize a village culture located within a state-supported chiefship system, one that retained a robust commitment to "tradition," but also to understand the ways in which various pasts shaped and haunted the present. It thus paid attention to the role of the state and the global in the making of the village, and it tracked the promiscuous hybridizations which characterized the Togolese cultural and political landscape of that era. More broadly, again informed by postcolonial theory (Said 1978; Mitchell 1988; Bhabha 1994; Prakash 1990, 1994; Young 1990, 1995; Chatterjee 1993; Gilroy 1993; Stoler 1995; Comaroff and Comaroff 1997; Chakrabarty 2000), this work sought to valorize the margins of Europe's colonial/postcolonial empire, to explore the ways in which capitalism's peripheries had remade its centers, and to disrupt episte-mological divides between modernity and tradition, global and local, core and periphery—divides which have long served as premise for the West's domination of its others. The remote village, I attempted to argue, was a generative site of the modern, as privileged as any other.

I remain committed to this theoretical orientation and to the politics of this earlier project. And yet I find the theoretical tools of that moment in-adequate to the present and feel that today's ethnographic terrain—with its new sovereignties, its emergent forms of power, its diffuse and still incho-ate resistances, its religious imaginaries, its refusal of tradition and hybrid culture[2]—calls for a different set of critical theories. I thus roam beyond anthropology and postcolonial theory—into Hardt and Negri (2001, 2005), Deleuze and Guattari (1983, 1988), Agamben (1998, 2000), and Mbembe (2003, 2005, 2006)—to assemble my toolkit.[3]

I find especially useful the way in which Hardt and Negri (2001, 2005) draw on a genealogy of modes of sovereignty—from transcendent to imma-nent—to think the passage from "modern" to "imperial" forms of power. They suggest that today we are undergoing a transition from the vertical sovereignties and fixities of the modern and colonial—of nation-state imperialism and its modernist imaginaries, institutions, and clear chains of authority—to horizontal, more flexible forms of sovereignty that are also more proximate to the social field. With the nation-state under siege, sovereign power in much of the world is vested in those horizontally linked supranational institutions—the IMF and the World Bank, the human rights and humanitarian organizations, the NGOs and the churches—organiza-tions which exercise "governance without government" (Hardt and Negri 2001:14).[4] These institutions regulate not only economic but also social policy, deciding who to support and who not to support, who will live and who will die. Today is also a moment, Hardt and Negri suggest, when the entire world has been subsumed by capital—in which all outsides have vanished and the commodity form has saturated the social field—and in which political opposition is immanent to the field of power. In a provoca-tive reversal of the usual view, they suggest that it is opposition or resistance that is originary and power reactive—and thus that the former drives change and global history.

While Hardt and Negri certainly did not have a small West African na-tion and its hinterland in their sights when they wrote *Empire*, I nevertheless find it a strikingly apt description of power's recent shifts in this area. With sovereignty no longer wielded by a metropolitan colonial country (or by a postcolonial dictator who did little more than reissue the colonial project in a new guise) and with today's shell of a state presiding over chiefships that no longer carry weight, it is the NGOs and the churches that have taken over the social and biopolitical fields. In demonizing tradition and urging a break with the past, the churches and NGOs not only recalibrate the relationship between citizen and sovereign, and between sovereignty and the biopolitical, but also refigure temporality—away from a past tied to, while also haunting, the present, to a preoccupation with the future. Space is similarly reconstituted—again by both Pentecostals and NGOs, though each in their distinct ways—with the distant metropolitan or global seemingly close and immanent, even at times appearing locally authored. Consonant with the shift from sovereign and chief to NGO and prosperity preacher is a turning away from relational dependency and the gift to a preoccupation with autonomy and the money/commodity form.

Consistent with these transformations in the shape of power and the biopolitical is a shift in the nature of those critical discourses that circulate today. There is a shadowy, elusive, nontransparent nature to today's commentaries that is different from those of the 1970s and 1980s that—often targeted at the state and at a "politics of the belly," to use Bayart's (1989) phrase—were able to name a clear source of opposition. Today's foes in this post-politics-of-the-belly (post-dictatorship) moment are less identifiable, more inchoate, and more diffuse.

It is these shifts—from verticality to horizontality, from pasts to futures, from transcendence to immanence, from meaning to affect, from a world with borders and outsides to one in which all outsides have been forever banished, from the gift to the commodity form—that Hardt and Negri, drawing on Spinoza and Deleuze, elicit and help to theorize.

At the same time, their theory stops short of enabling us to come to terms with the content and specificity of the cultural imaginaries that accompany these shifts, of the ways in which Togolese, and West Africans more generally, have responded to these shifts in global governance and political economy. I mean here not only the specificity of ways of doing politics—of grasping worlds in which power plays with the invisible, of the need for sovereignty to legitimate itself by demonstrating its capacity to act (rather than indexing a "contract" with its citizenry), of the force of rumor in constituting the political—but also of the ways in which Togolese have chosen to respond to the crisis of the 1990s—through Pentecostal and occult imaginaries, through a sacrificial logic that enables them to jettison the past and embrace the future, through acts of mimetic engagement with that which they desire. This social and political world may reside within Empire, but it does so at an angle and with a difference.

Moreover, taking seriously the view from this ragged edge of Empire may cause us to challenge aspects of the theory itself. For one, Hardt and Negri's periodization of the transition from modern to imperial rule—as coinciding with the end of colonialism—does not accommodate the case of Africa, where it is not until the 1990s that nation-state imperialism is replaced by postnational governmentality. For another, and more importantly, the *Empire* project is largely silent on religion, and yet the experience of Africa— where charismatic Christianity and occult imaginaries have transformed the cultural landscape in the last ten years—would seem to demand that we take seriously its influence on political culture. Thirdly, if supranational governmentality is the wave of the future, Africa, as one of its contemporary laboratories, perhaps its preeminent laboratory, may not only have something to teach about the next stage of global Empire but also provide a rich source of theorizing about global political futures (cf. Comaroff and Comaroff 2006a; Ferguson 2006; Mbembe 2006; Hoffman 2007a, 2007b, nd). Lastly, we need to ask what it would mean to take seriously notions of politics and political agency that do not emanate from European theory. Might they and the cultural horizons that produce them—those networked "singularities" that constitute the "multitude," to put it in Hardt and Negri's (2001, 2005) terms—potentially influence and transform that theory?

If theorists of the global need to be reminded of the anthropological truism that "*there* things are different," the new moment also poses challenges to longstanding anthropological sensibilities. It suggests that we see African "tradition" or "culture" as atavistic and Pentecostalism as progressive (and even locally authored), that we measure "agency" through engagement with rather than rejection of Euro-otherness, that we look for politics in unlikely places, surrendering familiar notions of the political, and that we commit to a position in which sacrificing the past and all that is known is the only way to the future.

## After Sovereignty

Africa has long been a productive site for the exploration of issues of sovereignty, and this well before those recent events—the neoliberal assault on the state and state modes of regulation in the 1990s, fortress Europe and its new immigrants, 9/11 and its aftermath, the global refugee crisis—that have occasioned much of the recent scholarship on sovereignty (Agamben 1998, 2000; Balibar 2003, 2009; Butler 2006; Hardt and Negri 2001, 2005; Rasch 2005). Indeed, questions of sovereignty and political overrule have been at the center of African studies since it was instituted as an area studies field in the 1950s.

From anthropology's early (1940s and 1950s) interest in the sources of political authority and solidarity in "stateless" societies (Fortes and Evans-Pritchard 1940; Middleton and Tait 1958), to that discipline's later focus on the relationship between the colonial state and those village societies studied by anthropologists (Asad 1973), to history's embrace of nationalist historiographies in the 1960s, to political science's more recent preoccupation with "failed" or "weak" states, issues of political sovereignty have informed, and often driven, scholarly interest in Africa. Moreover, the iconic nature of the colonial state in Africa, of Lugard's system of "indirect rule"—what Hannah Arendt (1951) referred to in her monumental study of totalitarianism as a naked version of modern sovereign power, the raw truth and racist underside of the modern state (Hansen and Stepputat 2005)—as well as the excesses and tyrannies of the dictatorial postcolonial state, have provided fertile ground for thinking the limits of sovereignty and have generated extraordinarily provocative work by Bayart (1989), Mbembe (1992a, 2001, 2003), and Mamdani (1996), among others, work that has been influential well beyond African studies.

Due to the constraints, fiscal as well as political, under which its states have had to operate during the postcolonial period, Africa has been the site of a range of creative adaptations and experiments in state sovereignty, causing scholars to generate a dizzying array of terms to describe its mutations: it has "shadow" and "minimalist" states, "quasi-" states, "para-" states, "rhizome" states, "patrimonial" and "criminal" states, states that are "invisible," states that are "privatized." Moreover, with state sovereignty in retreat—due to the reconfigurations and displacements that have taken place since the end of the Cold War and the onset of neoliberal reform—there is an emergent literature on non- or extra-state sovereignties, which has also produced its own (un-stately) lexicon. Thus, there are sovereignties deemed "partial," "fragmented," "multiple," "informal," "selective," "parastatal."

A branch of this recent literature that has particular relevance for my own work is one that focuses on zones now beyond state control, either those no longer regulated but poached or preyed on by states (Roitman 1998, 2005), or those that have been abandoned altogether. These latter—"gray zones," as Mbembe (2006:305) and Vergès (2007) refer to them—are often vast areas (in Congo, in Chad and the Central African Republic, in Somalia and the southern Sudan, in the countries of the West African Sahel) that have been left alone by the state and the international (cf. Ferguson 2006:27–28). They have become sites of abjection and disposability, areas of desperate poverty filled with people for whom the state and the international no longer care (Mbembe 2003:34). Without rights and protections, without infrastructure and healthcare, its inhabitants—like refugees and migrants in the new global order (Agamben 1998, 2000; De Genova 2009), like African AIDS patients (Comaroff 2007)—have been reduced to a type of "bare life" (Agamben 1998, 2000). Moreover, living in locales that can only be described as "necropolitical" (Mbembe 2003), its denizens are subject to violence two times over—the violence of neglect and abandonment, and that inflicted by those warlords and mercenary armies who prey upon such zones.[5]

Togo and its hinterland might be said to be a place that is "graying." Left alone by the state—thus, ironically, returning to its precolonial "statelessness"—this zone of unstable sovereignties has de facto become the charge of the churches and NGOs. It is they who have assumed the mantle of sovereign, deciding who to support and who not to support, and thus where to draw the line between life and death (Redfield 2005, 2009; Fassin 2007). However, unlike those earlier sovereigns who ruled the area, their intervention is erratic and anarchic. It comes and goes, hops in and out (Ferguson 2006:14, 38), at other times slithering snakelike (Deleuze 1995), targeting some and not others, omitting one village while including another. Its agendas are driven from far away and, despite widespread poverty and decaying local infrastructure, largely focus on things immaterial (education, human rights, elections). This, too, is an area being abandoned to bare life.[6]

But Togo's hinterland is far from unique. It shares the plight of much of the continent, where state withdrawal has left social and developmental fields to the NGOs and the churches. It is they—Médecins Sans Frontières, the Centers for Disease Control, World Vision, CARE, Amnesty International and Human Rights Watch, Assemblies of God and a thousand "prosperity" churches—who are remaking the face of African humanity, and deciding who to save and who to let die.

## Wagering on Rupture

Asserting that a crisis or rupture has occurred in global governance and political economy is necessarily fraught (Roitman 2009). Critical theory has recently wrestled with the question of momentous breaks—between mod-

ern and postmodern (Jameson 1985, 1991; Harvey 1989), between Ford-
ist and post-Fordist (Harvey 1989), between industrial and informational
(Castells 1996, 1997, 1998), between disciplinary society and societies of
control (Deleuze 1995; Hardt and Negri 2001), between nation-state imperialism and Empire (Hardt and Negri 2001, 2005), between Cold War
and neoliberal regimes of governmentality (Comaroff and Comaroff 2000,
2006a; Denning 2004; Harvey 2005, 2007; Ong 2006; Weiss 2004a, 2004b).
Nonetheless, there is no bedrock consensus that things today are qualitatively different than before—and this despite broad agreement that the end
of colonialism in the 1950s and 1960s, the advent of post-Fordist regimes
of production in the 1970s, the rise of informationalism in the 1980s, the
end of the Cold War and the collapse of the Soviet Union in 1989, and the
spread of neoliberal economic and political policy in the 1990s have produced significant new political-economic contours and have intensified and
accelerated processes of change.

Indeed, critics remind us that the world in the 1920s, among other periods, was as globalized as that of today (Trouillot 2003; Cooper 2001),
that, post-9/11, the nation-state appears to be as strong as ever (Hirst and
Thompson 1999; Thompson 2000), that continuities across each of these
divides may outweigh discontinuities (Trouillot 2003; Cooper 2001; Guyer
2007). Moreover, they warn that by jumping on the "today is new and different" bandwagon, scholars risk being taken in by the ideology of the moment, an ideology that serves the interests of global capital (Cooper 2001).

I find these reminders useful and agree with much of this critique—
namely, that there are broad continuities across epochal periods, that the
nation-state retains enormous political and economic importance, that
there were earlier moments of globalization and, indeed, that global history
since the 1600s has been nothing if not a series of crossings and re-crossings
of regions and cultures of the world. And, yet, I also remain committed
to the idea that a threshold has been crossed and that the contemporary
world is undergoing significant shifts in modes of sovereignty and forms of
political-economic organization, shifts that dramatically transformed Africa
in the 1990s.

In the absence of overwhelming evidence one way or the other that
things are indeed different—and I am not sure how one would settle such
an issue on empirical grounds, by, say, lining up statistics or testimony one
way or the other—the proof must lie in the heuristic value of the theory in
helping to account for the phenomenon at hand (in this case, the nature of
power and the biopolitical in today's world) and in whether or not it opens
up productive avenues of research and poses interesting questions. Each of

the aforementioned theorists of global change has hitched her or his theoretical wagon—and politics—to a sense that the contemporary moment is
new and qualitatively different, and with profit.[7] Moreover, the position that
there are large global changes underway is a familiar one in anthropological
writing. The anthropologies of Arjun Appadurai (1990, 1991, 1997), Jean
and John Comaroff (2000), and Aiwa Ong (1999, 2006), among others, all
presume dramatic contemporary change.

A commitment to rupture need not preclude appreciation of those continuities that persist during transitional times. Thus, authoritarian strains and
cultural hybridities remain etched into Togolese political and popular cultures. Indeed the ensuing chapters on political culture, on charismatic Christianity, on occult imaginaries in the villages are testimony to the complex
cultural mixing that endures amidst transformation. Despite the continued
presence of such hybridities—of the cultural mixing that is emblematic of
the postcolonial moment and celebrated by postcolonial theory—this is
nevertheless a world that has turned a new page.

In wagering on rupture, I also take my cue from those I know in Togo
who identify the 1990s with dramatic change in their lives, change that
has entered their everyday lexicon. The "changes" (lurusoro; lit., putting one
thing in the place of, exchanging it for, another), or simply "démocratie,"
designate a watershed greater than any in recent memory. Inaugurated by
violence (on the streets of Lomé, in the towns and farming communities
of the south), the 1990s brought the dictatorship to its knees and liberalized the public sphere. Its "democracy" and "rights of man" discourses led
an attack on longstanding authority figures, destabilizing communities and
families. A time of economic privation, it saw prices in the markets esca-
late, women take up farming for the first time ever, and—a small act that
nevertheless condenses an entire era—rural households pay for water from
government pumps. Finally, as if gathering together all the anxiety and frustration of the decade, this was a time when witchcraft imaginaries exploded
to consume the public sphere.

Taken together, these add up to a seismic shift in the lives of Togolese.
For better or worse, their world will never be the same.

## Periodizing Theory

By privileging the end of the Cold War as periodizing rubric, I do not ignore
the importance of influences that exceed that rubric—among them, the proliferation of new information technologies, transformations in global labor

and financial regimes, the spread of human rights and humanitarian ideologies. However, those factors more directly associated with the new geopolitics of the 1990s remain crucial to my narrative about West Africa. It
was the metropolitan abandonment of the dictatorships with the end of the
Cold War that led to the withdrawal of those monies that had supported
them, forcing the state to withdraw from social and development fields and
to turn its back on large-scale, top-down development projects (and the
linear teleologies that accompanied them). Moreover, as alluded to above,
the state's subsequent abandonment of chiefs and village tradition has effectively ended a century of indirect rule in the rural areas and reconfigured
relations with the past. A fragmented/pluralized/privatized sovereignty—
and a sovereign no longer able to rule by fiat and censorship—has been
accompanied by the liberalization of political, media, and religious spheres.
Symptomatic of these changes, and reversing the footsteps of those in the
1970s and 1980s who went to Europe and the US for schooling before returning home to seek employment, those who leave today rarely return and
those who remain behind dream of escape.

To be sure, there are specificities to the Togolese case, for it was Togo's
failure to hold "transparent" elections in the 1990s, unlike neighboring
Ghana and Benin, that produced a massive withdrawal of metropolitan
monies and exacerbated its economic and political crisis. Moreover, while
the end of the Cold War in Sierra Leone, Liberia, and Cote d'Ivoire led to
the proliferation of small arms among mercenaries (often recruited from
underemployed or underpaid military forces—whose weapons came from
the arsenals of countries once under Soviet influence), such has not been
the case in Togo, though civil war in those countries did have ripple effects
in Lomé (see chapter 1). Despite such differences, Togo still exhibits, and
indeed crystallizes, many of the changes that have accompanied the recent
shifts in sovereignty and their cultural entailments across the region—the
retreat of the state and the unraveling of the dictatorship complex, the turn
to Pentecostalism and the jettisoning of tradition, the proliferation of cultures of deception and the quest for exile.

As noted earlier, the shifts that are underway in West Africa also suggest
that we rethink our commitment to the term "postcolonial" and its attendant
theorizing. A label fraught from its inception with ambiguity and multiple
referents—indexing most straightforwardly the era that followed independence from colonial rule—it also refers to a mode of theorizing attentive to
the cultural politics of that period (albeit implying for some a moment that
was "anti-colonial" and for others "neocolonial"), while also leading some

historians to a rethinking of the colonial itself (Prakash 1990, 1994; Young 1990, 2001; Appiah 1991; Williams and Chrisman 1994; Ranger 1996). The postcolonial in African studies similarly references an era and a mode of theorizing—that moment of dictatorial politics, of (re)invented tradition, of cultural mixing, and of vernacular/alternative modernities and subjectivities (Appiah 1992; Werbner 1996; Mbembe 2001). Its theorists thus engage in a distinctive—and, for that time period, highly productive—type of theorizing that emphasizes African agency and inventiveness in reworking Eurocentric culture and in deflecting colonial design.

Again, I remain compelled by this project but feel that the end of the Cold War has changed the sociopolitical landscape in ways that demand new theoretical tools. Today, a diffuse and fragmented sovereignty is replacing authoritarian political culture; tradition is set aside and cultural mixing looked down upon; Africanity is rejected and Euro-modernity embraced; futures are replacing the past as cultural reservoir. Postcolonial theory's focus on hybrid culture, on the ways in which pasts haunt the present, on the cultural impulse to appropriate and indigenize that which is outside, stops short in analyzing this new—post-postcolonial—terrain.[8]

It is this emergent culture and its attendant politics that I set out to theorize in this text. I aim for something like a "cartography of the present" (Rose 2007:4–5), a mapping of an emergent form of life (Fischer 2004; Maurer 2005), a description that tracks the unmaking and remaking of an entire social world and takes seriously the wager of a people willing to trade a past for a future still unknown.

## Sites of Study, Situating the Story

My archive in tracking the moment in Togo after the Cold War consists of chapters on the state, the charismatic churches, the visa lottery, village witchcraft imaginaries, and the NGOs. The text tacks back and forth from city to countryside, not only mimicking my own movements as researcher but also attempting to span sites that are themselves intimately connected, in which a string pulled here produces an unraveling there—in which a panic in the village affects life in the city, just as a death in the city will occasion a return to the village.

In bundling the domains of state, church, development, occult, and lottery into a single text—domains that are often studied separately—I aim to explore the ways in which they constitute a common sociopolitical field. I thus connect the dispersal of state power to a burgeoning Pentecostalism, to development's new initiatives, to cultures of exile, to the explosion in occult imaginaries—and theorize their co-emergence in relation to the long history of colonialism and postcolonialism in the area. In what ways do Pentecostal and occult imaginaries produce one another, and how are they related to the withdrawal of Cold War monies and the evacuation of the state? Is there something about the contemporary moment that mandates affective development *and* charismatic preoccupations with the body? How is it that state and lottery come to resemble one another? Why is "performance" central to so many of these domains? [9]

While sited in a sliver of a country, I nevertheless see this study also having broader salience, describing a set of transformations common to much of West Africa today. It goes without saying that this larger region is enormously diverse—encompassing Anglophone and Francophone countries, containing states with vastly different colonial and postcolonial cultures, possessing ethnic and religious constituencies that vary significantly from one country to the next. Moreover, the democracy moment has produced countervailing—localizing—tendencies in some places (Geschiere and Nyamjoh 2000; Ndjio nd). Still, there are fundamental features of the period after the end of the Cold War that are shared across the entire region— the pullback of the state and the advent of neoliberal reform, the transfer of the biopolitical to the NGOs and the human rights organizations, the rapid spread of charismatic Christianity, the retreat of tradition in the villages, the rise of cultures of deception and identity fabrication, the desire for exile. It is these commonalities—ones at the heart of my analysis of Togolese political culture—that I have in mind in suggesting that ethnography conducted in a single place might also stand for the larger whole. A simple index of my point: the sketch of the contemporary Togolese political-economic and cultural landscape with which I began this chapter could have been written about any country in West Africa—or across the continent for that matter (see the essays in Weiss 2004a)—with only minor changes, and each of the book's chapters, despite local inflection, also describes conditions in Nigeria, Ghana, Benin, Cameroon. [10]

In thus recalibrating the standard anthropological unit of analysis, I also jump scales throughout the text—from village, to village cluster, to capital, to Togo as a whole, to neighboring Ghana, to the Ghana-Togo-Benin-Nigeria coastal corridor. In so doing, I aim to resist ethnography's incarceration by the local. The localizing effect of much anthropological work and writing (Ferguson 2006:3–4), and mine has been no exception, is anthropology at its best but also at its most limiting. In carefully cataloguing cultural nuance and detailing local history, anthropologists offer rich portraits of social life's complexity in out-of-the-way places. But in so doing we often render ourselves illegible to the world beyond—not only to those journalists and policy makers who ought to find something of value in our work but also to colleagues in kindred disciplines (cf. Mamdani 2002, 2009). It is for this reason too that I draw on theories of the global, seeing the local as both saturated by and laboratory for the global. Here I follow in the footsteps of recent work in African studies (Bayart 2000; Comaroff and Comaroff 2000, 2004, 2006a; Ferguson 2001, 2002, 2006; Weiss 2004a; Buggenhagen, Jackson, Makhulu 2010) that attempts to rescale the ethnographic and speak to Africa's "place-in-the-world" (Ferguson 2006:6).

Much of my text is filled with stories, stories people tell about their everyday lives, about power, about the occult, about the visa lottery, and stories I recite about those stories. Thus, the chapter on the state is replete with storytelling about Eyadéma and his "barons"—anecdotes told on the streets and in the villages. The chapter on charismatic Christianity centers on Pentecostal narratives about the village, about sin, about End Times—narrativizing that lies at the heart of charismatic Christianity's contemporary appeal. The chapter on the visa lottery is told through the eyes of a lottery entrepreneur and brilliant raconteur—who typically narrates his clients' interviews at the US Embassy in story-and-punch-line form. "Guess what trick question the consul asked today!" he'll ask rhetorically as you enter his Lomé "bureau." The chapter on witchcraft imaginaries, too, is replete with rumoring—about occult encounters, about the provenance of baboons plaguing village fields, about the ongoing drama between charismatics and village religion— suggesting that it is these narratives that grab the imagination and account for occult inflation as much as anything else.

But why the story form, and why the proliferation of stories today? Oddly, perhaps, given modernity's conceits, stories appear to be particularly conducive to current times—to a time in which power seems more diffuse and less transparent than ever (evidenced in those conspiracy theories that fill the global imagination today), a time of runaway financial speculation (with its storied boom-busts, its Ponzie frauds, its futures trading, its pervasive lotteries and casinos), a time of necropolitics (in which death has become ubiquitous—through war that knows no end, through the AIDs pandemic, through pervasive structural violence). Benjamin ([1936] 1969a), in an essay lamenting the disappearance of storytelling in his time, suggested that death begets storytelling—that death's mysteries and silences necessitate narration and elicit the storyteller (and that modernity's sequestering and avoidance of death was in part responsible for the death of the story). Today death has returned, and with it the story. The hidden nature and indeterminacy of power and the spectral nature of contemporary wealth production

(Comaroff and Comaroff 2000) would also seem to demand rumoring and narration.

The crisis of the West African post-Cold War moment only amplifies the effect. This is a time when rumoring is the only form of politics available, when extravagant money-making alongside abject poverty suggests fraud or occult practice, when the gap between a known but rejected past and an unknown though desired future appears unbridgeable, when death sees no end. "Death is our currency now," a friend in Lomé said in summer 2008 after attending her sixth funeral in three weeks, half for people still in their twenties. "It happens all the time, striking young and old, and often those you least expect. A friend of mine says it is because Africa has been cursed with the plague of witchcraft. Perhaps, but I told him this was also what the Bible predicted would happen at the End of Time." Benjamin's point exactly: death demands explication—and here elicits competing stories—attempting to render meaningful the inchoate, snatching life from death, offering laughter alongside melancholy. But far from stabilizing meaning and bringing closure, storytelling produces its own excess—more stories, more versions of the same story, more ambiguity in any story's "true" meaning.

Moreover, as the following chapters evince, this is a landscape wired for "dramaturgy" (Comaroff and Comaroff 2006a, 2006b) and "affect" (Deleuze and Guattari 1983, 1988). From a withered state that has to "perform" itself to convince its subjects that it remains powerful, to the charismatic churches' preoccupation with embodied states of possession, to the Latin American soaps that light up living rooms across Lomé, to villages that attempt to attract NGOs through performatively staging their need—drama, affect, and storytelling fill the everyday lives of Togolese.[11]

Finally, the story form would appear to be ideally suited to ethnography as knowledge practice. Stories have a situated, experience-near quality, in principle retaining something of the context in which they arose. They also evoke the relationality of ethnographic practice, the fact that ethnography is conducted with others and forever consists of exchange. For Benjamin, the relational was constitutive of storytelling: "A man listening to a story is in the company of the story-teller" ([1936] 1969a:100), engaging in the exchange of experience (84). Moreover, the best stories have an open-ended, indirect, even mystical quality to them—which opposes them to "news" or "information," to that which is verifiable, transparent, understandable in itself, if also fleeting. "It is half the art of story-telling to keep a story free from explanation" (89), to ensure that "the connection of events is not forced on the reader" (89), to make sure that the story does not "expend itself" (90). Such has also long been said to be the hallmark of all the great classical ethnography.

---

My text attends to the inventions of everyday Togolese under crisis, exploring what the crisis is producing rather than strictly what it has taken away or what is lost (Weiss 2004b). Put otherwise, I aim to examine the ways in which the current moment's two faces—privation, invention—inform and feed off one another. In drawing attention to peoples' inventiveness, I intend not to belittle the all-too-real privations of the contemporary moment or to romanticize what it means to live under crisis but rather to acknowledge those worlds that Togolese inhabit in the only way they know how, imagining, against all odds and despite enormous privation, that today might be their day, but if it isn't, surely tomorrow will be.

If ever there was an imagined iconic site of tradition, the African village would surely be near the top of the list. Flush with ceremonies, nurtured by ancestral custom, gifting and bartering their surpluses, living close to nature, the village would seem to demand a sense of continuous time and an inalienable connection to the past. It is thus arresting to see those who have embraced such traditions—from both city and village—jettison their past and commit themselves to a future without a telos and be willing to evacuate a space they call home. Moreover, I struggle to reconcile such desires for displacement—of the past and of home, the one temporal, the other spatial—with the hustle and laughter that fill the streets and the everyday, with the fact that those I know seem fully in their skin and infused with hope and dynamism, with the cultural innovation that speaks back to privation, with the pride of place Togolese share despite the political disappointments of recent decades. Such are the paradoxes of everyday life in contemporary West Africa.

My title, *Nostalgia for the Future,* indexes Togolese longing for a future that replaces untoward pasts, both political and cultural. Such longing is represented not only in Christian End Times narratives and the universal quest for exit visas but also in the embrace of a thousand development initiatives that hail youth and leave elders behind. It also evokes the disjunctive temporalities of a moment when not only futures are exchanged for pasts but also diverse sovereignties—some horizontal and episodic, others top-down and temporally linear—jockey for supremacy. But such desires for a different future and a new political, as with all nostalgic longing, are already elusive before they can be attained.

# ONE

# States of Emergency

This chapter explores transformations in the Togolese state apparatus from early independence to the present. The Cold War years were marked by dictatorial rule, a mode of governance fully supported by Western metropolitan countries preoccupied with anti-Soviet geopolitics. With the end of the Cold War and the abandonment of Africa by the world's superpowers, local democracy movements were joined by Western embassies in seeking an end to the dictatorship and the inauguration of neoliberal reforms. To the surprise of most, the dictator survived and his family remains in power to the present day, although the state today bears little resemblance to its Cold War predecessor.

In addition to exploring shifts in state logic, this chapter aims to unsettle several reigning interpretations of Togolese politics, interpretations shared by many Togolese as well as those in the international community. One is that the ethnic divide between north and south remains key to understanding the larger political landscape—and is responsible for the nation's ongoing political impasse. Another is that Togolese politics has been held hostage since the early years of independence by a rivalry between two families—that of Sylvanus Olympio, the country's first president, and that of Gnassingbé Eyadéma, the soldier who assassinated Olympio and replaced him in power (where he remained until 2005). A third, more obsession than explanation, is the focus on the figure of Eyadéma—as if understanding him explains Togolese politics *tout court*, and getting rid of him was the answer to breaking the ongoing impasse. While all three contain elements of truth, each also obscures more complex political realities and power's other sources, in the process helping to reproduce power itself.

My own analysis places less emphasis on these explanations than on those shifts in global geopolitics and national-transnational governance that have taken place over the last forty years (Hardt and Negri 2001, 2005; Harvey 2005, 2007; Ong 2006), and on the emergence of a small ethnically mixed political class that has come to dominate Togo's political economy and that has siphoned the country's resources for its own profit (and, paradoxically, has increased its economic standing during the crisis of the past ten years). Because of the fixation on north-south politics, on the Shakespearean melodrama between the Eyadéma and Olympio families, and on the exploits and excesses of Eyadéma himself, the international community and this ruling elite have been able to operate in the shadows, largely beyond critique.

In drawing broadly on theories of the state and postcolonial governance in Africa, I owe much to the writings of Achille Mbembe (1992, 2001, 2003) and Comi Toulabour (1986, 2005).[1] Their work takes us beyond conventional accounts of the state, to acknowledge the locally inflected nature of power in the African postcolony while also recognizing the ways in which (dictatorial) power deploys culture as technology and instrument of rule. Eyadéma was the very embodiment of such a politics, brilliant at both wrapping himself in and eliciting/manipulating local cultural signifiers. Both theorists, though especially Mbembe (2001, 2005, 2006), also productively theorize African postcolonial politics as surfeit and expenditure (cf. Bataille 1985, 1993), as rooted in excesses of consumption, waste, bodiliness, sexuality, spectacle, cynicism, laughter, narrative. Indeed, in that Eyadéma was largely invisible to his subjects, his presence—and his claim to power and sovereignty—was forever mediated and made real through proxies, often through narrative and rumor. Much of the chapter is an assemblage of stories and rumors about the dictator and the political—culled from conversations on the street, in bars and beer huts, in bush taxis, on village paths—stories and popular imaginings that constitute their own theory of the political.

A central preoccupation of the recent sovereignty literature has been the relationship between sovereign power and "state of exception." Thus, Agamben (1998, 2005) draws on Schmitt ([1922] 2007, [1927] 2006) and Benjamin ([1939] 1969b) to suggest that it is the sovereign's ability to decide who will live and who die, rendering himself purveyor of but also party to "bare life," that constitutes the essence of sovereign power. While hesitant to bring all of Agamben on board in an analysis of a West African political system (which, despite its origins in colonial-authoritarian systems of rule, has also evolved in locally distinct ways), I nevertheless find this aspect of his analysis useful in thinking through Eyadéma's long hold on power. The potentate was a master at proclaiming sovereign privilege in declaring states of emergency and suspending the law—because of imagined/real threats, both without and within. And in a stroke of evil genius, he even conjured emergency states, staging coup attempts that allowed him to declare states of siege and consolidate power in moments of vulnerability. Moreover, he carried the notion of exceptional state to capricious extreme, making of his own body a site of excess (and object of desire)[2] in a sea of desperate poverty, and, by hinting at his deadly supernatural powers, reminding all of the sovereign's ability to let live and make die.

## Politique du Ventre

Togo's military dictator of four decades, Gnassingbé Eyadéma, came to power in independent Africa's first coup d'état. Having fought for the French in Indochina and Algeria during the late colonial period, Eyadéma returned home at independence expecting to find a station in the independent nation's military. However, his request, and that of a small group of ex-combatants, most hailing from the north of Togo, was refused by those in power. In 1963, Eyadéma and his compatriots overthrew the government—and killed Togo's first president, Sylvanus Olympio, so the story goes, on the steps of the US Embassy, where Olympio was seeking refuge.[3] Eyadéma and his colleagues initially handed power to a more moderate southerner, Nicolas Grunitzky (a brother-in-law of Olympio), before taking full, formal control in 1967, with Eyadéma as president.

Throughout the 1970s and 1980s, Eyadéma ruled in textbook patrimonial fashion, playing favorites and rewarding those who were loyal with riches and special perks (Toulabour 1986). This "politique du ventre" (belly politics), in Bayart's (1989) evocative phrase, lined the pockets and filled the bellies of those in power at the expense of the rest of the nation—and made itself visible in the body of the dictator and the padded stomachs of members of the political class. The beneficiaries of Eyadéma's largesse were not only supportive individuals but also ethnic groups and regions. Those who showed proper respect were rewarded—with money gifts, with development projects—and those (individuals/groups/regions) who did not were denied and discriminated against. A trivial though revealing example of the patron-client system at work: when traveling on the national highway during the 1980s, one could immediately identify which préfectures were pro-Eyadéma and which not by whether or not the road had been maintained in that area. I remember a 20 km stretch just outside Atakpamé, an obstacle course of giant potholes that took an hour to traverse and left a thick film of dust on all who ventured there: the district of a disrespectful préfet.

1. Eyadéma c. 1980

Eyadéma's geometry of power also entailed ethnicizing the national pol-ity and the military. While he strategically appointed southerners to high position within his government (thus cleverly dividing elements of the po-litical opposition), all of the most important ministries were headed by trusted northerners, and the country's single political party (Rassemblement du Peuple Togolais [RPT]) was dominated by northern loyalists. Moreover, 80 percent of Togo's soldiers (10,000 out of 13,000) were from the north, with 7,000 from Eyadéma's Kabiyé ethnic group and 3,000 from his home village (Toulabour 2005:3), the latter often hand-picked by the president himself at the annual wrestling matches that are part of male initiation cere-monies in his home region (Piot 1999:91–92). For many southerners, the mono-ethnic military became the public face and icon of the north's mo-nopoly on power, and it served as constant reminder of the violence that inaugurated the dictatorship and maintained it in place.

Indeed, most Togolese experienced the state most directly through the presence of the military in their daily lives. All who took the roadways—and most Togolese are prolific travelers (riding minibuses, route-taxis, and motorcycle-taxis to and from work, between markets and centers of com-merce, to and from their villages of origin)—have had experience of the random roadside check: olive-green uniform rifling through their bags, AK-47 swinging carelessly from a shoulder, the interrogation and insults of the vehicle's driver, the inevitable bribe, the feeling that there is nothing negotiable here. These roadside searches are stagings of state presence as much as anything else, dramaturgical performances (Comaroff and Comaroff 2006a, 2006b; Hansen and Stepputat 2005; Mbembe 2001) intended to impress and intimidate—and to create the effect that one is in the presence of absolute authority, albeit an authority that is under siege and in constant state of emergency. Few ever forget such an encounter, no matter how infrequent. Indeed, the irregularity of the search and the element of surprise—the checkpoints remain for weeks and then disappear, sometimes for months, before migrating to another location unannounced—is one of the secrets of their effectiveness (Mbembe 2006:319).

Another technology of rule during this era: the periodic imprisoning of ministers and high military officials, including occasionally those close to the dictator himself and indeed those from his own ethnic group, on charges of embezzlement, of plotting to overthrow the government, of insubordination. The message was a simple but effective one: you were never safe nor beyond suspicion; absolute loyalty and perpetual uncertainty remained the order of the day. Yet another strategy of control: Eyadéma made a habit of sleeping with the wives of male ministers (and, needless to say, with those few female ministers he appointed), a practice clearly rooted in power politics as much as in the sexual appetite of the dictator. Note at the same time a poignant example of power breeding resistance. One minister with an especially attractive—and also professional—wife went to extremes to prevent the dictator from sharing her bed: he had her resign her professorship at the university and left her at home whenever state dinners were held, so that Eyadéma would never set eyes on her.[4]

Like military dictators across the continent (Mbembe 2001; Schatzberg 1988, 2001), Eyadéma sought to identify himself with the nation and the nation with himself (Toulabour 1986). His praises, as Togo's progenitor and savior, were sung whenever he appeared in public by dancing "animators" wearing cloth emblazoned with his image.[5] His name was invoked at the inception of all development projects, whether large or small, whether in city or remote locale ("even a well or latrine in a distant village was thanks to Eyadéma," a cynic commented). His picture was hung from the walls of offices throughout the country and was daily displayed on the front page of Togo's single (state) newspaper: the potentate greeting an ambassador, hosting a development expert, convening the cabinet. The lead image on state television's nightly news, an image borrowed from Mobutu (de Boeck

1996:36), showed Eyadéma descending from heaven on a cloud. The blank face of a watch sold on the street morphed into a picture of the dictator in military uniform, appearing and disappearing, phantomlike, every thirty seconds. A popular comic book told the story of his life and his rise to power.

Personalizing power also entailed fashioning a spectacular presidential biography, replete with foiled assassination attempt and plane crash survival—real events that were nevertheless fetishized and fictionalized in the telling. The attempt on Eyadéma's life—the first of many (van Geirt 2006)—took place in 1973 at the presidential palace, with the assassin, a Kabiyé soldier from a village near Eyadéma's own, somehow slipping past the president's bodyguards. When he fired at Eyadéma from close range, however, the bullet was intercepted by a small book—some say a Bible—in the dictator's breast pocket. Imprisoned, the attacker was released a year later and invited to dinner by the man he had tried to kill, a touch—part charm, part sadism, all power—that was trademark Eyadéma. Despite the ruthlessness and sadism of many of his political tactics, Eyadéma also had his charming—and even generous and gentle—side. He was constantly surprising visitors in unexpected ways with his friendliness and gifting—giving to people, even rivals, when there was no apparent political gain to be had. Like a strict/punitive but by turns indulgent/generous father, such kindness could be deeply affecting, especially for someone expecting the opposite.

The second mythical biographical moment, the plane crash, occurred a year later when the president was returning to his home village in the north. The small plane in which he was traveling went down, killing all except him and one other. The event immediately came to stand for more than itself, with Eyadéma claiming divine protection, and the crash site (Sarakawa) becoming a national monument and pilgrimage destination—to which the potentate returned each year, entire cabinet in tow, to narrate the event and his miraculous survival. "Sarakawa" also became a day of the week in the north and the name of a five-star hotel in Lomé, and the dates of both events—the assassination attempt and the plane crash—became national holidays.

Indeed, in perhaps the ultimate instantiation of this cult of personality, all state holidays celebrated during this period were associated with Eyadéma: January 13, the day of the 1963 and 1967 coups; January 24, the plane crash; February 2, the post-crash return to Lomé; April 24, the assassination attempt; June 21, the death of a "martyr" from Eyadéma's natal village who was killed fighting the first Germans (a critic's commentary: "as if no village other than his own resisted the colonial order!"); June 28, the day (in 1986) when the president's mother died; August 30, the call (in 1969) to

2. The remains of the 1974 plane crash, Sarakawa 2009

found Eyadéma's political party (the RPT); September 23, the 1986 defeat of an invasion force from Ghana (purportedly organized by Gilchrist Olympio, the son of the man Eyadéma killed when he took power); September 28, the inauguration of the RPT (also in 1969). A notable omission in the holiday cycle: April 27, the day of Togolese independence from colonial rule—excluded because it was also the birthday of Eyadéma's political rival, Sylvanus Olympio.[6]

Like other African presidents during this time period—and, needless to say, another powerful technology of rule—Eyadéma cultivated the image of himself as someone with heightened mystical powers (Toulabour 1986). Stories embellishing his reputation as a witch—as someone possessing the ability to kill with mystical power—were legion, and indeed he was rumored to have ensorcelled his parents as a child. He claimed also to be protected by powerful deities. Thus, when he survived the 1974 plane crash, he insisted that he had been saved by the spirit Gu (Ogun), to whom he sacrificed all-white animals—the color demanded by the spirit—when he returned each year to the site of the crash. He periodically consulted powerful diviners and had a live-in southern savant—an old man (an Ewe from Notse, origin and sacred center of southern Togolese culture) who had been close to

Olympio, and who, many insist, was the power behind the throne, counseling Eyadéma on how to defeat his southern opposition. "He revealed all
our secrets and is the reason Eyadéma's still in power," a southerner once
told me. The dictator was also famous for calling meetings—with ministers,
with visiting dignitaries—in the middle of the night, cultivating the impres-
sion that he didn't sleep, thus enhancing the image of someone who possessed superordinate powers.

Another source of Eyadéma's power and charisma: throughout his years
in office, the dictator's body was a fertile site of semiosis, a text that was read
and re-read, coded and decoded—one way by his followers, another by his
opponents. A massive man, 6'4" tall with athletic build, he was referred to
as the "giant," the "baobab," the "dinosaur"—monikers which for some
indexed his enormous power, for others his brutishness. His handsome
looks, dapper suits, and dozens of mistresses—"concubines," as they are
referred to in Lomé, with many of whom he fathered children: both Faure,
his filial successor, and Kpatcha, his would-be successor, were the children
of mistresses—produced myth-making about his sexual prowess, which
only seemed confirmed when, three years before his death, he married and
had two children with a woman five decades his junior. On the flip side,
the ubiquitous sunglasses and high shirt collars that marked his later years
produced endless speculation—anxious for supporters, hopeful for detractors—about the throat cancer and degenerative eye disease from which he
was said to be suffering.

But it was not simply the deployment of such patented (pan-African
dictatorial) modes and technologies of power—patrimonialism, ethnic politics, control of the means of violence, a personality cult and occult personality of epic proportions—that kept Eyadéma in power. The international
community played a pivotal role as well, and in the last instance this era
needs to be read in terms of the ways in which the international community was itself also responsible for producing and maintaining a distinctive
Togolese political culture.

The Cold War years were ones in which the superpowers, the United
States and the Soviet Union, played checkerboard politics with the African
continent (Clough 1992). What mattered most, more than ideology or the
conduct of domestic politics, was whether one was friend or foe. Thus, the
United States supported any and all who were in its camp, including some
of the most notoriously wicked and corrupt dictators—Zaire's Mobutu, Somalia's Siad Barre, Chad's Hissène Habré, Liberia's Samuel Doe, and Togo's
Eyadéma.

Although a tiny country, Togo was nevertheless strategically important during the 1970s and 1980s. Surrounded on all sides by socialist-Marxist (and thus Soviet-friendly) regimes—Benin to the East, Burkina Faso to the north, Ghana to the west—it was the only pro-Western country in the immediate area. It also held a seat on the United Nations Security Council during the early 1980s, thus casting an all-important vote during this era of Cold War politics. As well, France maintained ongoing interests in Togo, both economic and affective, attachments derived from its half century of colonial rule—interests that served a sizeable postcolonial resident French population of entrepreneurs, shopkeepers, advisors, and soldiers.

The strong interests of the United States and France in ensuring Togo's continued loyalty translated into ongoing economic aid—aid which, unlike during the 1990s, was all funneled through the state. As a result Eyadéma's regime was flush with income, money that supported its expenditures on the military and the political class as well as on infrastructure and rural development—and that gave Togo the reputation of being West Africa's "little Switzerland" (van Geirt 2006:15). It bears repeating: none of the state's expenditures during this period, nor the distinctive political culture that was nurtured by them, would have been possible without Cold War monies from its patrons.

Moreover, as noted in the previous chapter, relations of authority that were established during the colonial era—especially the compact between metropole, state, and local community (Mamdani 1996)—remained largely unchanged during the first thirty years of independence. Thus, a distant metropolitan power (France, the United States) retained ultimate control (via financial subsidy and the threat of military intervention) while nevertheless ceding significant authority to its intermediary and proxy, Eyadéma's postcolonial state, in managing local subjects. The state's mode of control of rural areas, where 70 percent of Togolese lived, followed closely in the footsteps of the colonial system of indirect rule. All canton chiefs, and many village-level chiefs (especially those in the Kabiyé north), were approved by Eyadéma, and recalcitrant ones deposed.[7] Chiefs at every level were expected to implement state projects in the village—serving as conduits for information from above, opening the door to development, recruiting children to attend school and engage in "animation," modeling obeisant citizenship for their subjects. As quid pro quo, they received small salaries and invitations to state events.

Just as the colonial needed and "invented" tradition (Hobsbawm and Ranger 1983) in the rural areas to provide crucial and less costly social services in reproducing its labor force (Meillassoux 1981), so too Eyadéma's Togolese state, now taking its cue from Zaire's Mobutu, sought to reinforce and celebrate "tradition" in the villages, not only because the villages remained a vital source of labor power but also because state support of local tradition was a means of ensuring local support for the state. Thus, in addition to government proclamations supporting village traditions and ceremonies— ceremonies that were written into tourist brochures as part of a "Togolese" festival cycle—Eyadéma himself returned to his home village in the Kabiyé area of northern Togo every year to participate in local ceremonies and consult with village chiefs and elders (Piot 1999:91–92).

This Cold War mix of triangulated (metropole/state/local) power relations—of monies (and ultimate control) flowing from Europe and the United States, of a strong state centered on the person of the dictator, of ongoing indirect rule in the villages—would all begin to come undone in the 1990s.

## Démocratie

With the end of the Cold War in 1989 and the withdrawal of the Soviet Union from the global geopolitical field, American and European interest in Africa shifted dramatically (Clough 1992). The United States, especially, saw little of remaining value in West Africa and largely abandoned it. With little at stake politically, and because of the massive failures of investment in economic development across the region, it redirected development monies toward Eastern Europe and, when Apartheid ended in 1994, southern Africa. Indexing this shift, the Agency for International Development, the development arm of the State Department, an office that operated a multi-million dollar annual budget in Togo during the 1970s and 1980s with development projects up and down the country, closed the doors to its Togo office in 1994. Between 1990 and 2001, development aid to Togo fell from over $200 million to $50 million a year (World Bank/UNDP Report 2004:13).

France continued to have ongoing interests in West Africa, but these too underwent major shifts during the 1990s. France's aid package to Togo dropped from $192 to $44 million a year between 1991 and 2001 (Banque de France 2003), and for the first time there were whispers that it might end its century-long relationship with the continent (Smith 2003; Glaser and Smith 2005). The 1994 genocide in Rwanda, and the former colonial power's much-criticized role in that catastrophic event—if not abetting, at least failing to act—further damaged its reputation and alienated many of its former colonies and allies. And this was only a prelude to the debacle in Cote d'Ivoire at the end of the decade—and the abiding sense that the relationship between France and its former colonial empire had changed forever.

At the same moment as these withdrawals of economic aid were occurring—aid that, in Togo as elsewhere, had previously flowed through state coffers—the large international lending institutions, the World Bank and the IMF, stepped up pressure—pressure begun in the mid-1980s, as quid pro quo for the restructuring of debt—to liberalize and privatize the economies of countries throughout the region. A small dose of short-term austerity, they imagined, would release large amounts of long-term economic/entrepreneurial innovation. Thus, at the insistence of the large lending institutions, state-owned industries were sold to private investors, lands previously inalienable were put on the market, and currencies were devalued, to bring them into line, the economists argued, with their "real" value.

For francophone countries, currency adjustment was a particularly bitter pill to swallow. In 1994, at the World Bank's urging, France devalued the CFA franc by 50 percent,[8] doubling the cost of imported goods and thus removing them from the budgets of most households. In addition to reducing buying power and domestic savings, devaluation effectively doubled the national debt, so that debt service consumed state monies previously directed to domestic spending. Moreover, the privileged classes' decreased ability to buy directly affected markets and households in rural locales, locales which subsisted in part on selling their products to the urban market. The mid-1990s was a time, market women in northern Togo commented, when the markets lost their usual animation and when sellers would return home at the end of the day with what they had brought that morning—a moment, then, with origins in Paris and Washington, which had dramatic effects even on rural household economies (Piot 1999:111).

Coterminous with these shifts in geopolitical and global economic policy, social protest movements across the West African subregion began to shake the Cold War state from within. In Togo in summer 1991, after months of clashes on the streets between dissidents and the military, Eyadéma capitulated to calls for a national conference to discuss steps toward democratization. In so doing, he exposed himself to an extraordinary three-week period of public denunciation, a cascade of commentary condemning the dictatorship years, that surprised everyone with its directness. Critics—lawyers, academics, politicians—stepped forward to voice their complaints openly: of northern favoritism, of patrimonialism gone wild, of a runaway military apparatus that had become the dictator's private army, of disappearances. Many from the north as well, including those from Eya-déma's own ethnic group, joined in the criticism. A Kabiyé acquaintance commented at the time: "There is little difference between north and south. We are all victims of the regime."

---

Let me insert a parenthesis here. It is tempting to read much of Togolese politics in ethnic (north-south) terms. And indeed there is truth in such a reading—namely, that there is a great divide between north and south, a separation deemed ethnic-tribal-even racial. Thus, Togolese from the north distrust those from the south, and those from the south are similarly con-temptuous of those from the north, finding them "backward" and uncul-tured, and myriad stories attest to the acts of exclusion and violence carried out on the streets of Lomé and in workplaces every day in the name of tribalist sentiment.[9]

While not denying the all-too-real—and sometimes deadly—effects that "tribalist" thinking has on the lives of many Togolese, we should neverthe-less be cautious of ethnic/tribalist interpretations. There are many accounts of northerners and southerners living and working together for generations. Moreover, both north and south are diverse and far from politically mono-lithic: witness the 2003 presidential election, in which 25 percent of the electorate in Eyadéma's home region voted for the southern opposition candidate. In addition, both northern and southern elites deploy "tribal-ist" terms to marshal political support. Thus Eyadéma repeatedly played the ethnic card (Toulabour 1986), attempting to instill fear in northerners by suggesting that if a southerner came to power, all northerners would be chased from the south. Southerners similarly fed anti-northern sentiment to marshal support for their own political cause.

Most importantly, however, such a reading deflects attention from the fact that it is a small—ethnically mixed—political class that has run Togo for four decades, a northern-southern elite that has stolen the country's re-sources for personal profit. It is this elite—Eyadéma's "barons," as they are referred to in Lomé—that would have us think that Togo's problem is one of unbridgeable north-south divides rather than one of a small privileged elite dominating the vast majority of (southern *and* northern) Togolese. On this reading, then, the real conflict—Togo's real problem—should be un-derstood as class rather than ethnic conflict.[10] Moreover, the ongoing fixa-tion of Togolese and those in the international community on north-south politics—like that on the rivalry between Eyadéma and Olympio families,[11] or on the exploits and excesses of Eyadéma himself—has enabled this ruling elite to operate off-stage and avoid critique. I read my acquaintance's pithy comment, "we are all victims of the regime," as an astute perception of this political reality.

––––––––––––––––––––––

At the end of the national conference in 1991, Eyadéma cleverly headed off an attempt by the political opposition to strip him of power (Ellis 1993), but agreed to hold presidential elections. Virtually everyone thought the end of the dictatorship was at hand. But the president with nine lives survived once again, this time standing for election, and, when all the main opposition parties boycotted (because of anticipated fraud), coming away with 96 percent of the vote. This was the first in a series of post-Cold War election adventures—needless to say, each with the same outcome. Thus, in 1998, just when it appeared that Eyadéma might be defeated at the polls by his lifelong political rival Gilchrist Olympio (the son of the man he had assassinated in 1963), the minister of the interior impounded the ballot boxes, counted the votes himself, and declared Eyadéma the winner—with 52 percent of the vote, just enough to avoid a runoff. The irregularities surrounding these and legislative elections, and the government's poor human rights record, led the international community to punish Eyadéma's regime, with the European Union suspending all funding in 1993. Still today, sixteen years later, most of the funding—now in the hundreds of millions of Euros—has not been released.

Despite these electoral embarrassments, and the de facto continuation of the dictatorship, the 1990s left the Togolese political scene forever changed. Liberalization spread across political and cultural fields like brushfire—a genie that, despite the best efforts of the regime, could not be contained. By mid-decade, a dozen political parties cluttered the political scene, and a score of opposition newspapers appeared on the streets, often running daring exposés of government malfeasance. So too was the religious domain liberalized. The ban on churches other than Roman Catholic and Presbyterian, those of longstanding colonial-era pedigree, was lifted, and a flood of new Christian ministries, mostly Pentecostal-charismatic, entered the social field and began to displace state sovereignty in the national imaginary. Moreover, the privatization and liberalization of radio/television—no longer censored, channels proliferating—and the revolution in information technology, led to an explosion of the popular-cultural field. Now MTV, France's TV5, international soccer, and Mexican and Brazilian soaps filled the social space and evening hours of families throughout Lomé, and cyber-cafés were crowded with youth surfing the web and connecting with friends and relatives overseas. The borders of the nation, both real and virtual, became porous as never before.[12]

For most Togolese, however, and despite the often-exhilarating gains of the era of liberalization, the post-Cold War mix of political and economic reforms was largely experienced as a massive withdrawal of money and a steady worsening of the economy. Not only did the promised benefits of structural adjustment fail to materialize, but World Bank/IMF austerity measures pushed Togo, already teetering on the brink, into an ongoing state of crisis. With earnings/savings cut in half, with a state budget that was a fraction of what it was in the 1980s, with the disappearance of social services, with the steady increase in the cost of essentials like gasoline and medicine, everyday life for most Togolese became a never-ending struggle. Every year living standards in Lomé were ratcheted down yet another notch, with more people out of work, more beggars and homeless on the streets, a higher rate of crime (and its corollary: more security firms protecting businesses and residences), and ever-greater levels of everyday frustration. In the rural areas, too, money became scarcer and budgets were pushed to the limit—with surpluses evaporated, with fewer able to afford the fees of sending their children to school, with more unable to buy needed medicines, and with a dramatic increase in disease and death (and their corollary: an increase in witchcraft claims and counterclaims).

In short, life in the era of "démocratie" was—and continues to be—experienced by most Togolese as life under crisis, a crisis not only political and economic but also of the spirit. In Lomé today, the loss of hope and of a sense of political possibility is palpable.

## The Empty State

The flight of Cold War monies, the fallout from the national conference, and the effects of neo-liberalization eviscerated the strong patrimonial state. As a result, the state had to reinvent itself, and reinvent itself it did.

Lacking funding, the Togolese state retreated from social and development fields, leaving the latter to the NGOs, and sought new sources of income. It thus renewed and deepened its relationship with the expatriate communities in Lomé, especially French and Lebanese business interests (in used cars and hotels, in grocery and merchandise stores), trading state protection and tax-free standing for kickbacks. It opened its doors to the international underground, becoming a West African *plaque tournante* (turntable) for the global arms and drug trades (Labarthe 2005)—and thereby providing elite state actors (generals in the army, high-ranking police officials, commissioners at the port) with new and often extravagant sources of income. It supplied the Angolan rebel leader Jonas Savimbi with arms in return for ("blood") diamonds. And, most importantly, when civil war broke out in Cote d'Ivoire in the late 1990s, it won the bid, as it were, to replace that country's port as point of disembarkation for goods bound for the "enclave" countries—Mali, Burkina Faso, Niger—of the West African interior. With taxes of over 50 percent on incoming merchandise—the purchaser of a used car costing $2,000 paid an additional $1,200 in tax—the Lomé port became Eyadéma's major source of post-Cold War income and filled the pockets of members of his family and coterie, most notably those of his imposingly corpulent son and port director, Kpatcha, who purchased his own jet with earnings from the port.

Low-level state functionaries—many entirely de-salaried, others receiving paychecks only intermittently—also engaged in novel and often ingenious modes of revenue capture. Recognizing that the only international monies now entering Togo flowed through NGOs, state employees created their own NGOs, of which they were sometimes the only member (Hibou 1999). Schoolteachers, long accustomed to putting schoolchildren to work on their own fields, now began generating added income by hiring them out to local farmers and/or having them manufacture products to sell. A particularly outrageous example from Kuwdé, the village in northern Togo where I have worked: parents began buying straw for roofing their houses from a local school, straw cut by their own children—now working for the schoolteachers instead of themselves. And police and soldiers, remarkably restrained during the years of the Cold War, began padding their incomes with bribes, thus taking their pay directly from the citizenry, and hired themselves out for special services, thereby using the state's uniform for personal profit (cf. Hibou 1999, 2004; Roitman 2005).

While Togolese state income had long served as the private fund of the dictator—with all monies passing through Eyadéma's hands before being disbursed to state functions and clients—the new moment took state privatization to new extremes (Hibou 1999, 2004). Now potential earnings were immediately privatized, with sources of state revenue becoming avenues of private income for multiple state actors. State revenue thus no longer entered the national treasury, nor even—the treasury's surrogate under the dictatorship—"Lomé 2" (Eyadéma's private residence), but went directly into the pockets of state employees, albeit employee-citizens dressed up as state actors.

The privatization and "banditization" (Bayart, Ellis, and Hibou 1999; Hibou 1999, 2004; Toulabour 2005) of the state during this period was complemented by its remilitarization. It is said that Eyadéma realized—only for the first time after the national conference in 1991—that he was not liked by a majority of Togolese. His response to this "enemy within" was to strengthen and further elaborate what was already one of the most loyal and disciplined armies and best systems of intelligence in West Africa. He increased the size of the military to over 13,000—one soldier for every 300 citizens (Toulabour 2005:2)—and multiplied the number and types of military units (cf. Mbembe 2006:322). Thus, special commando units were created—a "green beret" presidential guard, an elite quick-strike force ("Force d'Intervention Rapide"), a "red beret" paratrooper unit (this latter the charge of Eyadéma's infamous son Ernest, known for his ruthlessness and baroque torture techniques, applied especially to dissidents from his own [Kabiyé] ethnic group in the north) (Toulabour 2005:12).[13]

Note here how the role of the military is internal to domestic political life. Soldiers rather than police patrol the neighborhoods of Lomé and man its checkpoints at night, and soldiers occupy the stops on the highway to the northern border. This inversion of the customary role of the military (as defender of the nation beyond its borders) is justified by those in power in the name of security. "We are a small country, easily invaded—as we have been several times by mercenary forces from Ghana. This requires perpetual vigilance, and the army is best trained to repel an invading force," a soldier told me. This view, however, is belied by the fact that those Lomé neighborhoods routinely patrolled by soldiers, especially Bè, are strongholds of the political opposition, not of foreigners.

Eyadéma's security apparatus also extended into nonstate organizations. A dozen private security firms appeared during the 1990s (Toulabour 2005:4–6), many headed by former army officers or intimates of the regime. These companies remained tethered to the state, serving as de facto reserves—called upon in 2005, for example, to assist the military in suppressing opposition neighborhoods when violence broke out during the elections. Their agents, stationed in neighborhoods throughout Lomé, also served as potential "ears" for the regime. Another paramilitary organization, HACAME, a militant student group at the university, emerged after the national conference to promote northern interests and to keep opposition student groups under surveillance (Toulabour 2005:4–5). One example of the tight set of connections among these organizations and the regime: HACAME's president during the mid-1990s was appointed Togolese ambassador to Washington in 1998, before he became head of cabinet when Eyadéma's son Faure came to power in 2005. One of his best friends, also a student leader of HACAME in the 1990s, today runs one of the largest security firms in Lomé. Associations of northern civil servants resident in Lomé ("Amicales") also formed during this period, meeting monthly to discuss ways to develop their home communities and to provide mutual aid for one another (see chapter 5). While less overtly concerned with security, these groups nevertheless consolidated and extended northern networks, thus tightening the reins of those in power.

There were now government snitches everywhere, reporting on suspicious activity. Some were hired as such but others stepped forward on their own, offering information about those opposed to the regime in return for money. One state-hired informer I heard about went incognito as a village crazy, nakedly wandering the streets of a northern town (and Eyadéma stronghold), hair long and matted—and reporting dissidents to Eyadéma's vengeful sons. (The image of state intelligence represented by a madman with no clothes strikes me as brilliantly capturing some of the absurdities and ironies of the moment.) A northern chief I know routinely reported names of dissidents to the ruling party and prevented all other parties from holding rallies in his canton during electoral campaigns—in return for a boost to his earnings.

State paranoia was matched by conspiracy thinking from below. "Radio trottoir" (sidewalk radio) was awash with rumors about the private lives and machinations of those in power: of secret organizations—the Freemasons, the Rosicrucians—to which they belonged, of human sacrifice, of sorcery killings, of subterranean passageways connecting military camps and Eyadéma residences, of plots against, and deals cut with, members of the opposition, of "ears" everywhere. Whether the latter was true or not—whether there were really government informers behind every bush—was beside the point. People thought there were, and the state wanted people to think there were. As such, the belief alone served state interest.

The chilling effect of this culture of paranoia on public discourse was near-total. One simply did not voice one's politics in public if they were in any way construable as anti-regime. An illustration: I once gave a lecture on African Culture Ministries to an English-language class at the American Cultural Center in Lomé, and, by way of illustrating the way in which states can influence local culture, I discussed how Eyadéma's return to the north each year to celebrate Kabiyé wrestling and initiation has turned this event into a state spectacle and transformed the ritual complex with which it is associated. I was told afterward by a friend that my use of that example was foolhardy—that it could be construed as critical of the regime and that a paid informer in the class, or someone just looking to make money, could turn me in to the authorities and have my head. Again, whether this was true or not was beside the point.

As with those new regimes of accumulation that accompanied the neo-liberal/post-Cold War moment, so too new logics of violence emerged during this period. The state monopoly on violence that typified the Cold War years was broken and—with the emergence of new criminal networks, the proliferation of security firms, and the rise of uniformed state (police/military) actors seeking personal gain—was replaced by regimes of violence that were more diffuse and privatized. Moreover, as noted above, state violence itself was transformed, becoming more intensified and specialized—as with the creation and proliferation of new military units with discrete functions (the red and green berets, the rapid strike force).

A privatized, remilitarized—leaner, meaner—state was nevertheless still a state largely without resources, and, importantly, one with fewer resources than it had in the 1970s and 1980s. It was thus a state whose presence was experienced in the everyday lives of its citizens as an absence—all the more so because the developmental state of the 1980s (West Africa's "little Switzerland") had been active in communities throughout the country, building schools and clinics and sponsoring family/community education through the ubiquitous government agency Affaires Sociales.

How to fill this gap? One solution, a Eyadéma staple, was through performance and conjury. Witness the following from August 1998.

At dawn on a Sunday, gunshots rang out in the Lomé neighborhood of Kodjoviakopé, which abuts the border with Ghana. Soldiers rushed to the scene, filling the streets, going door-to-door, shooting wildly in the air. By mid-morning, calm had been restored and state radio announced that eight mercenaries had been captured—mercenaries, the radio asserted, who had crossed the border from Ghana with intent to overthrow the regime. The next day, as life returned to normal in the capital city, the political opposition claimed that the previous day's "coup attempt" had been staged by the government. I spoke to many, northerners as well as southerners, in the weeks immediately after, and most agreed that the opposition theory was probably accurate.

This event occurred two months after an election marked by massive fraud—the second post-Cold War presidential election in which the interior minister had declared Eyadéma victor by fiat—and after a series of strikes and marches organized by the opposition to protest the election results (with the marches often ending in front of the US Embassy, which, unlike the French Embassy, had allied itself with the anti-Eyadéma forces). These protests were notable for the way in which Eyadéma's government parried and effectively undermined the tactics of the opposition. Thus each time a strike—"ville morte" (dead city)—was announced, the government cleverly declared a national holiday. As a result, no one ever knew how widespread was the opposition's support. And another type of government parry, this with the international community as much as with the opposition: a series of Amnesty International human rights reports appeared during the late 1990s documenting the role of the Togolese state in torturing and "disappearing" members of the opposition at the time of elections. Each time Amnesty sent a delegation, however, the state would convene its own commission to investigate—and, needless to say, would present another version of the facts, challenging the evidence and testimony on which the Amnesty reports were based. At the very least, the state showed itself adept at recognizing that there was a new game in town—of international monitors convening commissions and generating reports—a game which it also had to play (cf. Comaroff and Comaroff 2006a:23–24), while at times exposing an overzealous Amnesty investigation.

After the "coup attempt" in mid-August, and following two months of vigorous opposition activity, the streets were surprisingly quiescent. Moreover, despite the fact that there was widespread consensus that the regime had staged it all, many also felt that the event itself had succeeded in at least neutralizing the opposition. But how so? A coup attempt staged by the government to discredit the opposition achieving its end despite widespread consensus that it might have been staged? One part of the answer is quite straightforward: the coup attempt, whether staged by the regime or not, showed that the military, always the backbone of Eyadéma's power, remained firmly behind him. The unrest of the early 1990s had been marked by defections. When this did not occur in August 1998, people knew that the opposition's chances of success were slim at best.

But equally important to the apparent "success" of this event was its value as spectacle (Comaroff and Comaroff 2006b; Mbembe 2001, 2005, 2006). Eyadéma's rule had long been tied to making himself, the state, and the military "visible" to his subjects. The coup attempt and its "suppression" was another in a long string of staged spectacles—large government construction projects (like the towering, and often empty, Hôtel 2 Février), the performance of "animation" for visiting dignitaries, the daily high-speed motorcade from the presidential palace to the military camp, the annual pilgrimage to the site of the plane crash, the cabinet's televised trek to Eyadéma's home village to witness the wrestling matches of Kabiyé initiates. All were performances intended to impress, as if seeing/witnessing conveyed power to the author of the performance. The uncertainties of the post-Cold War moment, demanding new inventiveness, took spectacle to a novel register.

Just after the coup attempt, I had several conversations with an official at the US Embassy in Lomé whose job it was to report to the State Department on the Togolese political scene. On the morning after the coup attempt, this official and a counterpart from the German Embassy, both strong critics of the regime, had been taken to the border by a Togolese government official to examine the site where the invasion had occurred. They were shown a set of jeep tracks in the sand leading up to the barbed wire fence that divided Ghana from Togo—the tracks, they were told, of the vehicle used by the mercenaries. Since the government would not let these officials speak to the imprisoned mercenaries, this was the extent of the "evidence" they had that there had been a coup attempt.

When I asked the American official what he thought had "really" happened—whether the government had staged the coup attempt or not—he simply shrugged his shoulders. "It's impossible to tell. Both sides claim the other was responsible, but other than those tire marks in the sand there's no evidence that would allow anyone to decide. I don't know in this country anymore where the truth lies. Look at this," he said handing me a flyer that had been circulating in the streets. Unsigned, it claimed to have been written by someone recruited by the political opposition to dress up as a soldier in order to trash the house of a member of the opposition. The opposition claimed, of course, that it was a government fabrication. "But these things work on the streets," he said. "They affect people. Eyadéma's very clever at winning the battle for public opinion."[14]

Notice how the "time" of the political during the post-Cold War period becomes more punctuated (Guyer 2007) and episodic, organized around "events" like the staged coup attempt, the dramaturgy of elections, the detention of journalists, most recently the gunfight at Kpatcha's house (see below). These events swallow the nation's attention, diverting state projects into gossip and rumor, disappearing the national interest into petty disputes. Evanescent power in the contemporary era, like evanescent development (see chapter 5), now appears and disappears, staging itself when it sees fit, subverting the linear time of the Cold War state (which was organized around the succession of holidays and teleologies of development). This is also the temporality of Pentecostal Christianity—of the unforeseen event and a radical interruption of time and the everyday.

It bears noting, too, that many of these "events" have to do with bodies—threats to the life of bodies, the detention and torture of bodies, the absence of the dictator's body at death (see below). Moreover, as already alluded to, Eyadéma's body became a national obsession, especially during the post-Cold War years. Such body fetishization, here sutured to imaginaries of the state—thus perhaps standing in for the diffusion and decentering of power today—is also central to other domains explored throughout this book: to charismatic worship (which celebrates the chaste body and calls on the Holy Spirit to enter the believer to speak in tongues and exorcise demons), to "affective" development (which connects two "hearts" a continent apart and focuses more on the bodily integrity of the aid recipient than on infrastructure), to occult imaginaries (that are rooted in preoccupations with the diseased or dying body), to the lottery (in which the visa applicant's moment of truth entails presenting her "real" body for the embassy interview, convincing the consul that the body before her is the same as that represented in a dossier of documents). Moreover, preoccupation with the body seems a global phenomenon in the contemporary era, and this despite—or perhaps because of—increasing virtualization. Popular culture seems positively enamored of the body—in fitness and beauty regimes, in proliferating sexualized cultures, in pornography, in video games (Allison 2001; Piot 2003). Critical theory, too, has recently devoted significant attention to the body (Bordo 1993; Butler 1993; Grosz 1994; cf. Jameson 2003).

Eyadema's "politics of illusion" (Apter 1999, 2005) enabled him not only to discipline subjects at home but also to speak back to the international community, and this in more ways than one. The August coup attempt aimed not only to convince everyone that there were real threats to Togolese national security, justifying perpetual state of emergency measures, but also to intimidate members of the diplomatic community who sided with the opposition. A simple example, though far from unique: on the morning of the August coup attempt, the house of a political officer with the US Embassy who had dined with an opposition leader the night before was surrounded by soldiers shooting in the air. This embassy official later told me that he and his family pasted themselves to the floor of the third story of their house, imagining the worst.

But this staged coup d'état performed a different type of work as well. At a time of ongoing crisis, when there were no resources at all, when there was little for the regime to do other than preserve itself in power, when the state had been emptied of content, these spectral phantasms were ways in which it could manufacture and invent itself, thus demonstrating its capacity to act. This act of conjury—"the resort to drama and fantasy to conjure up visible means of governance" (Comaroff and Comaroff 2006b:292)—said nothing so much as "we are still here and in power."[15] Note, moreover, the way in which power attempts to legitimate itself through demonstrating its capacity to act—and through making itself visible for all to see—rather than, as with liberal conceptions of power and the state, through upholding a rights-and-obligations "contract" with its citizenry.

As Mbembe (1992a, 2001, 2005, 2006) has remarked—and Togo is a textbook example (and indeed was the country he referenced, along with his native Cameroon, in his early writings on African postcolonial governance)—the culture of the postcolony is one of excess: of performance, rumor, deception, the double-coded message, talk that masks as reality, appearance and disappearance/s, paranoia and conspiracy, utter cynicism and uproarious laughter—all tethered to the figure of the dictator, himself a figure of extraordinary excess (of appetite, sexuality, paranoia, violence, generosity). Here, too, unpredictability and state of emergency are norm rather than exception.[16]

---

Eyadéma's life of fiction has, perhaps not surprisingly, been fictionalized. The Ivoirean writer Ahmadou Kourouma's prizewinning 1998 magical realist novel, *En attendant le vote des bêtes sauvages*, about a Cold War-era African dictator—the president-for-life "Supreme Guide" of the "République du Golfe"—is a barely disguised portrait of Eyadéma.[17] Like Eyadéma, Kourouma's protagonist, Koyaga, hailed from a remote mountain culture, where he was a champion hunter and wrestler. Recruited into the French colonial army, Koyaga fought in Indo-China and Algeria, winning numerous medals of honor and securing the perpetual loyalty of the French. Upon returning home at independence, he assassinated the country's first president (like Togo's Olympio, a "Brazilian"), put himself in power, and built an extravagant cult of personality—insisting that performers greet him whenever he appeared in public and erecting statues of himself—the "Father of the Nation"—throughout the country. Surviving a plane crash and multiple assassination attempts, flaunting his sexual appetite by taking mistresses and fathering children all over the country, consulting marabouts and diviners, imprisoning associates as well as enemies, creating a vast spy network to keep the population under surveillance, and seeking advice from dictators across the continent—"the caiman" (Houphouët-Boigny), "the leopard" (Mobutu), "the hyena" (Bokassa)—this fictional/real Eyadéma is the very embodiment of dictatorial delusion and excess.

And yet, while Kourouma's novel scathingly satirizes the figure of the dictator, it also renders Koyaga human and portrays him as product not only of local but also of continent-wide and global forces. Moreover, through-out the text condemnation and mockery bleed into voyeuristic fascination, hinting at the ambivalence and even seduction which also attends the figure of the dictator, a repulsion-attraction which suggests that such political cultures were not only produced from above but also from below (Mbembe 1992a, 2001; Werbner 1996).

---

A grand irony of the late Eyadéma years: that, in adapting to the new realities of the post-Cold War moment, the potentate oversaw and even engineered his own deconstruction. The patrimonial state—centered on the person of the dictator who retained absolute control over power, money, development, and violence—disappeared into the ether of the neoliberal moment. Yes, Eyadéma was still wealthy beyond belief, and members of his family continued to strut around Lomé like little kings—"barons"—but privatization and NGO-ization meant that monies formerly flowing through the state now bypassed it altogether, with the result that Eyadéma and his clients skimmed less and less. Cynics insisted that Eyadéma's exchanging of military uniform for suit—as was common practice among African dictators during the 1990s—was nothing but a charade, that he was still the same all-everything potentate. But this was far from the case, for he retained less and less control. The pervasive sense that Eyadéma remained omnipotent, and the way in which the fetish of Eyadéma lived on, was another of the mirages of Togolese political life.

The figure of the "empty" state would appear to be at odds with several recent analyses of the state in Africa (Hibou 1999, 2004; Bayart 2008; Roitman 2005; Comaroff and Comaroff 2006a). These works acknowledge that the state has undergone dramatic transformation since the end of the Cold War but nevertheless suggest that it retains enormous efficacy. While agreeing with many of the claims of these authors, and indeed my account has drawn attention to the ways in which the Togolese regime has reinvented itself in multiple ways over the last fifteen years, my characterization of the emptiness of that state draws on local perceptions that the strong patrimonial state of the 1970s and 1980s has abandoned its role as provider of social services and largely withdrawn from the biopolitical production of life, in city and village alike. Despite its remilitarization, and despite the fact that state actors continue to plunder the social field for private profit, the Togolese state today subsists more than ever on performance, on presenting an image or simulacrum of itself—largely to itself. But more to the point, my analysis is less concerned with the question of whether or not the state exists as such than with what Mitchell (1988) has referred to as "state effects"—with the ways in which the state and its actors make themselves known/visible, and today ever more invisible/absent, to an increasingly disaffected population.

## After the Death of the Dictator

When, in February 2005, after thirty-eight years in power, Eyadéma died of a heart attack—midair, en route to Israel for treatment—a new start seemed possible, if only for a brief moment. I was with a Togolese friend in North Carolina when the news broke, and his cell phone kept ringing and ringing—a call from Newark, another from Raleigh, a third from Minneapolis, a fourth from Paris, another from Vancouver . . . Munich . . . Barcelona. All from Togolese throughout the diaspora, passing the news, congratulating one another, imagining a fresh start and a different future. The excitement was palpable, and, after four decades of pent-up anger and frustration, deeply visceral. It was also short lived.

Despite the suddenness and unexpectedness of his death—Eyadéma's seeming invincibility was one of his defining traits—those in the inner circle acted quickly and decisively. They immediately sealed the borders and moved government troops into opposition neighborhoods. They rerouted a plane returning from Paris with the speaker of the national legislature—the constitutionally recognized successor of a deceased president, but a known reformer. (He remained in Cotonou, in neighboring Benin, denied entry to Togo, until Eyadéma loyalists had chosen their own successor.) They cut communications with the diaspora, blocking cell and landline access and shutting down Internet servers, while nevertheless leaving the electricity on—for fear that a dark city might better conceal subversive activity.[18] And they appointed one of Eyadéma's sons, Faure Gnassingbé, head of state, announcing that he would complete his father's mandate (due to expire in 2008).

The selection of the thirty-eight-year-old Faure was a brilliant, if surprising, move. Despite the fact that he had spent much of his life overseas in French and American schools and had little political experience, the fact that he was cut from a different cloth from his father (unlike the redoubtable Kpatcha, who looked and acted the very embodiment of the African dictator) made him acceptable to a post-Cold War international community eager to move beyond the dictatorship era. But also Faure's youthfulness and inexperience ensured his dependence on older members of the ruling elite. Indeed, four years later, many see him as little more than a puppet of members of the ancien régime.

This "government coup," as the opposition was quick to label it, triggered an outbreak of violence in Lomé's opposition neighborhoods and swift condemnation from the international community. The Western embassies, as well as the Economic Community of West African States (ECOWAS) and the African Union (AU), warned that Togo risked new sanctions and hinted at military intervention if Faure remained in power without an electoral mandate. "The era of dictatorships and coups in Africa is over," declared South Africa's Thabo Mbeki, speaking directly to the Togo crisis on behalf of the AU. Not willing to risk the disapprobation of the international community, the regime ceded to the pressure and scheduled an election for late April 2005.

The three-month interregnum turned out to be another classic moment in Togolese politics—a moment of disorder and state of emergency from which the ruling elite was once again able to draw advantage. New elections and the uncertainties of the moment simply presented them with another opportunity to consolidate their strengths and exploit opposition weakness. This they did by (now) nominating Faure to run for president, and then putting all the resources of the Eyadéma fortune at his disposal. Attempting to present himself as presidential, Faure flew around the continent in his father's jet to solicit "advice" from other heads of state—Qadhafi, Bongo, Obasanjo, Kufuor, Campaoré; he embarked on an American-style whistle-stop campaign throughout the countryside, with large entourage in tow; he blanketed towns with billboard pictures of himself promising "a new beginning" and "change within stability." Meanwhile, the opposition not only was unable to keep up—for want of funds—but also, once again, seemed in disarray, unsure whether or not to boycott the election, disagreeing over candidates—and in the end putting forward a seventy-three-year old Olympio proxy, Akitani Bob, who failed to inspire, especially among the younger generation.[19]

Election day itself showed the regime in full command of its usual tricks in steering the election toward a single predetermined outcome. They foiled an opposition party attempt to track the vote in select precincts by closing the party's bureau and confiscating its computers—arguing that the opposition had not applied to the national electoral committee for permission to monitor the vote. (Here serendipity also played into the hands of the regime, for the EU refused to send monitors on less than three months' notice.) They engaged in fraud in polling stations throughout the country.

(An acquaintance who volunteered at a polling place in the north—a young democrat whose civic pride drove him to want to help usher in the new dispensation—said he was so discouraged by the vote-switching he witnessed—members of the ruling party changing votes for Akitani Bob to votes for Faure—that he would never volunteer again.) In Lomé, in a widely publicized moment—aired on France's TV5 and circulated on the Internet—a French film crew captured Togolese soldiers rushing a voting station in the opposition neighborhood of Bè and carrying off ballot boxes. Cleverly, again showing its ability to play the new international game of parrying with critique—and indeed demonstrating a flair for deconstructing the apparent transparency of meaning conveyed by the image—the government responded by suggesting that the footage failed to show what happened *before* the soldiers rushed in, namely an attempt by members of the political opposition to stuff the ballot boxes. Thus, they argued, the soldiers were protecting rather than stealing the boxes. Other government sympathizers asked whether the soldiers had been positively identified as such. "It's easy to obtain a soldier's uniform, so how do we know the 'soldiers' in the video footage were not really members of the opposition dressed up as soldiers, attempting to discredit the government?"

Not surprisingly, when Faure was announced "winner" of the April election, violence erupted again. In the opposition neighborhoods of Bè and Kodjoviakopé, protestors erected roadblocks with tree trunks and burning tires—and engaged in pitched battle with government troops. In the same neighborhoods, the houses of French and Lebanese expatriates were sacked (while those of Americans and Germans were spared)—actions motivated by the calculus supporters/opponents of the regime, and indicative of the widespread perception that local electoral outcomes were also driven by international agendas. In another, more tragic example of local populations standing in for international interests, eight immigrants from Mali, mistakenly thought to be from Niger, were killed by a mob in apparent retribution for the fact that the Niger-ien president of ECOWAS—widely believed to have been bought off by the regime—endorsed the electoral outcome.

The overriding topic of discussion amongst Togolese in the weeks immediately after the election was the international community's muted response to the fraudulent outcome. The United States and Germany, strong critics of the dictatorship during the 1990s, met the announcement that Faure had won with the tepid insistence that he form a coalition government, set an early date for legislative elections, and continue to work towards reform—read by all as de facto support of the election's outcome. Most outrageously for many Togolese, French President Chirac congratulated Faure on the vote and promised French support of the new regime—a follow-up to his February lament that, with Eyadéma's passing, he had "lost a close friend," a comment that, needless to say, generated disbelief in Togolese quarters.[20]

French loyalty to Eyadéma has long puzzled and infuriated many Togolese, and has provided endless fodder for discussion. Conspiracy thinking provides the most common explanation for France's enduring support of the regime: that the original crime, the death of Sylvanus Olympio in 1963, was a French crime—they wanted Olympio out because of his strong ties to Britain, and a French soldier, not Eyadéma, killed Olympio on the steps of the US Embassy; thus, as quid pro quo for Eyadéma's taking the fall for the assassination, the French promised eternal support. Another popular theory is that France has long used Togo as a staging ground—a "laboratory," as one critic put it—for its experiments in political overrule in Africa, especially during the post-Cold War era when the Elysée continued to support dictator-friends against democratic-populist movements. Thus, Togo was one of the first African countries to hold a national conference in the early 1990s and became the test case for how to finesse a democratic (anti-French) opposition; Togo was the first to parry the international human rights inquiry with the counter-inquiry; Eyadéma was at the front of his class (of African post-Cold War presidents) in agreeing to and then abandoning a commitment to the two-term limit; Togolese security forces (with the help of French advisors) excelled in developing advanced techniques of intelligence, torture, and border control.

Whatever the merits of these explanations, it is clearly the case that France's attachment to the regime, and especially to a stable Togo, is also due to the economic and affective ties built up during a century of colonial and postcolonial rule and to the ongoing presence of a sizeable French population in Lomé. "Dictatorships are business's best friend," a Togolese acquaintance commented recently in discussing the bond between Eyadéma and the Elysée. "They provide stability and a knowable environment."

The geopolitics of the larger region, and the shifts of the post-9/11 period, were also clearly in play at this time, informing not only France's reaction but also that of the larger international community. The Ghana-Togo-Benin coastal corridor—bookended by war-torn Sierra Leone-Liberia-Cote d'Ivoire on one side and unpredictable/unruly Nigeria on the other—is an island of stability in a subregion otherwise racked by conflict and ruinous civil wars. Civil war in Togo, a virtual certainty if Gilchrist came to power, would put the entire subregion at risk. Such fears were fueled in summer 2005 by rumors that decommissioned Sierra Leonian and Liberian child soldiers in search of the next war were being recruited by members of the Togolese opposition to overthrow the regime.

Finally, post-9/11 reasoning—and something of a return to the politics of the Cold War—was informing metropolitan policy toward Africa as well. Today, when the United States looks at West Africa, it sees a vast impoverished region filled with weak or "failed" states and a sizeable Muslim population, and imagines it as a possible terrorist training ground. Not coincidentally, the US renewed economic aid and sent military advisors to the Sahelian countries Mali, Niger, Mauritania, and Chad in 2004 (Smith 2004; Kaplan 2005), and sent naval ships to patrol the Gulf of Guinea in 2006 (Miles 2006). In 2007, it created AFRICOM, a Department of Defense initiative focusing on diplomatic, economic, and humanitarian aid to African countries, with the larger aim of creating a security toehold in the area (www.africom.mil/). Then, too, West Africa has significant oil reserves, with projections that it will provide the United States with 30 percent of its crude by 2015 (importantly, oil that is also coveted by global rival China). For all these reasons—the security and stability of the region, the knowability and predictability of the regime—the international community was willing to tolerate, if not secretly celebrate, the continuation of authoritarian rule in Togo.

## 2008–2009

If the international community's attitude toward West Africa in the current (post-9/11) conjuncture bears similarity to its orientation during the Cold War era—when the enemy/friend distinction, more than the nature of the political system (democratic/authoritarian), defined the political field and determined political allegiance and support—the same cannot be said of the state itself. During the 1990s, the strong state inherited from the Cold War years, centered around the person of the dictator, became a shell of its former self, and a diffuse and elusive entity. Starved of money, privatized and criminalized, the post-Cold War Togolese state withdrew from the social field, leaving that to the NGOs and the churches.

The death of the dictator continued and amplified these trends. Throughout 2007 and 2008, it was common to hear people comment that today, unlike during the time of Eyadéma, when everything went through the dictator, no one knows who is in charge. "Some decisions are made here, others there, with competition among all and confusion everywhere," one put it. It is tempting to read this apparent diffusion of power—and corresponding shift from vertical to horizontal structures of authority (Hardt and Negri 2001; Ferguson 2006)—as due to the fact that a young and inexperienced son, with little force of personality and shallow ties to the ruling elite, has replaced a father who spent four decades building his personality cult and power base. And there is certainly some truth in this view. Faure *is* young and seems at pains to distance himself from the cult of personality that defined his father's reign—with consequence for his ability to govern effectively. There is also truth in the widespread belief that jealousies and power struggles among Eyadéma's sons have hamstrung Faure's ability to carry out reform and have narrowed his horizon of possibilities. One hears a frequent refrain on the streets of Lomé: "Eyadéma's sons think Togo is their cake, the inheritance their father left them. And they all want their share."

The widely publicized scandal—and international embarrassment—over the Togolese soccer team at the 2006 World Cup provides a case in point. The national soccer federation's failure to pay its players the going international rate, producing a near-boycott, was due to the fact that the federation's head, Rock ("Rock and Roll") Gnassingbé, a Eyadéma son, wanted to pocket the money FIFA had allocated Togo for qualifying for the Cup—since he saw this as his chance to cash in his inheritance. Moreover, and most tellingly, Faure's inability to reign Rock in was due to the fact that Faure was indebted to his brothers for being in office in the first place. "It was us who selected you and ensured your election," Rock is said to have told Faure when the latter attempted to bring him to heel.

The same is true of Kpatcha, the bullying son who was minister of defense during Faure's first three years in office and who oversaw Lomé's tax-free zone. When Faure tried to loosen Kpatcha's control of the port, the latter responded that it was their father who gave it to him and that Faure had no right to deprive him of his inheritance. Tensions have continued to mount between the two and, when rumors circulated in summer 2008 that a Kpatcha-led coup was imminent (and another: that Kpatcha would run for office against Faure in the 2010 presidential election), Gabon's Bongo was called in to mediate.

In April 2009, the plot thickened even more. Faure received a tip, some say from US intelligence, that Kpatcha intended to stage a coup attempt while his older brother was away in China. Faure responded quickly, sending the military's "quick-strike force" to Kpatcha's house on a Sunday night where a gunfight broke out, killing five. Under house arrest, Kpatcha nevertheless managed to escape to the entrance of the US Embassy (the same site, not without irony, the Togo blogs were quick to point out, where his father had killed Sylvanus Olympio in 1963). The embassy denied him access, and Kpatcha was arrested by security forces and imprisoned, along with a cadre of high-ranking military officers. In the ensuing weeks, the rumors continued to pile on top of one another: Who else was involved and how deep into the military did the plot go? Did this episode signal a recursive north-south split within the Eyadéma clan itself—Kpatcha's mother is northern, Faure's southern—that foreshadows a return to ethnic politics? Did Faure stage the entire event to remove his main rival in the upcoming 2010 election? Again, whatever the "real" of this incident, it was another "event" in Togolese politics, with all the Shakespearian dramatic twists to which its citizens have become accustomed, dominating the airwaves and, once again, deflecting attention from more pressing issues.

Despite these power struggles among the sons of Eyadéma—and the diffusion of authority and control they index—as well as Faure's youthfulness and inexperience, the horizontality and diffuseness of state power at this time owes even more to those broader global processes associated with the neoliberal post-Cold War moment—the privatization and criminalization of the state, and the circulation of new sources of income beyond the state's control. Political control and sovereignty today lie as much in the hands of the NGOs, and the World Bank and IMF (Hardt and Negri 2001, 2005; Ferguson 2001 2006), as in the Togolese state apparatus, and the state itself has in many ways become another individual—or rather a loosely connected, often incoherent, set of individuals and interests—in search of income, fleecing international agencies and actors, in pursuit of their own ends. Indeed, focusing on the ongoing soap opera of the Eyadéma children, like fixating on the melodrama of the two families (Eyadéma/Olympio) that have dominated talk about Togolese politics for four decades, or investing too much explanatory power in north/south (tribalist) splits—as do many Togolese themselves, as well as Togo watchers in the international community—once again fetishizes and distracts attention from power's true nature and source.

---

Sidewalk radio in summer 2006 was busy adding a final ironic brushstroke to the Eyadéma legend. Piqued by the fact that, unlike at the funerals of other African heads of state, there was no open casket at Eyadéma's, those on the street had it that he had died not, as the official version suggested, on a plane to Israel but rather in his own chambers and of his own doing. On the evening of his death in February 2005, rumor had it, he dined and then returned to his quarters in an intoxicated state, locking the door before going for his bath. After turning on the hot water, he slipped and hit his head, falling into the tub. Unconscious, he was scalded to death. (Another version: that an electrical device fell into the bath water, electrocuting him.) The water mixed with the potentate's blood and seeped under the door, alerting a servant to enter, where she discovered Eyadéma's grotesquely scalded body—a body so disfigured that it had to be withheld from viewing at the funeral.[21]

There seems something entirely fitting about this story from the street of the death of the dictator, organized as it is around a string of Lévi-Straussian inversions: one who had been impervious to multiple assassination attempts and who claimed superordinate powers of protection is brought down in the most banal of ways, slipping to his death in the bathtub; he who spent his political life torturing others tortures himself to death, with his own demise announced by a trickle of blood under the door; the body of this man, so much a part of his charisma while alive and a symbol of potency throughout (because of its size and excessive sexuality) was so absent from his ceremonies at death, with the final image of the dictator's body one of putrefying flesh. And, yet, for all these inversions, these subaltern renderings of the death of the potentate, a constant of his reign remained the order of the day after his passing: the narrativizing and rumoring that constituted one of Eyadéma's most powerful technologies of rule—the fact that he was always "good to think"—continued to operate, rendering him as multiple, elusive, and present/absent as ever.

# TWO

# The End of History

It would be hard to overestimate the significance of the new Pentecostal churches in the post-Cold War cultural life of Ghana and Togo, especially among the middle classes in the capital cities.[1] In Accra and Lomé alone, there are hundreds of new charismatic churches, some with thousands of seats. On Sundays, the city is dead and the churches, large open-air buildings with booming sound systems, are filled with smartly dressed congregants. Many partake during the week as well—in daily prayer meetings, in Friday "all-nights," in counseling sessions—and, periodically, in "conferences" and "seminars" with visiting pastors, in "crusades" to heal the sick and win converts, in "deliverance" sessions to exorcise demons. If you visit the University of Ghana at six in the morning on a school day, you'll find the soccer pitch filled with thousands of students praying and speaking in tongues. Board a plane in Accra or Lagos, and you'll bear witness to collective prayers before takeoff and landing. Moreover, as Birgit Meyer (2004a) has suggested, Ghana's public sphere is now a "Pentecostalite" one, in which films and soaps routinely index Pentecostal themes and radio talk shows casually reference the Holy Spirit. Increasingly in the bars and nightclubs of Lomé, the music is church disco ("Jesus is the only one, he's my true love"). "The charismaticization of Lomé's nightlife?" I suggested to a friend as we walked by a string of bars on the Boulevard Circulaire all blasting religious-pop. "Yes," she replied, with an approving smile.[2]

It is no accident that the charismatic churches burst onto the scene during the 1990s when the Cold War state was in eclipse—and this not simply because the potentate was no longer able to censor the political and religious life of the nation as before but also because of the new churches' fit with the antiauthoritarian spirit of the times. In important ways, the churches stepped into the gap left by a state that was forced to withdraw from the social field, thus also usurping the place of the dictator in the national imaginary. Moreover, through their attacks on tradition and gerontocracy in the villages, the new churches have played a crucial role in the unraveling of the indirect rule system that tied state to rural. This chapter explores the ways in which charismatic Christianity opens a space for the constitution of a new public sphere, reconfiguring sensibilities and attachments away from older forms of authority and familiar modes of thought to produce a fresh vision of the political and of a world not yet born.

## Sociology

An initial, more sociological, reading of the Pentecostal phenomenon in West Africa is to see the new churches as proxy for an eviscerated post-Cold War state, in part filling the gap left by the state in providing social services (cf. Bornstein 2003; Meyer 2004b; Bornstein and Redfield forthcoming; Comaroff forthcoming). In Ghana, there will soon be more church- than state-owned universities, and the ubiquitous orphanages are largely church-funded. In Togo, the new churches are coming to be seen as development agencies, responsible for the building of new clinics and elementary schools, and sponsoring AIDS research and treatment. Significantly, the financial base of the churches is built up less through foreign donations than through tithing within the congregation—from one perspective, a new form of "taxation." An interesting squabble took place in summer 2004 in Accra when it was revealed that one of the large Nigerian charismatic churches there, Winner's Chapel, was repatriating tithes raised from its Accra branch to the parent church back home—a not insignificant sum of $200,000 a month. One of the principal commentaries about the repatriation scheme, commentaries which dominated the public sphere in Accra for several weeks, was to ask what effect such capital flight might have on the economic development of Ghana. "So now Ghanaians are paying for the development of Nigeria?" one talk-radio call-in listener asked rhetorically.

But the churches do much more for their members than merely provide state functions. They offer a type of total institution or total culture which stands in for the family in otherwise anomic urban conditions (van Dijk 1997; Meyer 2004b; Englund 2007). Many of the churches in Accra and Lomé are organized into "neighborhoods," so that networked members of the church who live near one another can meet during the week for prayer sessions or call one another when in need. Singles and youth groups go on weekend outings at least once a month. And the church serves as proxy for

3. Charismatic church, Lomé 2009

family and village in regulating marriage, encouraging believers to marry within the church and insisting on premarital chastity. In one church I attended in Accra, several couples were discovered (during the counseling sessions that precede marriage) to have engaged in premarital sex and were paraded before the congregation, before being banished to the back pews for a full year. Extramarital sex is also considered a serious sin, especially when a woman sleeps with the husband of another.[3]

Most significantly—here still within the ambit of a sociology of the new churches—these communities of believers instill codes of conduct and orientations toward the everyday that provide a virtual blueprint for disciplining the post-Cold War citizen-subject into the neoliberal economy (cf. Comaroff forthcoming). Believers are expected to be hardworking, honest, frugal, sexually chaste, abstemious, and—textbook Weber—to see evidence of their faith as success within the new economy.[4] "I want everyone to pray for success this week—that you will get the job you have been looking for, find the flat you've been seeking, get the money you need. . . . Praise the Lord . . . This is your reward for living a Christian life," sermonized a prosperity pastor at Action Faith Ministries in Accra in June 2004. A Lomé family

4. Lomé prosperity pastor, 2009

I know, that rises at four in the morning to pray together, asks daily for the success of family members—that a son will receive the job he has applied for, that a nephew will succeed in school, that a daughter will pass her baccalaureate, that a land dispute will be favorably resolved. Literacy, too, and middleclass-ness, is everywhere performed and on display.[5] Thus, church members are urged to take notes on the sermon (in small notebooks tucked into purses and breast pockets) and to write down Bible passages to study and reflect upon during the week, and services are simultaneously translated from the vernacular (Twi in Accra, Mina in Lomé) into English or French, or vice versa—not only an attempt to draw in multiple constituencies but also to project an educated, cosmopolitan, internationalist image.[6]

## Narrative

The new churches are narrative-machines as much as welfare societies and new economy interpellation devices. They generate stories—often fantastic stories—about the world today and the place of West Africa in that world. These are stories that appeal especially to those who are weary of the old narratives that have for too long defined Africa as victim of forces and histories beyond its control. They are also ones that undermine the authority relations of the old regime that sutured a Cold War state to chiefs and elders in the rural areas. I mention here three such narratives, each a tale of rupture—of a "break with the past" (Meyer 1998, 1999a; van Dijk 1998, 2001a; Engelke 2004; Robbins 2007)—whether collective or personal.

The first is about development and its corollary, the disavowal of village religion/tradition. West Africa is underdeveloped, members of the church say, because Satan inhabits the villages. Extirpate the Devil and all his manifestations (the worship of spirits and ancestors), and West Africa will develop quickly. A pastor who missionizes in the village where I conduct research in northern Togo gave the following example: were it not for a sacred forest that climbs the highest ridge in the community (and whose taboos forbid human intervention—cultivation, house construction—within its boundaries), they could build a road that would, as he put it, "develop the community overnight. It is pagan beliefs like this that are the cause of Africa's poverty today." When I asked whether it wasn't instead Europe that had "underdeveloped" and further impoverished Africa (Frank 1971; Rodney 1981), he admitted familiarity with such an explanation ("oh, yes, they taught us that at the university") and acknowledged that that might also be true, but he said that Togolese needed to get their own house in order first and then Europe would make up for past sins.

This "blame tradition" story was reiterated in a different register by a Togolese schoolteacher from the north. In describing the extravagant spending that went into a recent funeral in which three cows were sacrificed, he upbraided the family for putting their limited means to such ends rather than toward development and material wellbeing—and blamed "tradition" for obligating them to do so. "One cow would have been enough to honor the dead man *and* give everyone a piece of meat. Three was totally unnecessary, and, even worse, much of the meat rotted because there was too much to give away."[7] His commentary came as a surprise, for despite being Christian he has always been partial to village religion—thus indicating how widespread is the view today that development and tradition are antithetical.

A lecture by the visiting American charismatic pastor T. L. Osborn, at a conference of pastors in Lomé in March 2006, drew the distinction between village religion and Christianity sharply. The difference between the "sacrificial" religion of the Old Testament and Christianity, Osborn asserted, is that in the former sins were merely "covered over" for a short period of time ("until the next communal sacrifice"), while in the latter they were removed once and for all. "The religion of the Old Testament was a false religion, a religion that prevented people from doing God's work. They had no way of protecting themselves from the Devil. Sacrificing animals does nothing but deceive. The only meaningful sacrifice in all of history was that of Jesus, who gave himself up so that we could be saved, who spilled his blood to take away our sins. Animal sacrifice is wrong; the sacrifice of Christ, history's final sacrifice, is what has saved us and makes living without sin possible." Osborn never mentioned Africa, but his point was transparent to all. The "religion of the Old Testament" was code for village religion in Africa today.

The rejection of tradition, especially animal sacrifice, is not merely intellectual and distanced but also deeply visceral. In 2001, when I took a group of US study abroad students to the village in northern Togo where I work, we were greeted by the killing of a chicken and a goat. The Ghanaian bus driver who accompanied us, a devout Pentecostal, was beside himself at the prospect of animals being offered up. "My church forbids animal sacrifice and won't allow me to witness it," he said nervously. Then, abruptly, and despite assurances that these were nothing more than welcoming gifts (because not offered to spirits or ancestors), he snatched one of the students' cameras and snapped a dozen close-up pictures of the bloodletting. He wouldn't discuss his actions afterward, but he seemed to be drawing on local representations that associate cameras with the capture and neutralization of spirits—thus preventing efficacious ritual action. Similarly, a Togolese friend, a fervent charismatic whose origins are in these same northern villages, is reluctant to return to her homeland for fear of witches and of excessive contact with the sacrificial acts of her northern brethren. These refusals go beyond a simple desire to avoid condoning behaviors with which they disagree. In both cases, there was something deep and embodied—as if a fear of bodily contagion—about these individuals' abjection of village religion.

---

In demonizing tradition and waging "spiritual warfare" against it (Meyer 1998; Shaw 2007), the Pentecostal imagination spares no violence—attacking manifestations of the Devil with a virulence that recalls nothing so much as the way in which the dictatorial state dealt with its subjects. Witness the following passage from the popular pamphlet, *Delivered from the Powers of Darkness*, an autobiographical account by the Nigerian charismatic Emmanuel Eni (1988) of his life with the Devil before being reborn as a Christian. As an agent for a Satanic spirit of the sea, Eni is sent on a mission to his home village:

The Queen of the Coast [a demonic spirit of the sea] gave me what she called her 'first assignment'—I should go to my village and kill my uncle, a prominent powerful native doctor who was responsible, according to her, for the death of my parents. I obeyed and went but having not killed before, I hadn't the courage to kill him, rather I destroyed his medicines and rendered him powerless. As a result of this act he lost all his customers till this date. I came back to give a report of my assignment but she was wrath with me. She said, the consequence of disobeying her instructions was death, but because of her love for me she would send me back to the same village to kill two elders who she said gave a helping hand in the killing of my parents. Whether this was a punishment for disobeying her or not I did not know; however, I obeyed and went back to the village and 'managed' to kill these men and sent their blood to her. (Eni 1988:20)

A few pages later, he is sent on another deadly mission:

I had no human feelings nor mercy in my heart any longer. I went into operation immediately and destroyed five duplex at a go. They all sunk inside the ground with all its inhabitants. This happened in Lagos in August 1982. The contractor was held responsible for not laying a good foundation and he paid dearly for it. A lot of destructions happening in the world today are not man made. The devil's duty is to steal, kill and destroy. I say it again Satan has no 'free gift.' (Eni 1988:23)

To counter Satan's temptations, followers of the Holy Spirit wage their own "warfare" against the Devil and his allies—among them, "demons" of the village and those who patronize them in village ceremonies. Indeed, despite the fact that a not-yet born-again Eni was here working for a demonic spirit, these passages are easily read as emblematic of the way in which the Pentecostal imaginary itself wages spiritual warfare against village religion. The assault on spirits/ancestors/witches during exorcisms is palpable and bodily, with pastors shouting at and sometimes striking congregants who are possessed by "demons." In visits back to the village, devotees not infrequently desecrate spirit shrines and uproot ancestral stones from family homesteads. Accused witches are beaten and sometimes exiled to witch camps, where their incarceration is total and prison-like. Inhabiting a culture that has long normalized dictatorial modes of violence in policing and disciplining subjects—though now reversing and disavowing the potentate's embrace of tradition, here punishing the village for its attachment to spirits and the ancestors—charismatic consciousness is no stranger to the necropolitical (Mbembe 2003). Borrowing state sovereignty's toolkit, it too suspends everyday norms, creates exceptional states and carceral regimes, and wages war on those who defy its authority.

---

As mentioned earlier, and as Birgit Meyer (1999a, 1999b, 2004a) has described for southern Ghana, the "Pentecostalite" demonization of tradition is written into Nigerian and Ghanaian popular cinema. A theme repeated over and over in these films is that of the urban middle-class family with ongoing ties to the village, ties invariably of an occult nature. As the plot unwinds, the family is destroyed by jealousy and village sorcery (and viewers are implicitly instructed to leave tradition and the old deities behind). The round of Nigerian films airing in Accra in summer 2004 went a step further, transforming these more secular Pentecostal themes into overtly religious ones, with conversion/baptism/rebirth and encounters with the Holy Spirit built right into the narratives themselves.

The brilliance of the Pentecostal metaphysic is that it allows believers to have their cake and eat it too: distancing themselves from village religion—and, not coincidentally, from the social obligations that accompany ongoing ties to the village (van Dijk 1998; Meyer 2004b)—while nevertheless remaining thoroughly within its logic and animating categories. Not only do charismatics fully believe in the ongoing existence and efficacy of the spirits and witches of the village, albeit demonizing them, but also they continue to inhabit a village world of opaque signs (that index the machinations of invisible forces) in need of constant hermeneutical attention. Those urban charismatics I know search their everyday worlds as well as their dreams for signs of the workings of malevolent forces, as well as of the Holy Spirit. When a friend experienced a close call while driving home in Lomé traffic on the anniversary of her father's death from a car accident, she said it was the work of demons—"spirits of death trying to steal my life"—and thanked Jesus that she had been protected. When she dreamt of apparitions hovering over her bed one night, presences that she was able to chase away, she again claimed triumph over evil spirits.

Meyer (2002, 2003) reports a fascinating phenomenon among film-watching Ghanaians: that many offered as evidence for the existence of the occult the fact that they had seen such phenomena in popular film itself. Indeed, in the dozens of Nigerian films I watched in Accra theaters in summer 2004, the one moment when people stopped talking and cell phones went unanswered was the moment when a compact with a spirit or demon was shown or a witch's actions were exposed. The cinematic here serves to visualize and make public that which, in a pre-cinematic world, had remained concealed (for the world of spirits is invisible to the human eye) and could only be accessed through the imagination—thus also, ironically, making the occult seem more "real." Moreover, the story that locates Satan in the villages generates a thousand urban legends about the inner workings of the occult in those locales, stories that circulate and feed the imagination and voyeuristic impulses of the urban middle classes, again holding close that world they otherwise strive to keep at a distance.[8]

Here, then, is a textbook example of Foucault's (1980, [1978] 1990) reworking of the repression hypothesis: Pentecostalism's demonizing of village religion has done nothing so much as lead to an efflorescence, a promiscuous proliferation, of images of spirits and witches—in the popular imagination, in local films and soaps, and in the churches themselves, where sermons go into graphic detail about encounters with demonic forces. A sublime irony, however, for much of this occurs in the cities and among those elites intent on distancing themselves from the religion of the villages.

Note, too, the mapping of the West African landscape that accompanies Pentecostal views of the village. In representing West Africa's vast rural spaces as Satanic, the Pentecostal believer constructs a spiritual cartography that opposes village and city as those who are lost to the Devil and those saved by Christ. This map cuts longstanding connectivities between rural and urban, replacing them with relays among Pentecostal nodes in Lagos-Lomé-Accra-Abidjan. Moreover, national borders seem to matter little, not only because they are transgressed by Christian flows along the coastal corridor but also because mission work in the Satanic rural areas is no longer strictly contained by national borders (as during the early independence period): the Assemblies of God in Lomé today sends missionaries to Mali and Niger, into the Satanic (also Muslim) north, as well as to rural villages in its home country. This is a mapping that complements that of the NGOs (see chapter 5), who see the rural village as site of poverty in need of "saving"—focusing, however, on the poverty of the soil rather than of the spirit.

While this "blame tradition" story echoes earlier modernization theory narratives about African development and the obstacles posed by "traditional culture," and while one might thus be tempted to see the latest round of globalization and its ideologies as little more than a recycling of that earlier (1960s) moment, there are also significant differences. For one, the orientalizing impulse has been utterly indigenized and domesticated, and has a mass popular-cultural appeal that it lacked in the earlier moment.

For another, the contemporary narrativization is empowering in a way that the earlier one was not, precisely because it is seen and experienced as self-authored. Moreover, while not easy for the anthropologist to admit, the church's rejection of tradition—of local ritual and cosmology—might also be read as a rejection of the colonial, and, ironically, because done in the name of a religion with Euro-American roots, as an attempt to decolonize the mind. To wit, it was colonialism that "invented" chiefs and village tradition as technologies of power, projects and technologies that were reissued by postcolonial dictatorships. Charismatics see themselves as attempting to free themselves from the weight of this (to them) oppressive tradition.

One of the most telling aspects of the Pentecostal phenomenon is its refusal of the old structures of authority and mediation. Not only do the new churches see themselves as working outside the chain of colonial/postcolonial authority structures, which connected a metropolitan country to a colonial-and-then-postcolonial state to a hinterland, but also there is a large-scale rejection of the two main colonial ("orthodox" or "mission") churches in Togo and Ghana—the Roman Catholic and the Presbyterian—both because of their association with the older structures of authority *and* because of their liturgical reliance on the mediating power of the church (in administering the sacraments). The Pentecostal church is precisely about a more direct/spontaneous connection between believer and deity (van Dijk 1998), a nonmediated experience of the Holy Spirit (as exemplified through healing or speaking in tongues). A charismatic friend commented that her confessional moments are now only between herself and God. If she has sinned, she owns up to God alone, in a moment of prayer in the quiet of her room, asking forgiveness. A West African Protestant reformation this.

In refusing the older authority structures—and the strong identifications with nation and locality that accompanied them—the new religious affiliations are generative of identities that are translocal (here, globally Christian) in nature (cf. Meyer 1998, 2004b; van Dijk 1998, 2001b; Maxwell 2008; Marshall-Fratini 2001; Englund 2003). The visiting American pastor T. L. Osborn's lecture in March 2006 made the point explicit: "The born-again Christian has no nation or region that he calls home. He is a member of a single world-wide community, and speaks one language. The different religions and cultures of the world cease to exist for this Christian." Sunday sermons routinely make the same point, offering accounts of the defeat of tradition/Satan in diverse locales across the world—the Philippines, Mexico, Russia, Kenya, Rwanda—and the entry of remote communities into the global community of Christ. Notice, then, the very different orientation of these churches toward tradition from the earlier colonial mission

(Catholic and Presbyterian) churches, which worked within existing state and local contexts, and which accommodated local beliefs, even hybridizing their own. This earlier "postcolonial" sensibility—of accommodation and hybridization—is roundly rejected by the new churches, which seek a transcendence of the local in favor of a Christian global identity.

But the new charismatic churches also resist contemporary transnational structures of hierarchy/centralization and influence—acknowledging roots in the US or Nigeria, perhaps, but resisting obeisance—and see themselves as radically autonomous. Why else are there a thousand differently named charismatic-Pentecostal churches in Accra alone, all raising their own money through a system of tithes? "Our way of worshipping God is being imitated by everyone now, including you in America," a Lomé charismatic responded when I asked whether she saw her mode of worship as derivative. Indeed, in a striking historical reversal, US pastors are now traveling to Africa to be ordained—because they see African Christianity as a purer form—before returning "home" to engage in "mission" work (Jenkins 2002). To repeat, those I know see themselves as engaged in independent and autonomous cultural/religious authorship; Christianity, for them, is not something originating elsewhere that they have remade or enhanced. They see a direct connection between God and West Africa, and God and believer, that requires no other form of mediation.

The new churches' resistance to centralized hierarchical forms of organization and their embrace of radical autonomy or democracy have produced a decentralized networked form of organization (Castells 1996; Hardt and Negri 2001, 2005). Churches are horizontally—informally, loosely—tied to other churches across a vast field of charismatic worship that spans the West African countries of Nigeria, Benin, Togo, Ghana, and Cote d'Ivoire. Pastors and "prophets" travel across this terrain, moving from country to country, visiting churches, delivering sermons, and counseling congregants. Pentecostal pamphlets, cassettes, and videos—many in English, originating in Nigeria—circulate throughout the region as well. Sometimes congregants' attachments to a particular church run deep, but often not. I know many who migrate from church to church, spending a few months at one before moving on to another. "All of the churches I attend are charismatic and open themselves to the Holy Spirit," one told me, "so I feel at home in any of them. I am just looking for those pastors and churches that will inspire me and make my life better."

Caveats are in order here. While much in the Pentecostal moment suggests a positive break with the past—a displacement of the fascist state, a refusal of patriarchal authority, a move beyond often stultifying local identifications, an agentive seizing of the current moment—there is nevertheless also a significant way in which many of those identifications are smuggled back in, and indeed in which the necropolitical (Mbembe 2003) might be said to be at the center of charismatic consciousness. Those imaginaries that describe the work of Satan in the villages, and that seek to extirpate him therefrom, are inordinately violent, as are the commentaries on, and the unblinking endorsements of, US policy in the Middle East, a site of the necropolitical if there ever was one.[9] Moreover, the surveilling, tithe-extracting church strikes one as nothing so much as the surveilling, extractive postcolonial state, and libidinal attachments to the church as drawing on and recycling similar attachments to the sovereign dictator. Are these not authoritarian imaginaries, and is this not also the world of the necropolitical?

It is thus tempting to interpret the turn to the Holy Spirit in the 1990s as little more than compensation for loss of the dictator. Indeed, the church has not only taken on state functions (building schools, clinics, orphanages) but also partially fills the space in the public imaginary previously occupied by the sovereign. Moreover, God, church, and pastor serve as authority figures in the regulation of everyday life and are celebrated in ways—with singing and dancing—not unlike those previously reserved for the potentate. A connection between the two sovereignty regimes was nowhere drawn so explicitly as in sermons in Lomé at the moment of the electoral crisis in 2005 that compared God's to the state's "sovereignty," albeit finding the latter wanting. Nevertheless, while borrowing from state imaginaries, charismatic Christianity also transforms them, displacing identification with sovereign and nation onto modes of belonging that are transregional and global, and horizontally rather than vertically linked. Moreover, despite the strong authority of God and pastor, the churches encourage broad-based participation and identification across ethnicity (cf. Englund 2007), and divine sovereignty, while transcendent and absolute, is also immanent, global, and available to a broad public.

A second narrative with strong appeal to Ghanaian and Togolese charismatics, and one that is related to the first (as psychology to sociology or history), is that of the fall of humanity and its subsequent rescue by Christ—and of the bearing of this narrative on personal histories of wrongdoing and sin. The tale of Satan tempting humanity into sin and desire, followed by humanity's rescue by God—through Christ's crucifixion, death, and resurrection—appeals to those living in a world, like that of the urban West African, that is saturated with temptation and longing, on the one hand, and with morality and discipline, on the other. This is a world of strong desires and limited means, of pleasure and responsibility, of commitment to and inevitable betrayal of family and friends, of guilt over personal pasts best left behind. It is here that the Pentecostal story of forgiveness has considerable bite, promising liberation from past misdeeds and a new start. "I know that my God will forgive my sins if I confess them to him with sincerity and humility. He is above all a compassionate God," a congregant told me. "I can then move on and begin anew." She went on to contrast the liberating effect of the Christian doctrine of sin with what she perceived as its opposite in the culture of the village, where sins were admitted and forgiven but—because of vicious village rumor mills—never forgotten. Is not this narrative of and desire for a personal rupture—a leaving behind of unsavory and sinful pasts—also related to the narrative of cultural and historical rupture and forgetting to which so many seem drawn in this millennial moment? And, indeed, what a powerful set of intersections—of the personal with the cultural and political—Pentecostal Christianity brings together in furthering its cause and attracting adherents.

A third narrative which captures the imagination of West African charismatic communities is that of the End Times—in which those born-again Christians will ascend to heaven to sit beside Christ and those sinners who are "left behind" will be condemned to a world of war and suffering ruled over by the Antichrist.[10] Thus, one must do all in one's power to resist the forces of Satan and live the Christian life, in preparation for the End, an end which may be right around the corner. This is a topic that routinely comes up in sermons: in predictions as to when the Rapture will occur (and in lengthy discussions of false predictions), in exhortations to believers to ready themselves ("if the world ended today, would you be ready?"), in discussions about the Antichrist (and his many guises and temptations).

This End Times narrative also provides a template for reading global politics. Thus, the Iraq war and the ongoing Israeli-Palestinian conflict provide/d endless fodder for discussions about biblical predictions as to when the Rapture would occur. Moreover, End Times thinking enters into readings of local history as well. A devotee explained the co-presence in Nigeria of megachurches and monstrous crime (outrageous Internet fraud, corruption beyond belief, serial murder, sorcery killings) in the following way: "Wherever you find true Christians you also find the Devil hard at work trying to undo the work of the Holy Spirit. Once Satan loses someone to Christ, he will try that much harder to win him back. This is why so many Christians are involved in sorcery. And it is why big thieves and strong Christians are found side by side in Nigeria." (She then added: "Someone like yourself who is not born again, you are already in the Devil's camp. So he doesn't have to work hard to keep you, and he doesn't need to give you the gifts of sorcery.") "But these are also signs that the end of the world is at hand—when thieves abound and the world is in chaos. And another sign: I recently saw on television that missionaries from Kenya have been sent to England to evangelize. Is this not what the Bible predicted would happen at the End—that the 'first shall be last, and the last first'?"

Again, a narrative of radical rupture—in this latter case, the most extreme of temporal breaks: an end of history as we know it.[11]

While the End Times narrative certainly operates in the most literal of registers, it works in others as well. One is as injunction to live the moral life, thus disciplining the everyday of the believer: Are you living like a Christian? Would you be ready if Christ returned today? Another is as template/exemplar of the way in which rupture and radical indeterminacy define a Pentecostal view of event and history more generally—not only of Christ's appearance at the end of time but also of the quotidian. Thus, those micro-encounters of the everyday—a chance meeting with a stranger, an unexpected phone call, a sudden flash of insight—are potentially pregnant with meaning and might lead to a radical shift in the life of the believer, even changing everything that went before. While a more dramatic version of historical rupture, to be sure, the End Times story is nevertheless no different in kind from those interventions of the Holy Spirit into the everyday. Its narrative prominence in the life of the church thus serves to condition congregants into an openness to a radical/millennialist orientation toward time and the everyday.

Such a nonlinear punctuated temporality (Guyer 2007) also resonates with those in other (non-Christian) domains described in subsequent chapters—in occult imaginaries (whose aim is to account for the unexpected), in development practice (where NGOs appear and disappear without apparent rhyme or reason), in the visa lottery (where "luck" or occult/charismatic manipulation is as important to success as methodical preparation). Immersed in a time and rhetoric of crisis, everyone, it seems, is hedging their bets—on the afterlife, on the lottery, on the miraculous appearance and capture of an NGO—hoping for an intercession that might be life-transforming.

I am suggesting that it is these fantastical narratives—about underdevelopment as sinfulness, about personal sin and redemption, about the End Times and the everyday—that animate the imagination and account for the charismatic moment as much as the more prosaic sociological indicators. Moreover, I see the appeal of these narratives as related to peoples' exhaustion with the older (Cold War) narratives that connected West Africa to the metropole, on the one hand, and celebrated (and connected the urban

5. "Keep watch because you do not know the day or the hour"
(of the End of Time), Lomé church 2009

middle classes to) tradition and the village, on the other. These new Pentecostal stories—stories of personal and cultural forgetting, and thus stories
that are fundamentally anti-hauntological in nature (cf. Nora 1972, 1989;
Connerton 1989; Gilroy 1993; Gordon 1996; Cole 2001; Shaw 2002, 2007;
Baucom 2005)—are very much about the death of such earlier narratives
(and the political-economic conditions that accompanied them) and about
the birth of a new (post-Cold War) world.[12] As such they are accounts that
empower and attempt to redefine historical agency—as less about a relationship to or debt with the past, or to a colonial/postcolonial other in the
present, and more about a nostalgia for the future.

## Affect

The charismatic experience also draws on another deep reservoir, on what
Deleuze and Guattari (1983, 1988) refer to as "affect." Affect is linked, to be
sure, to the social and semiotic, but it also escapes and transcends these. It is
something other than and beyond meaning alone, and something not simply reducible to psychological state. An affect is a disposition or orientation,

something between a feeling and an idea: an experience, an attitude, a sentiment, an intensity. Moreover, in Deleuzian terms (Hardt 1993, 2007; Holland 2002), it is something that "affects" or changes you, and those around you, something that moves you to action—and, in the charismatic case, something that breaks down boundaries of body-self and subjectivity.

West African charismatic religion strikes me as a brilliant generator of intensities and affects: of joy and happiness, of confidence and pride, of feelings of empowerment and importance (and, in the extreme, of narcissism), of vitality and vitalism, of optimism and hope, of humility, of fearlessness, and of intoxicating, even eroticized, attachments to the Holy Trinity (the words of a song popular in 2005: "Darling Jesus, take me in your arms . . . ").

At a Sunday service I attended in March 2006 at Friends of Christ Church in Lomé, the pastor deviated from the sermon to implore: "God loves you. Christ loves you. The Holy Spirit loves you. He is happy for you. God is happy for you. You are happy. You will be filled with happiness when you are next to God. You are special. God tells me you are special. Know that you are special. He will help you . . ." With each injunction, the thousand-strong congregation swelled, voicing its support, releasing ever-more-enthusiastic cries of approval. Ad-libbing, the pastor then led his followers in a fifteen minute prayer session during which congregants prayed out loud, each on their own, making requests of their God, palms open skyward, some gesticulating animatedly in the air, others pounding their sides, some falling to the ground in the aisles, all opening themselves to the power of the Holy Spirit, imploring the Spirit to enter them. "The power of God is in us. Allelujah," the pastor bellowed as he segued back to his sermon. "Amen," boomed the congregation.

A schoolteacher and recent charismatic convert put it like this:

The new churches make people feel good about themselves and give them the willpower to take control of their lives. This is especially important in the face of fatalistic attachments to spirits and witches. Here is a simple example. Mahatom [a non-Christian villager] had a pain in his lower stomach, which turned out to be a hernia. He refused to go see a doctor because he thought there was a mystical cause. But after spending months visiting diviners, and still not getting better, we convinced him to go to the hospital and have an operation. Now he is fine. But look at all the time and money he wasted along the way. And remember the time when Palabei was seriously sick and thought he had been bewitched and refused to go to the clinic [because medicine is not efficacious when witchcraft is involved]? Day after day, he went to diviners, looking for a supernatural cause. Finally, near death, we took him to the clinic, where they discovered that he had pneumonia and gave him antibiotics. Within a week he was back to normal and lived twenty more years. His resistance was the fear of the villager in the face of invisible forces. Yes, the Christian believes that witches are real, but he doesn't give them power over him. If he gets sick, he will turn to Jesus right away and ask for help. And he will go to the hospital to get medicine. But this is only a small example of how Christianity empowers. It gives people the feeling that they can take hold of their lives and make them better, something that is lacking in the religion of the villages.

Another put it this way: "When I walk down the street as a Christian, I hold my head high. I know I have something that others don't. I am not wealthy and I am not classed *(classé)*, but I have something even better. I have Jesus on my side, and with Jesus anything is possible. Others look at me and wonder where this confidence comes from, because they don't see money or class. But this is what Jesus does for you. Every day I get out of bed and feel that today will be even better than the day before."

I have accompanied this person to church on many occasions, and I am always struck by the pure joy and utter enthrallment she seems to experience during the service, especially when praying and singing. "Once you've felt the power of the Holy Spirit, you are never the same. There is nothing else like it," she exults. Such rapture and embodied affect, in its most noted form, "speaking in tongues," is the figure of immanence itself—of the presence ("in-filling") of the Holy Spirit in the life and body of the believer.

Immanent globality also manifests in a merging of the Holy Spirit and commodity form. In that worldly success is taken as a sign of the divine, charismatics celebrate and offer church testimonials not only to healings and the defeat of spiritual adversaries but also to the acquisition of things material (cell phones, televisions, cars, money). Such testimonials of the coming into commodities offer proof positive of the proximity between believer and the Holy Spirit, suggesting that she is one of the elect. Note, however, that church members also often refigure commodities in Christian ways—watching strictly Pentecostal programming on television, putting only religious songs on an iPod, configuring cell phones with Christian visuals and messages.

These are affects—of joy and pleasure, of confidence and boldness, of worldly accomplishment, of personal empowerment—that certainly sit well with the neoliberal moment (and with the current global conjuncture, dominated as it is by the "immateriality" of labor and the production of affective experience [Hardt and Negri 2001, 2005; Hardt 2007; Clough and Halley 2007]). But also, and even more importantly—doubling its effectiveness—the church is producing bold, confident, vital subjects in a postcolonial environment that, like its colonial predecessor, has long thrived on instilling inferiority, humiliation, and fear in the populace.

---

Brazilian and Mexican soap operas are currently all the rage among women, especially charismatics, in Lomé—and have been since the mid-1990s. It is not unusual to see women running through the streets at seven in the evening to get home before the soaps begin or to find women congregating in workplaces or market stalls to discuss a previous night's episode. Moreover, Lomé clothes fashions increasingly follow those in the popular soaps. Similar to soap operas elsewhere, these shows are filled with scandalous love affairs—between a girlfriend's best friend and her fiancé, between a wealthy woman and her chauffeur, between a mother and her daughter's lover—and with scenarios of those caught between attachments to money/class and romance.

But why are these shows so popular right now? And, given that the relationships therein are the inverse of those promoted by the church, how to account for the fact that much of the viewership is born-again Christian? A male acquaintance and occasional churchgoer to whom I put the question said that the charismatic family celebrated by the church is an ideal image of family, while soap operas represent the everyday reality of peoples' lives (and especially, given the inequalities in Lomé's sexual culture, of women abandoned by husbands or partners for other, usually younger, lovers). Soaps, on this reading, allow women to reflect upon, and discuss with friends, the travails of their own lives. Indeed, a female acquaintance, in describing a friend's estranged wife's affair with a security guard at her house, compared it to an ongoing, widely discussed affair in a 2006 Brazilian soap *Terra Nostra*, in which an older aristocratic woman was sleeping with her much-younger chauffeur. Then, too, as with the simultaneous push-pull (repulsion/attraction) in charismatic views of witchcraft, the scandalous (sinning) soap opera family would appear to be another example of the Pentecostal imagination producing an intoxication with its opposite. Moreover, these soap operas, and their obsession with romantic love, articulate well with neoliberal notions of personal freedom/individualism, on the one hand, and with the Pentecostal pursuit of "affect," on the other. Romantic love, and the endless searching and emoting that accompanies it, strikes me as all about the quest for experience, intensity, and affect.

## Prosperity/Politics

Two questions linger in my thinking about the contemporary charismatic moment in West Africa.

The first concerns the issue of "prosperity," which is so central to the appeal of these churches—that health, wealth, and success will accrue and attend to the believer. This is the "prosperity gospel" message delivered weekly from pulpits and promised in the charismatic literature. "Pray for success—that you will get the job you have been looking for, find the flat you've been seeking, get the money you need. . . ."[13] But, how, in an environment of privation—of inordinately limited means and ongoing crisis—does such a message retain its traction? What are its limits, both material and representational? The social scientist imagines a near future when the promises will remain unfulfilled and the new churches will empty out (Maxwell 1998:366; Meyer 2004b:460).

My experience with Togolese and Ghanaian charismatics suggests otherwise. Consider, for instance, how elastic the concept of "prosperity" can be—how it lends itself to almost any definition. When something, virtually anything, good happens in a believer's life, it is taken as a sign of prosperity: not only when a person gets the job she has been looking for or turns a handsome profit, but also when she succeeds at an exam, or when her health turns for the better, or even when her spirits pick up after she has been down. When I attended a new church in a small village in the north and doubled the collection with my $2 contribution, it was taken as a sign of the church's prosperity. When a pastor friend received a small money gift when an unexpected need arose—having to buy additional tin roofing for a house he was building—he interpreted it as a sign of prosperity. When someone succeeds at one thing while failing at all others, they may nevertheless see themselves as prospering. Moreover, a direct experience of the Holy Spirit such as speaking in tongues or having a healing not only provides auto-validation of God's presence and the truth of religion but also offers proof that one is prospering. Even membership in the charismatic community itself might be taken as a sign of one's prosperity, this because of the church's popularity in contemporary cultural life (thus, syllogistically: the churches are prospering; I am a member of this popular phenomenon; therefore I am prospering). Prosperity is not necessarily, or even principally, a material thing or a money reward, though it can certainly also be that.

Moreover, when things go against one, it is taken not so much as a sign of God's impotence as of one's own.[14]

Certainly some believers experience a sort of ground zero and leave the faith when promises made go unfulfilled and when riches desired are unattained, but many are drawn into the community of belief for affective and narrative reasons, and semiotic systems have a way of protecting themselves from these sorts of critiques. I remain skeptical, then, of the suggestion that there are threshold material conditions that will eventually undo prosperity gospel systems of belief—and more broadly of theories of religion that see religious practice as little more than compensatory and constituted by lack.

The second question that lingers in my work on the charismatic phenomenon relates to its politics (Gifford 1998; Meyer 2004b; Englund 2007). The question retains some urgency, for the charismatic phenomenon has not only swept across the West African landscape but also counts some 500 million adherents worldwide (including over 100 million in Africa), with many million new converts a year (Jenkins 2007; World Christian Database 2008). By any reckoning, global Pentecostalism is the most successful social movement of our time.

Of course, there are many ways of thinking the politics of a social movement. And, indeed, the charismatic phenomenon suggests a failure of the political as we know it. The old collective struggles have not worked, especially in Togo where, after all these years, an authoritarian regime remains in power. Charismatic Christianity proposes a personal project—a project of personal transformation—in place of these more conventional political projects, an antipolitics politics if you will, that charismatics themselves see as having world-transforming potential. Still, the question of Pentecostalism's politics remains paramount for me, for charismatics—and indeed the Holy Spirit itself—inhabit social worlds, and beliefs have political entailments.

On several scores—especially in terms of its gender and sexual politics— West African Pentecostalism is undeniably conservative. Thus, the charismatic church is emphatically homophobic, and men always take the lead at home as well as in the church itself (where the head pastor is invariably male, with women occasionally filling the role of second or third pastor and of translator/interpreter). Moreover, the church explicitly aims to reproduce, and indeed fetishizes in the extreme, the hetero-normative family: sermons invoke the sanctity of the heterosexual couple (as do youth group and marriage counseling sessions); marriages between church members are announced at Sunday service with the couple called on to stand and be recognized; and parents parade newborns in front of the entire congregation at the end of service to receive the pastor's blessing.[15] (At the same time, as suggested above, there are arguably progressive effects to such family values, in that they protect women from philanderers and predatory sexual practices in workplaces.)

The relationship between the new churches and local/national politics is a less straightforward matter. In Togo, where a dictatorship has been in power for four decades, overt political commentary must remain muted, and, as a general principle, the churches eschew any direct engagement in the political life of the nation. Then, too, Eyadéma himself consciously courted pastors and priests—gifting them and drawing them into the patrimonial state apparatus—for he knew the power of religion and its potential effect on the politics of the nation. But the new churches, unlike the older mission churches, are instinctively anti-authoritarian and are widely associated with the 1990s democracy (anti-dictatorship) moment (cf. van Dijk 1998 and Englund 2007 on Malawi).

Though critique can never be overt, it is often only thinly veiled (cf. Marshall-Fratini 2001:100; Shaw 2007:84). Osborn opened his crusade in Lomé in 2006 by announcing that "only you, the people, can save Togo; true government must come from the people, not the state"—a clear, even bold, attempt to open a space of critique of the dictatorship. At the time of the presidential election in April 2005, when expectations for a transition to post-dictatorial rule were high, sermons were filled with parables and commentary about governance and rightful rule—thus, implicitly, with critique of authoritarian politics and the authoritarian state. In a lengthy sermon in Praise Chapel Church just after the election, and following a week of street violence and brutal military reprisal in the opposition neighborhoods of Bè and Kodjoviakopé, the pastor told a story about soldiers entering a neighborhood church—his account alliteratively peppered with the imitation of gun shots ("pop-pop-pop"), provoking uneasy laughter from an audience all-too-familiar with the sound. These soldiers, he opined, came to impose their authority but were transformed in God's sanctuary, putting down their guns and leaving peacefully. The message: faith trumps military rule and suggests a different political future. And in a sermon the following week at an Assemblies of God church, at a moment when disappointment and cynicism over the election results were at an inordinately high pitch, the pastor criticized all forms of "sovereignty" that were not divine while also asserting that God's sovereignty works in sometimes mysterious ways—this latter an attempt to address the pessimism of the moment and the widespread feeling that God had abandoned the Togolese in their time of need. "In God's Kingdom, the first shall be last, and the last shall be first," he concluded.

Mild critique by left political standards, perhaps, but critique nonetheless. And, after forty years of dictatorship, during which any public mention of politics was unthinkable, it at least marks a beginning, not only opening a new discursive space within the church itself but also generating discussion and commentary beyond, in households and on the street.

Note also that at the time of elections local and national politicians are increasingly mindful of the presence and importance of the charismatic churches—not only in the politically instrumental sense of casting for votes but also in remaining cognizant of, and sometimes capitulating to, church policy on public issues. Thus, during the 2004 presidential campaign in Ghana, John Kufuor carefully courted Pentecostal pastors and endorsed their positions on several issues, even changing his own to accord with theirs. And, despite being a committed Catholic, he also began attending Pentecostal services. In Togo, when a presidential hopeful, Dahuku Péré, was asked during the 2003 campaign whether or not he was a "nouveau né" (born-again), he responded that he was a "Chrétien apprentis" (apprentice Christian, which meant: not yet born-again, but on the way)—a response that not only drew universal laughter and made the rounds for months but also served notice that religious affiliation was very much on the table during the election (as well as of course serving to redefine the very meaning of the term "Christian" in Pentecostal terms—as only someone who is "born-again"). Here, then, is an emergent "Pentecostalite" political sphere, with national politics increasingly tied to charismatic Christianity.

Still indirect, there is also political critique in a more Pentecostal idiom. Eyadéma and many close to him were members of the Freemasons and the Rosicrucians, secret societies widely thought by charismatics to be Satanic cults whose members engage in sorcery. Such cult membership, combined with Eyadéma's reputation as one who since childhood possessed witchly powers, amplifies into the charismatic (and Bayartian 1989) view that the state itself is witch-like, its civil servants converting public monies to private ends, consuming the nation without giving back.[16] Though cryptic, such readings of the dictatorship constitute their own form of biting critique.

A stronger—more overt, progressive—critique of ethnic politics held sway in many of the churches in the aftermath of the 2005 election. In two instances I heard about, pastors were publicly reprimanded for making anti-northern, ethnic-essentialist comments during sermons. One was sacked by his church (for what a friend referred to as his "tribalism"), while the other was silenced in front of a large congregation by the church's head pastor, who took the microphone from the offender (the church's second pastor), telling the congregation that his church would not tolerate ethnic politics, and that everyone—regardless of ethnicity—was a member of the Kingdom of God. As elsewhere across the continent (Englund 2007), the new churches remain committed to multi-ethnic, democratic participation.

Beyond the charismatic churches' positions on such standard identity markers (gender, sexuality, ethnicity, nationalism)—positions that, needless to say, are also heterogeneous within the charismatic community itself—there is another set of orientations that figure as well and that strike me as holding out more interesting political possibilities. In concert with the anti-authoritarian impulse of these churches—an impulse that finds its genealogy in the anti-imperial politics of the early Christian community— and their critique of all local (tribal-essentialist, national, regional) identities is their embrace of a transcendent globalism. While not overtly political, this global sensibility asserts the immanence of the global-transcendent in the body and community of the believer, and thus an end to all structures of mediation. Tethered to an organizational structure that is horizontal and networked (and that thus stands as a critique of centralizing state projects) and expressing a worldview that is utopian and world-transforming, this sensibility involves a veritable "deterritorializing" and "recoding" of identity (Deleuze and Gauttari 1983, 1988), an unsettling of the known in order to become other than what one was before and discover life anew.

And this, needless to say, amidst a crisis of debilitating proportions that has lasted a lifetime and sees no end. Here the charismatic offers hope and possibility, a phoenix rising from the ashes of Afro-pessimism.

## Coda

The world of the charismatic Christian appears to embody much that Hardt and Negri (2001, 2005) describe as emblematic of the contemporary global moment. The born-again Christian inhabits a world of postnational sovereignty, of non-state-centric idioms of belonging, of horizontal networked forms of sociality, of nonlinear modes of temporality, of global immanence, of affect and intensity. This is also a world thoroughly saturated by commodity desire and the commodity form—in which proximity to the divine is also measured through the "prosperity" of the believer.[17] In breaking with the past—with the parochial nationalisms and vertical hierarchies and linear time of the dictatorial state, and with tradition and its patrons in the village—the figure of the Pentecostal attempts to reach beyond the present impasse and create a new future.

In the end, I remain undecided about West African Pentecostalism's possibilities and its politics, and tend to see it as something of a figure in transition. While attempting to abolish cultural difference, it nevertheless also reissues such difference and indeed subsists off it. While escaping capture by the state, and informed by a politics from below, it remains haunted by a biopolitics from above. While acknowledging a global pedigree, it nevertheless also remains inextricably tied to the local. While committed to dramatic personal and global transformation—to bringing into being a world that does not yet exist—its politics remains unknown and indeterminate. While seeking an End of History as we know it, the future it anticipates remains largely inchoate.

Still, I am moved by the extraordinary energy I have seen in the new churches in Accra and Lomé. Amidst poverty and abjection beyond belief, believers are filled—as if seized—with a sense of agency and possibility. They walk with heads held high, proudly refusing the colonial/postcolonial lot they have been dealt. They lead lives of purpose and discipline, and find pleasure in worship. Moreover, the initiative comes not from without or above, but seems entirely theirs. This is a cultural production of stunning proportions. Is it not, again ironies noted, an example of a project that speaks to what Mbembe (2001:14) suggests is the central problematic of African philosophy today: "the problem of freedom from servitude and the *possibility of an autonomous African subject*"?

# THREE

# Exit Strategy

If charismatic Christianity represents one response to the current sover-eignty crisis, playing the visa lottery is another, providing a complement to the virtual form of surrogation or exit enacted by the Pentecostal.[1] It also represents a practice that is symptomatic of Togo's "abjection"—to borrow Ferguson's (1999) phrase—from today's global economy, and it might be read as a desperate attempt by Togolese at inclusion. "The dictatorship has robbed us of our dreams," a lottery winner said in summer 2006. "And now, with 'le jeune' (the 'young one,' Eyadéma's son Faure) in power, it may be another four decades before we are able to dream again. Playing the visa lottery gives us hope that there may be a life beyond Togo and that we can live like everyone else."

## Gambling Futures

*Lotto visa,* as it is referred to in Lomé, has become a major cultural event in Togo over the past ten years. According to a consular official I interviewed at the US Embassy in August 2003, there were more green card visa lottery applications per capita in Togo that year than in any other African country, and Togo had ten times as many applications as Benin, the similarly sized country next door—numbers that have held steady since.[2] An embassy em-ployee told me in summer 2005 that he heard that one million Togolese (out of six million total) played the visa lottery in 2004. This figure is cer-tainly exaggerated, but the statement nevertheless captures something of the cultural cachet that this event holds for many Togolese today. Adding to lo-cal interest in this phenomenon—and the focus of this chapter—is the fact that every lottery winner is permitted to also bring a spouse and children (who may not have been listed when the winner applied), thus opening a space of considerable play, with many marrying others' spouses/siblings or adopting their children in return for help in paying the embassy interview fee ($775 in 2009) and a plane ticket to the US (over $1000).

The involvement of Togolese in the green card lottery is a textbook illustration of the sort of "Atlantic African" economic practice that Jane Guyer (2004) suggests has characterized African economic history for centuries—and that Bayart (2000) refers to as "extraversion," that process whereby Africans have long appropriated various outsides to enhance their own economic and political fortunes. In her book, *Marginal Gains: Monetary Transactions in Atlantic Africa* (2004), Guyer argues that the domain of the economic in Africa has long been situated at the intersection of various crossroads and within a transcultural space between the local and that which lay beyond: the slave trade, the colonial, and, now, a differently globalized postcolonial. It has also straddled the material and the performative, the impersonal and personal, the formal and informal. Atlantic African economies are thus hybrid, improvisational border practices engaged in the ongoing negotiation and invention of registers of value and personal distinction, practices and negotiations that mediate (and are mediated by) an ongoing state of "crisis." Under conditions of perpetual turbulence, Guyer suggests, economic actors seek their gain by strategically accessing those multiple scales of value that are in play in such borderland spaces. As with Atlantic African economic phenomena generally, *Lotto visa* is an enormously inventive, entrepreneurial border practice, which has generated its own scales of value and pricing, and has produced far-reaching networks of debt, rank, and clientage. These borrow from, though also innovate upon, conventional scales of value/price/rank/debt.

*Lotto visa* is also a practice that bears the imprint of the post-Cold War moment in West Africa, a moment that has fostered, among other things, cultures of duplicity and identity fabrication (Hibou 1999). Nigerian 419—the now-(in)famous system of Internet fraud whereby an overseas client is duped by the promise of sharing vast oil (or other) profits in return for sheltering money in a personal bank account, a transaction which demands that the client pay processing fees and transfer an account number which, needless to say, is quickly emptied (Apter 1999, 2005; Smith 2007)—is one example of the sort of duping and identity fraud that has become ever more common. The Cameroonian "feyman" or con artist (Malaquais 2001; Nyanmjoh 2006; Ndjio nd) is another. Closer to home, Togolese friends insist that counterfeits and fakes are so common today in the stores and on the streets of Lomé that one can never be sure whether an object one has purchased is "real" or not—a real or a fake Nokia phone, a real or an imitation piece of designer clothing, a new or a used car part. Stories abound of those who purchased products that worked for a few days or weeks before becoming useless.[3] The visa lottery shares kinship with these practices. It is an act of conjury, an attempt to generate something of value (an identity, a proxy citizenship) out of nothing—a conjury that seems emblematic of the neoliberal moment more broadly—of "casino capitalism," as the Comaroffs (2000) refer to it—with its Ponzi/pyramid schemes and income-generating lotteries and financial market "futures."

In what follows, I explore the practices of the Togolese visa lottery largely through the experiences and narrations of a single *Lotto visa* entrepreneur or "fixer," as the embassy refers to them.[4] He is not only an impressive raconteur, with a keen eye for new practices and the latest invention, but has also himself been responsible for the introduction of key innovations into the larger system. He thus provides a privileged view of practices at once conventional and dynamic.[5]

### *Lotto visa*

The inventions of *Lotto visa* culture are quite extraordinary, and in some ways reconstitute kinship by other means. As mentioned above, once selected (by the drawing in Williamsburg, Kentucky), and before going for the obligatory interview at the US Embassy in Lomé, lottery winners will often attempt to add "dependents" to their dossiers. Sometimes these are legitimate relatives but usually not. (Indeed, they are often relatives of those already in the diaspora—who can more easily afford the quid pro quo: payment of the visa winner's embassy interview fee and purchase of his/her plane ticket to the US.) Since US immigration rules only permit the visa winner to be accompanied by a spouse and children, the winner must then "marry" his sponsor's wife (or sister or cousin) and "adopt" any children before the interview—and present proof that they are indeed his/her dependents. This in turn requires producing a file of documents—marriage papers, wedding photos, birth certificates. One somewhat atypical but nevertheless revealing example: a friend's wife recently arrived in the US as the "wife" of a friend of her brother. The previous year, the brother and the friend both received political asylum (needless to say, under false pretenses) and entered into a "sister-exchange" arrangement, whereby each would "marry" the other's sister and pay her way to the States. As part of the agreement, my friend's wife's "husband" spent over $2,500 returning to Togo to take wedding photos with his friend's sister—for her to present at the embassy as proof that she was married to him. Moreover, this man (the "husband") could not fly to Lomé itself—for fear that if US authorities discovered that he had been back in Togo it might jeopardize his asylum status. Instead, he flew to Accra, took a bus to the border—where they only check passports of non-West Africans—and crossed into Togo on foot.

Another area of play/invention: A visa lottery winner must either possess a high school diploma, the baccalaureate or "bac," or have several years of job experience in a profession that is on the US Labor Department job list. Thus, those without the baccalaureate who do not already fit the job profile are quickly "apprenticed" into the appropriate trades (and papers backdating the apprenticeship and subsequent work experience are manufactured). The US consular official who was conducting interviews of visa lottery winners in summer 2003 told me that as soon as tailoring was put on the list "everyone in Togo became a tailor!" And, in 2006, when "peintre en bâtiment" (house painter) made the list, the consul's office was flooded with applications of those claiming to be painters.

A cottage industry of *Lotto visa* entrepreneurs has grown up around these practices—of those who help others with the online visa registration, of those who know who to bribe to get false marriage or adoption or job papers, of those who arrange the taking of marriage photos, and especially of those who serve as brokers between those in the diaspora and those at home. Another friend of mine, Kodjo—the one mentioned in the introduction whose "wife" failed her interview and then inquired whether he might get a medical visa for an arm replacement—signed up over twelve hundred people for the lottery in fall 2005. He wrote me just after the new online registration season had opened in October to say that he was leaving for northern Togo to enlist what he hoped would be several hundred applicants. In the north ("an untouched territory," as he referred to it), he visited local high schools where he sought permission from the school principals to speak with those students in their last year—because most in "terminale" are single (more easily enabling dependents to be added to the files of winners) and because they sit for the baccalaureate in July (if successful, ensuring an easier passage through the embassy interview). An innovation here in repertoire: unlike other *Lotto visa* entrepreneurs, Kodjo does not charge any of his enlistees to help them register—he takes their pictures and fills out the online form for them, all for free—in return for his owning each one's file. If one wins, he will add "dependents" (and make money for doing so). He's quite level-headed about all of this, saying that he simply plays the odds. "If only 1 percent of my applicants are selected, I can live for an entire year."

The embassy is of course fully aware that all of this gaming is going on—the US ambassador went on television in 2006 to say that he assumed *all* who came for the embassy interview were lying and fabricating identities, and that the burden was on the interviewee to prove that he/she wasn't—and has developed a set of tests to attempt to detect real from sham winners and, especially, real from false spouses. Thus, a common embassy strategy is to interview spouses separately, asking about the habits and desires of the other: "what's your husband's favorite color?" "his favorite food?" "what did you eat yesterday?" "the day before that?" "what side of the bed does he sleep on?" The embassy also knows of course that as soon as they ask a particular question, it will circulate to those who are next in line for interviews. (Indeed, Kodjo showed me a file he keeps of all the questions asked of interviewees over the past several years—a file he shares with friends and clients who are prepping for the embassy interview.) Thus, a cat-and-mouse game develops between embassy and street, the embassy trying to stay one step ahead by springing new questions and those about to go for interviews making sure they know as soon as new questions appear. In 2006, for instance, an interviewee's doctor's report—it is mandatory to have a physical exam and AIDS test before the interview—noted that there was a scar on one of his legs. The consular official conducting the interview asked his "wife" which leg, and, when she guessed incorrectly, they failed the interview. The next day, all on the street knew why they had failed—and had begun to explore the intimacies of their own visa-spouses' bodies. During an applicant's embassy interview in January 2006, the consular official challenged the woman she was interviewing by telling her that she didn't believe the man who had accompanied her was her husband—and that she would give the applicant a visa while denying him. Without hesitating, the woman responded that he was indeed her husband (though in fact he was not) and that if he was not granted a visa, she would refuse hers. This seemed proof enough for the consular official, and both were granted visas. Kodjo's commentary: that it takes this type of "courage" to pass the interview.

As one telling sign of the importance the visa lottery is assuming in the cultural life of Lomé today, I have heard repeatedly from Togolese that the (low-ranking) consular official who conducts the visa interviews at the embassy is far better known than the ambassador. "We don't even know who the ambassador is," a friend said. "But Mme Johnson, we know her well. She's a celebrity here. We study her every move—for she's the one who will decide whether we have a life beyond Togo or not." The same consular official told me that one day she was playing golf with the US ambassador when a car stopped on a busy road nearby. The driver jumped out and ran across the golf course to greet her ("I have always wanted to meet you," she reported him saying), while entirely ignoring the ambassador. Before taking

6. Togolese magistrate marrying a visa couple, with Togo's President
Faure Gnassingbé looking on, Lomé 2007

leave, he asked if she knew yet when the next visa lottery enrollment period
would begin.

Kodjo's history with the visa lottery—especially his evolution from participant to entrepreneur—illustrates the often intimate connection between
privation and invention that is emblematic of the post-Cold War moment,
for it was his failure as a lottery entrant that led to his entry into and eventual success as an entrepreneur. After an eighteen-year-old friend whom he
helped apply was selected in the lottery, he spent a small fortune (and the
better part of a year) "marrying" her, apprenticing her into a job on the Labor Department job list, and prepping her for the embassy interview. When
she failed the interview—overcome by nervousness, she became tongue-
tied when attempting to respond to the consul's questions—he sank into a
near-suicidal depression. But he then realized that despite his failure he had
learned an enormous amount about how to put together a file and prepare
someone for the interview. He thus began counseling others going through
the interview process and met with striking success. Today, as one of the
most accomplished visa lottery entrepreneurs in Lomé, he claims that it

was his initial failure as an applicant that led to his subsequent success as entrepreneur.

## Border Economics

I turn now to the economics of this system, and do so by following the case of this innovative entrepreneur (Kodjo), exploring practices that are at once unique to him but also informed by and in dialogue with those of the dozens of other *Lotto visa* fixers in Lomé.

Kodjo's number of enlistees jumped dramatically between 2001 and 2005, from a few dozen, to several hundred, to eight hundred, to twelve hundred. This sharp increase was due both to the fact that his reputation has grown with experience—he has now successfully shepherded many dossiers through the maze of interviews and medical exams, through the local market in false papers and fictional identities, and through the complicated financing that must be put together to pay for interviews and exams and plane tickets (financing that is far beyond the means of most Togolese)— *and* because, unlike other entrepreneurs, Kodjo waives the up-front fee that other entrepreneurs charge (CFAF 1,500 = $3) for helping someone register. (It is important to note that because registration is now online and must include a digital photograph of the applicant, most Togolese who play seek the help of an Internet savvy *Lotto visa* fixer—or go to one of the many cyber-cafés in Lomé that, during the October-November sign-up period, offer help in completing the application and in taking the applicant's photo.)

Kodjo's success has been dramatically enhanced as well by his pioneering forays into the north, into this "untouched territory." And here his ethnicity is a factor. Although Kodjo himself grew up in Lomé and is in many ways more "southern" than northern, he spent childhood summers in the Kabiyé north, where his father was born. (It is common practice for parents to send their children back to their natal villages during summer holidays—"to teach them how to work"). Thus, it is through some of Kodjo's childhood connections, as well as those of his family, that he has been able to get his foot in the door of local schools (a summer playmate is now principal of one of the northern lycées), something that would be difficult for a non-Kabiyé. Note, too, the effect of Kodjo's recruitment practices: children in remote Togolese villages are now playing the lottery and dreaming of US green cards—a fantasy recently made all the more real by the fact that one of Kodjo's northern clients was chosen in the July 2006 drawing.

In 2006, six of Kodjo's enlistees were selected in the Kentucky raffle.

7. Lomé Internet café during visa lottery sign-up period, November 2007

Because he signed them up free of charge, he "owned" each of their dossiers and was free to add "dependents" to them—a spouse and sometimes children. It is these dependents, or more typically their brothers/spouses in the diaspora, who will pay the cost of the embassy interview, the cost of the plane ticket to the US for the winner and dependent(s), the cost of apprenticing the winner into a trade, the cost of obtaining marriage papers, marriage photos, and new identity papers (and sometimes passports), and the cost of having Kodjo broker the entire affair. However—another Kodjo innovation—the winner him/herself is asked to pay for the $200 medical examination that all must undergo before the embassy interview. Kodjo's reasoning here is that there must be some additional incentive for winners to perform at peak level during the interview, and having them spend their own money beforehand is the best way to ensure that.

If a particular entrepreneur does not want to do the work of shepherding a dossier through this maze, he can sell it to another entrepreneur or directly to a sponsor. One such case I heard about in summer 2007 had a price tag of $3,000, though in the end it fetched $1,500, and this just for access to the winner's dossier. The price was this high, I was told, because the person already had his "bac" and was seen as a sure winner. (There are thus categories/ranks of winners, from "certain" to "high risk," that affect pricing outcomes.)

This market in visas has brought new risks as well. In 2007, apparently for the first time, a fixer began counterfeiting winners' letters for clients of his—on imitation State Department stationary—and then selling the "winner's" dossiers to Togolese in the diaspora. After receiving his transaction fees, this fixer vanished, leaving those he had victimized to slowly realize (in the end, confirmed by email communication with the office in Kentucky that processes applications) that they had been had. But notice the recursiveness—fraud within fraud—that this new practice represents, and also the distinctions that emerge for players around the category "fraud" itself. Thus, Kodjo and others found this practice reprehensible—a type of "inauthentic" fraud—in contrast with those practices—more authentic fakes—they were engaged in (in helping Togolese achieve a better life abroad, they said). Notice, too, the way in which such a practice will generate new procedures and safeguards in *Lotto visa* culture. Kodjo is now consulted by other entrepreneurs' clients who seek to verify the authenticity of the State Department letter announcing their selection and, in summer 2008, he discovered two counterfeits—by noticing slight misspellings and incongruities in the "official" letter—and was handsomely rewarded by those near-dupes he had saved from disastrous debt.

This system is also filled with stories of monumental, even tragic, loss. I know some who, without friends or relatives in the diaspora to help them with the cost of the embassy interview, raised their own money locally—by selling land or family home, or by borrowing from family members what amounts for many to a lifetime's savings—only to fail the interview. Indeed, in fall 2006, after a particularly difficult interview season during which only a few—on one day alone, only three out of forty—were granted visas, several hundred lottery winners staged a protest in a local park, demanding that the embassy return the interview fee to those who were denied visas. The embassy capitulated in part, and it now returns the interview fee for a denied winner's spouse (though not the fee for the winner him/herself). Still not satisfied, these same protestors began a daily sit-in at the entrance to the US Embassy in April 2008, a sit-in that lasted five months—until early October when the embassy asked Togolese security forces to remove the protestors.

Price structure within this popular economy is the result of an ongoing dialectic between conventionalized practice and innovation. Practices among entrepreneurs become standardized, only to be partially unsettled by improvising individuals like Kodjo—who waived the entry fee for

8. Visa lottery protestors outside the US Embassy, Lomé 2008

applicants, and who began requiring winners to cover some of the costs of pre-interview expenses. But such improvisations quickly circulate and affect the practices of other entrepreneurs before becoming standardized—and before new innovations in turn unsettle them once again. These are pricing mechanisms generated "from below"—not only beyond the purview of the state but also only partially driven by principles of supply and demand. When the cost of the recent winner's dossier fell from $3,000 to $1,500, this outcome was the result of negotiation between those in the diaspora (with their varying means to pay such an entrance fee) and the needs of entrepreneurs in Lomé (needs driven by familial and network commitments as much as by any prior standardized pricing structure).

All told, the financing for one of these cases costs between $5,000 and $10,000, depending on the initial cost of access and the number of dependents added to a dossier. With roughly 1,500 Togolese going for embassy interviews each year (out of 3,000 selectees),[6] up to $15 million is spent annually on this system—a not insignificant sum for a small West African country in the midst of a prolonged economic crisis. Indeed this system might be read as a partial solution to Togo's development impasse, for it serves as a remittance magnet, drawing millions of dollars annually from the diaspora back home. Moreover, it has a significant spillover effect, redistributing monies along networks of kin and friends and supporting entire cottage industries of document fabricators, photographers, those apprenticing winners into trades, doctors administering the medical exams, and the entrepreneurs themselves.

This popular economy also informs, and is informed by, other informal economy practices around it. Lomé today is nothing if not a crowded intersection of hundreds of informal economy ventures. Everyone, it seems, is hustling and jostling for position within the limited means of the post-Cold War moment. Moreover, the players in many of these groups overlap, with information about pricing/credit/debt (and the latest innovations) circulating amongst them. For example, Kodjo also sells used German cars with a group of friends who work at Lomé's port, while another of his friends, who helps obtain false documents for his enlistees, is involved in the export of "exotic" animals (pythons and iguanas) to Germany, Japan, and the US. Money and credit, too, move between these circles, with a busted deal here drawing on potential future earnings there. I have spent hours trying to follow the baroque and bewildering movements of money and debt from venture to venture and party to party, and always come away feeling I have

9. Embassy protestors dressed in red—"to show our wounds," Lomé 2008

never fully gotten to the bottom of the system of exchange and debt that is being transacted.

## Kodjo's Three Wives

If Kodjo has been brilliant at helping others get visas, he has had less success himself. Three times he has sent a "wife" for the embassy interview, only to have her turned away and his chance for a green card slip through his fingers.

The first of his three wives was the eighteen-old-year-old who became tongue-tied when she found herself face-to-face with the American consul. When she was selected in the 2001 drawing, Kodjo married her and apprenticed her into batik-making, a trade on that year's Labor Department job list. After raising the money for the medical exam and interview, he spent weeks preparing her for the consul's questions, plying her with information about her trade, about their marriage and honeymoon, about when/where they met and "fell in love." On the day of the interview, however, her nerves got the better of her. Standing before the glass window that separates applicant from consul, straining with her own broken French to understand the equally imperfect French of the American official in front of her, struggling to keep straight the information Kodjo had crammed into her about their marriage and her profession, she froze up and failed to answer easy question after easy question: "When were you married?" "What is the name of your employer?" "How long have you been making batik?" Kodjo sat on the bench behind her jumping out of his skin but, as trailing spouse, could do nothing but remain muzzled and mute.

Two years later, aiming to maximize his chances, Kodjo signed up only female applicants. When the results were announced, he emailed me to say that this time he had a sure winner: a woman in her early thirties who was cool and unflappable. But disappointment awaited him again. At the medical exam before the interview, the doctor discovered that this woman had a rare heart condition—"gros coeur" (enlarged heart)—that prevented her from going for the interview and obtaining a visa.

Kodjo's third marriage in 2006 was to a lottery selectee who was attending university (and thus someone who, because she had the high school baccalaureate, presented a less-complicated pathway through the interview process). Hoping to avoid the consul in Lomé who had turned away over 90 percent of those interviewed that year, Kodjo decided to test the waters in Ouagadougou, the capital of Burkina Faso to Togo's north. He thus made a short reconnaissance trip there and inquired at the embassy whether

Togolese nationals could interview in Ouagadougou instead of Lomé—and was told that, with the appropriate papers (demonstrating local residency and employment), they could. Such documentation proved easy to come by: a Togolese friend agreed to let Kodjo and his wife list his house as their residence and to vouch that Kodjo's wife was employed as a secretary at his business; moreover, for a small fee (CFAF 5,000 = $10), Kodjo was able to obtain backdated residency papers at Ouagadougou's central police station.

After depositing their papers (proof of baccalaureate, marriage certificate, residency papers) at the embassy, they were told that the consulate needed to verify the documents before setting the interview date, and that, since such verification involved contacting offices in Lomé, that process could take several weeks. Wanting to return to Lomé for the interim, while nevertheless needing to maintain the ruse that they were living in Ouagadougou, Kodjo purchased a subscription to a local (*Burkinabé*) cell phone number and routed it through his Lomé phone. Two months later the call from the embassy came, asking them to appear for the interview the next day. Since Ouagadougou is a two-day bus ride from Lomé, Kodjo, always quick on his feet, told the secretary that his wife's boss had sent her "en mission" and that she would only return on the weekend. This seemed convincing to the embassy official and the interview was scheduled for the following Tuesday.

The interview itself went exceedingly well. Even Kodjo, ever the taskmaster, was impressed with his "wife's" calm and her ability to finesse the trick questions put to her—about her work, about their marriage, about life in Ouagadougou. After thirty minutes, the consul seemed satisfied and congratulated them, telling them to return on Friday to retrieve their passports (with visas), and urging them to work on their English before their departure for the US.

When they returned that Friday, however, the secretary told them they needed to come back the following Tuesday for more questions. After an angst-filled weekend—of trying to imagine what weakness had been detected in their file, and of boning up on local geography/politics and the details of their marital history—Kodjo and his wife returned to the embassy that Tuesday. Turning directly to Kodjo, the consul asked whether he had been married before. (On the applicant form, they ask about prior marriages and, not wanting to arouse suspicion, while also assuming that the embassy purged its records at the end of each year, Kodjo had left that section blank. When I first heard him advance the theory that the embassy did not keep records beyond a year, I told him I was skeptical a US Embassy with its big computers would do such a thing. But he insisted that his hypothesis had been confirmed by the experience of successful clients who had interviewed more than once and not listed prior visa-spouses.)

When Kodjo responded to the consul's question by saying that this was his only marriage, she countered that she had record of a prior one. Without missing a beat, he agreed that he *had* been married before but said it was a "customary" marriage, and that was why he had not mentioned it. The consul pressed him, asking for the customary wife's name, but also putting Kodjo in a quandary: which of the two prior wives' names did she have, the eighteen-year-old who had frozen up at the interview five years previously or the one who had failed the medical exam two years ago? Still assuming that the embassy periodically purges its files and that it was more likely that they kept their records from two than from five years ago, he wrote down the name of his second wife, the one with the heart condition, and passed it to the consul. She said that was not the name they had on file, to which Kodjo calmly replied that he had been married one other time as well but that that wife had died. The consul asked for her name and, when he gave that of the eighteen-year-old, she acknowledged that was the correct name, but—clearly skeptical now—wanted to know if he had a death certificate. He said he did but that it was back in Lomé. At this point, the consul said she was sorry but she was unable to give them visas.

Consider: in having to choose between his two prior visa wives, Kodjo had a 50/50 chance of answering correctly—and of likely being granted the visa. Moreover, his decision to give the name of his second rather than first wife made perfect sense, given his experience-tested (though in the end flawed) assumption that the embassy did not keep records in perpetuity. But why did the embassy have the name of the first wife and not the second? Apparently, since the second was eliminated after the medical exam and before the interview, her name was never entered into the embassy computer. Kodjo has often said that it takes intelligence, nerves of steel, and a good dose of luck to succeed in the lottery. Clearly Lady Luck has not yet been on his side.

By 2008, chastened by these failures but still upbeat about his chances— "the next time, it will work, I am sure," he said after the third setback— Kodjo had come up with a new strategy. He would marry his fiancée—his *real* fiancée—to one of his client-winners. "When they pass the interview," he said, "I'll send her to the US to get her green card. Then she'll divorce her husband and return to Lomé. We'll get married and leave for America together." "But this could take years," I countered. "Are you prepared to wait that long?" "I've been waiting fifteen years already. I can easily wait a few more," he said.

## Church and State

Both state and Pentecostal touch the visa lottery in ways that are revealing of some of the larger political-economic shifts currently underway—while also suggesting how these domains cross-fertilize and influence one another.

Not surprisingly, perhaps, prayer is routinely called on to enhance peoples' chances in the lottery. Entire Lomé congregations have even been known to engage in prayer—especially during the sign-up period in November and December, and when lottery results are announced in May and June—so that members will get visas.[7]

In an instance that brings tears of laughter to those who hear it, a notorious philanderer whose wife was selected in the lottery suddenly found religion and began to follow the straight and narrow in ways that left friends astonished. Apparently the man's cheating was such common knowledge that his wife's pastor once corrected her when she referred to his "three" girlfriends by saying that he knew of at least six. But this "born-again" Christian took so seriously the prospect of getting a visa to the US—and of the importance of being on the right side of the Holy Spirit in achieving that end— that he abandoned all his paramours, returned home from work every night at 5 p.m. to be with his family, and became a model member of his church. As if in confirmation of his actions, this couple's case number—in the high 50s (57,000), and thus normally out of range for an interview—was called for the first time since the lottery had been instituted, and, divine justice, he and his wife received visas.[8]

The lottery fuels not only church attendance but also visits to spirit shrines. One selectee I know hedged his bets and did both, stepping up church attendance while also returning to the village to consult a diviner. Careful preparation for the embassy interview is seen as a necessary though not sufficient condition for success, requiring the supplement of mystical intercession or "luck."

If the visa lottery has penetrated the churches, the reverse is true as well. Prayer was present at the embassy protest in 2008, where, three times a day, a charismatic pastor forcefully prayed for heavenly intercession for those who had failed the interview and been denied visas. And, in a more subversive register, while a friend of Kodjo's who is a devout charismatic assiduously applies for the lottery each year, she resolutely refuses to allow him to

10. Charismatic pastor at embassy protest, Lomé 2008

arrange a marriage for her with one of his clients, claiming that marriage is sacred and that if God wants her to get a visa, He will arrange a (legal) way. (On the flip side, notice how visa-like identity manipulation seeps into the wider culture and even into the churches. When this same charismatic's even more religious sister in California was in a tight spot and needed to go to court to challenge a finding that she had behaved negligently at a daycare center where she worked, her sister back home went to the head of Lomé's charismatic church council to ask whether he would write a letter stating that the departed sister was a model babysitter when she was in Lomé. The letter was a ruse—he had never met the sister before—but this man of God was willing to help, to fabricate an identity for a "sister in Christ" who was in need.)

The relationship between lottery and state is a complex one, and I can only touch on the surface of that relationship here. In general, Togolese courts regard the behavior of entrepreneurs like Kodjo as perfectly legal, and, if called on to adjudicate a dispute with one of his clients, they will consider signed contracts of his much like any other contract—as presumptive consensual agreements between parties for services rendered. Kodjo has thus used the courts to enforce clients' obligations to him—which, according to the contract they sign when he enters their name in the drawing, allows him to add dependents to their file and to collect transaction fees for his services. Of course, such endorsement by the law also has a normalizing effect, sanctioning *Lotto visa* within the larger culture.

But state actors collude with visa lottery practice in other ways as well. A judge at the local préfecture presides over the marriages Kodjo arranges and backdates the marriage licenses—needless to say, for a fee. He even enters the marriage in the registry at the appropriate (backdated) place—thus making it difficult for the consulate's "fraud officer," a young Togolese woman sent around to verify applicants' documents, to detect whether the marriage was recent or not. This judge also participates in the photo shoot of the wedding party on the steps of the courtroom—a session whose aim is to produce the pictures often demanded by the consul at the interview to verify the authenticity of the union.

The practice of state actors, here a jurist seeking private income while performing state functions—not unlike soldiers taking bribes on the roadways, or civil servants hijacking NGOs, or teachers making personal profit from the labors of school children—has touched Kodjo's practice in other ways as well. A disgruntled client who tried to force Kodjo's hand—so that Kodjo would agree to let him go for the embassy interview in a way Kodjo deemed ill-advisable (because, mindful of the recent high failure rate at the embassy, Kodjo wanted him to pursue a less conventional route)—hired two policemen to pay Kodjo a visit. They showed up in plain clothes at his "bureau" one day, introducing themselves as "family members" of the client who wanted to "better understand their relative's case." After an hour's conversation, Kodjo apparently won them over, and they left satisfied that he had engaged in no wrongdoing, and more, that he was correct in his assessment of the best strategy for his/their client to pursue. In parting, they revealed their identity as security agents of the state.

As Kodjo noted later, these policemen were off-duty—state actors (albeit in plain clothes) using their public positions to realize private gain. For these functionaries, the state is little more than an enterprise that facilitates personal profiteering, a resource to be plundered (Hibou 1999). Indeed there is little distinction between their behavior and Kodjo's, between licit and illicit (Hibou 1999; Comaroff and Comaroff 2006a; Roitman 2006), between state and lottery. Judges and policemen here are all engaged in identity manipulation—not only helping others present themselves as someone they are not but also presenting themselves as identities they are not. Moreover, there is little distinction between this form of identity switching and that engaged in by the Togolese ruling party (RPT) and its political opposition (see chapter 1), most dramatically in the state's staging of itself as opposition during the 1998 "coup attempt," but also in opposition members' dressing up as state actors to engage in acts that sully the state.

## Desiring the Global

What sort of popular practice is this? A remittance system? A system of redistribution? A citizenship-for-sale scheme? Or merely a clever set of income-generating devices for people like Kodjo? Certainly it is all of these. But I think it is more as well. For it draws on all the resources and imaginaries of the moment, those of the post-Cold War conjuncture—of its felt crisis, of the eviscerated though still-feared state, of social death and the emptiness of citizenship under such conditions, of a sprawling transnational diaspora and the desires and longings it creates, of informationalism and its new technologies—to produce a generative fantasy about exile and citizenship and global membership (Ferguson 2002, 2006).

But why do so many more apply from Togo than from neighboring countries Benin and Burkina Faso? Certainly, as those to whom I have put the question typically respond, Togolese enthusiasm for the lottery is due to the ongoing political and economic crisis in their country, a crisis exacerbated by the continuation of the dictatorship beyond the end of the Cold War. This political climate, combined with the privation brought on by structural adjustment and the withdrawal of EU funding, has created a near-universal desire on the part of Togolese to leave their country for what they imagine are greener pastures in Europe and the US. Moreover, things are worse in Togo, they add, than in these other countries because of the election fraud that has characterized the post-Cold war moment (as opposed to the more open—and surprising—electoral outcomes that have characterized the two neighboring countries' recent political histories). When Kodjo returned from his trip to Burkina Faso (to see whether he—and other Togolese clients—could go for the embassy interview there instead of in Lomé, where the failure rate skyrocketed in 2006), he reported that life in Ouagadougou was infinitely better than in Lomé. "The roads are all paved, the street lights work, and when it rains the water runs off in an orderly manner into large cement ditches beside the road. Lomé is years behind."

While political-economic factors may thus condition a longing for exile and explain the higher incidence of visa lottery participants than in neighboring countries, they nevertheless do not fully account for the extraordinary popularity of, or the specific practices entailed in, the lottery phenomenon in Togo. This popularity also needs to be thought in terms of the fact that this event, like cultural practices elsewhere (Baudrillard 1996; Weiss 2009), has taken on a life of its own and produced its own excess. "These things start small and spread through the streets and, when successful, get taken up by others," Kodjo said. "Then they grow and grow, and, if some are successful, others follow. And, you know, each country has its own thing. With Nigerians it's 419; with Togolese it's *Lotto visa*."

This phenomenon, like economic entrepreneurialism throughout West Africa more broadly, also needs to be thought in terms of the "performative" (Guyer 2004:101–14). As an event that collects stories around it, that feeds a collective fantasy, and that produces reputations and markers of distinction, it is as much cultural performance as economic practice. Moreover, its dramatic growth and popularity among Togolese depends on the multitalents of entrepreneurs (or performers) like Kodjo. Not only must he be Internet savvy and have impeccable interpersonal skills (for example, counseling people how to treat one another as "spouses," calming those who may be short of cash—and/or those who squandered their money [because they failed the medical exam or the embassy interview]), but also he must be able to broker deals with people all over Lomé and draw on networks throughout the diaspora. As well, he needs to know the ins and outs of the lottery system and US immigration law.

A bizarre case presented itself in summer 2005, in which a Togolese national in Minneapolis, who had sponsored one of Kodjo's winners in return for the latter's marriage to his wife and adoption of his son, sued the winner for child support. (The Minneapolis man had remarried his wife after she arrived in the States but had not yet re-adopted his son, and felt that the winner, still the son's legal father, should help pay to support him.) Kodjo, because he had brokered the original deal between the two men, was contacted in Lomé by both sides to help resolve the dispute. He thus had to take a crash course in Minnesota family law and then weigh in as mediator. He was of course outraged at the hubris of the sponsor bringing the suit, and the case was finally resolved and the child support claim withdrawn when the winner threatened to go public with the illegalities surrounding the obtaining of the wife's and child's visas. "All in a day's work," Kodjo concluded with a wry smile in recounting his tale.

# MISE EN SCÈNE

The next two chapters, "Charismatic Enchantments" and "Arrested Development," follow the effects of the "changes" of the 1990s into the villages of the north where I have conducted research since the mid-1980s. Unlike much work today in my home discipline and in African Studies, I retain a commitment to the rural. It is in the villages that some of the most dramatic changes have occurred—and that new forms of sovereignty and biopower are in play. It is here that the unraveling of the dictatorship complex—its pact with village chiefs and its support of the ceremonial apparatus—is most urgently felt. It is also here that the new NGOs are most active and that the conflict between charismatic Christians and village religion is out in the open. And it is here that witchcraft imaginaries have exploded in the last ten years, animated by claims and counterclaims, by extravagant stories about night flyers and wealth seekers, by speculation and panic that touches virtually everyone.

To contextualize these transformations, I briefly describe the ritual-authority complex that was built up during the colonial and early postcolonial periods—between 1920 and 1990, from the period of French indirect rule to the end of the Cold War—in the Kabre villages of the north. It is this nexus of authority relations and its cultural habitus that is now fraying under the strains of the new dispensation.

Terrace cereal farmers spread across two massifs north of the Kara river and 400 km from the coast, Kabre were recognized early on by the French as industrious and hardworking and were targeted as a source of labor for the nascent colony (Piot 1999:40–43). Aided by chiefly allies who collected tax and recruited labor, the colonial state relocated small groups of Kabre men to the south during the 1920s and 1930s to build the roads and railroads that transected the colonial landscape. Despite relocation, disruptions to the northern villages were minimal, as it was French policy to quickly return departed workers to their home communities and replace them with another cohort—so that the villages themselves would bear the costs of social reproduction (Meillassoux 1981).

A second wave of migrants in the 1930s and 1940s, drawn by soils that were less rocky and more fertile than those in the north, settled on sparsely populated southern land to farm coffee, cotton, and cocoa for a colonial-international market. Their early success and relative autonomy turned a migrant trickle into a stream—producing a steady flow of youth out of the north, an exodus that continues into the present—and established hundreds of Kabre villages across Togo's southern plateau. These emigrants nevertheless retained strong ties to the north, returning to initiate their children and bury the dead, and to remit some of the proceeds of cash-cropping. A busy diaspora emerged around the back-and-forth between northern homeland and southern terminus, crowding the roadways with those heading south in search of money and with southerners returning home for ritual sustenance (Piot 1999:40–42, 156–71).

The northern villages, rolling expanses etched into the hillsides of the two massifs, were presided over by colonial-era chiefs and organized into a vast ritual system that regulated agriculture and initiation. Eight ceremonies cycled from village to village each year—beginning in Farang, they moved to Kuwdé a week later, then to Wazilao, then to Asiri, and so on—reiterating rank among the different communities (Piot 1999:136–43). When I began work in this area in the mid-1980s, the male elders who ran the ceremonies reigned supreme and were treated like royalty. Vernacular intellectuals, they endlessly debated and parsed the esoteric knowledge that veined through the system, thus also maintaining their control over it. In supplicating the spirits that gave life to human society—that brought the rain and fertilized the fields—they stood at the center of their world, and saw those in the diaspora and the cities of the south, including the country's native son president, as living on its margins (*nietoda*, lit., in the bush).

It is important to note that this was not some timeless ritual system, outside of or resistant to history. It was resolutely dynamic and underwent significant transformation throughout the twentieth century. During the early colonial period, rituals were diverted to address colonial labor practice (Piot 1999:89–90), and, to accommodate the comings and goings of its diaspora, some ceremonies were shortened or dropped altogether while others came to assume greater importance (90–91). Ironically, Kabre expansion into the south produced an amplification of northern ritual—for it was ritual that mediated long-distance relations among kin and that anchored diasporic spread. "We do more ceremonies today than in the past," a northern ritual leader observed in the 1980s, "because of family in the south who return with their problems [that require the intervention of northern diviners], and their dead, and their uninitiated children."[1]

Two Christian churches—Roman Catholic and Presbyterian—established themselves in the area in the 1950s and, unlike today's Pentecostal churches, struck up an easy alliance with local religion. Not only were villagers who attended church not discouraged from engaging in local ritual but also the churches themselves incorporated Kabre elements of song/speech/belief into their services and in many ways came to resemble village religion.

The Kabre ritual complex—and the elders who ran it, who controlled ceremony, and the chiefs with whom they were allied—was also yoked into Eyadéma's Kabre-nationalist project. The dictator, born in a village located on the southern of the two massifs, returned to the north each year, making the rounds of villages in his helicopter to witness the wrestling matches that keyed male initiation ceremonies. This Mobutuist gesture—showing support for "tradition"—also provided an occasion for Eyadéma to recruit a new generation of soldiers into the army from the ranks of newly minted champion wrestlers (Piot 1999:91–92).

To reiterate, the dictatorship complex—in many ways a continuation of colonial authority relations of indirect rule—stood behind and sustained this ritual-authority system deep into the independence period. Eyadéma both supported tradition and the ruling gerontocracy in the villages, and provided stipends for chiefs. Though the arrangement was never free of conflict, there was nevertheless a settled solidarity and clear line of authority that knit together these mountain communities and their southern diaspora throughout much of the twentieth century.

The changes of the 1990s burst onto this socio-cosmological stage like a comet from the sky. Disconcerted by the violence against Kabre in the cities of the south, puzzled by those strange new keywords *démocratie* and *droits de l'homme*, attacked by the Pentecostal churches, stung by currency devaluation and state withdrawal, and increasingly neglected by cash-strapped diasporics, this authority system was shaken to its roots.

No longer respected or receiving state stipends, its chiefs and ritual leaders became shadow figures, and many chiefships have remained vacant years after the death of officeholders. In a melodrama (described in chapter 5) that brings together many of the themes of the moment, Farendé's still-reigning albeit de-salaried canton chief has sought new income by encouraging litigation of witchcraft rumor—and, according to his detractors, by often hearing cases of questionable merit. Feeling that he has fanned rather than doused the flames of witch panic, Lomé's "Amicale" (village association) of emigrant civil servant sons and daughters has been trying to wrest power from him, most recently proposing that he be replaced by a mayor. His comeback: that he has a notable track record in detecting witches and bringing them to heel—and that, with the state in retreat, he is the villages' last hope against this epidemic. (Notice the way in which state eclipse has led a chief to seek private profit from a public problem, in the process inflating occult imaginaries and providing the occasion for a takeover of the rural by urban *petit fonctionnaires*.) Struggles over chiefship are not new, of course, but the current dispensation is challenging this institution in unprecedented, perhaps fatal, ways.

Authority is also under attack in households. Teens now demand money before working their fathers' fields and invoke the "rights of man" when upbraided by parental authority. One extreme albeit emblematic example: a recalcitrant sixteen-year-old who stayed out nights and slept until noon (while her parents and siblings worked the fields and completed household chores) responded to her exasperated father's suggestion that she move out and fend for herself with the riposte that the homestead belonged to the children and it was rather her father and mother who ought to move. As the disconsolate father put it, "this is what 'les droits de l'homme' has taught our children."

If this northern system of authority is coming undone, so too is the local economy under increasing strain. Household production has been hobbled not only by recalcitrant children who demand pay in return for labor but also by the departure of its most able-bodied teens for plantations in Nigeria (see chapter 5). The 1994 devaluation of the CFA franc not only emptied the markets and sent women into the fields for the first time but also led to price increases that further gouged already strapped family budgets. A small but telling moment: A middle-aged woman I know used to be able to pay the CFAF 250 (50 US cents) to ride the cattle truck to market in Ketao each Wednesday, but a rise in gasoline prices sent the fare to a budget-breaking CFAF 350, and she now walks the 30 km round trip—as she did during childhood.

While incipient, a new set of sovereignties, and a new biopolitical relationship between power and its subjects, is taking the place of those vertical sovereignties that defined the dictatorship era. Dispersed and partial authority—a vestigial state and its band of dispirited chiefs, salaried school teachers and civil servant émigrés, freelance entrepreneurs and NGOs, Pentecostal pastors—now clutter the social field and jostle for control. Today's

Kabre—less citizens than bare-life subjects (Agamben 1998) inhabiting a zone of abandonment (Mbembe 2006)—attach themselves to these actors while also seeking independence from authority. In the same way that southern Pentecostals strive for embodied self-possession, and visa lottery entrants aim to become sovereign accumulators (through possession of a US visa), northern farmers pursue their own autonomy—a privatized sovereignty—by hoping to create or capture an NGO or, more nefariously, through occult accumulation.

The next two chapters explore this unsettled moment in the villages of the northern massifs by focusing on the new religious dispensation and the NGO scene in two of Farang's offshoot communities—Kuwdé, second-ranked in the village hierarchy (and the mountain locale where I have worked since the mid-1980s), and Farendé, administrative and marketing center at the foot of the mountains. In these northern villages, charismatic Christianity and the new NGOs march hand in hand in producing a sense of crisis and in defining a new biopolitical after state sovereignty.

# FOUR

# Charismatic Enchantments

If in southern Togo (and Ghana), charismatic Christianity offers a sense of possibility and agency—and a turning away from authoritarian and patriarchal imaginaries—it is perceived quite differently in the villages of the north. There it is experienced as an attack on local values and as an attempt to usurp the ritual/authority system that is the base of northern power within the Kabre diasporic system. Not surprisingly, those in the villages have generated a series of commentaries on and pointed responses to the new religious dispensation. At the same time, many of these commentaries further enmesh them within the logic of that which they aim to reject.

This chapter explores the parry-and-response between churches and villagers over the new religious dispensation and the occult imaginaries that have emerged at their intersection.[1] These imaginaries and the panics that accompany them have come to embody, and indeed to constitute, a sense of crisis—a crisis as much epistemological as political-economic (cf. Weiss 2004b:16–19). Examining the content of these imaginaries, the chapter explores the meaning of cultural forms that appear both resistant and subsumed at the same time and that seem, despite their appropriation of things Euro-American, as much self- as other-constituted.

This is a landscape inhabited by strange new shapes, with churches that organize as totemic groups and are seen as witch factories, with Pentecostals coded as predatory apes, with local workgroups (only a few years ago, the site supreme of nonalienated labor) retooled as finance machines and mini-bureaucracies, with computers and cell phone towers that are co-opted by witches, with sorcerers who fly to Europe in airplanes and mimic capitalist financiers. These figurations, I suggest, are local translations of twenty-first century commodity logic, and evince neoliberalism's and Empire's expansion into and thorough saturation of the social field.

In its assault on local religion, Pentecostalism not only begins to shift religious imaginaries from "traditional" to Christian—from spirits to the Holy Spirit—but also fashions an interiorized subject who turns away from village authority and relational dependency. Untethered from local gerontocracy and the state, this new biopolitical subject—a subject and its social in perpetual "crisis"—seeks its own autonomous salvation.

## Millennial Totemism

When in the mid-1990s the new churches—Assemblies of God, Church of the Pentecost, Neo Baptist, Croix Blanche ("White Cross")—arrived in Farendé, administrative/market town at the foot of the northern Kabre massif and beachhead of the charismatic movement in the area, they created an immediate stir by broadcasting their opposition to local religious practice. They insisted that followers renounce the worship of spirits and ancestors—refraining not only from animal sacrifice but also from participating in initiations and the dances that accompanied them. Animal sacrifice, charismatics suggested, was Satanic, and initiation dances were seen, despite their largely social and aesthetic nature, as seducing Christians, as one church member put it, "back into the religion of the villages." Provocatively, the new churches also accused the two mission churches that had been in the area since the 1940s—the Roman Catholics and the Presbyterians—of "paganism," this because of the set of compromises they had made over the years with local religion.[2] Tellingly, by summer 2005 both of these mission churches were feeling the heat of the new churches and had become more critical of attendees who continued to worship local deities. They also began to incorporate charismatic elements into their services.

The new Farendé churches are largely shoestring operations, presided over by a single pastor sent from a parent church in the south. Sunday services attract between twenty and thirty devotees (though one church, Croix Blanche, regularly draws several hundred) and follow a familiar charismatic format—an hour of singing, dancing, and praying, a second hour of sermon and collection. Doctrinally, there is little to distinguish one church from the next. They all hew to the absolute authority and literal interpretation of Scripture, to the need to accept Christ as personal savior (thus as someone who died for human sins and through whose grace believers are saved), to the efficacy and concrete embodiment of the Holy Spirit in the life of the believer, and to the End Times narrative. They also see the Devil at work in the villages, especially in village religion.

These churches' appeal derives in part, as in southern Togo and Ghana, from their novelty and from the promise of a break with older narratives and structures of authority. Their drawing power also comes from the promise of success and wealth—the "prosperity gospel" for which they are well known, and a message with strong appeal during the contemporary period. But, as with religious movements elsewhere, the reasons for attraction are diverse. For many of the women in these churches—two-thirds of the congregation at each service I attended—they provide an expressive outlet and alternative to the male-dominated ritual system of the villages. For some of the men, the churches provide a welcome escape from the demands of tradition—a tradition which requires heads of families to engage in repeated and often large expenditures on animals and beer for ceremonies. Others, both male and female, mentioned the release from the psychological toll of the constant fear of witches—for prayer is said to ward off witch attacks. One man told me that after he started going to church the village rumor mill no longer got under his skin. "I don't care what people say anymore. God will be the judge of my actions."

The most successful of the new churches in Farendé, Croix Blanche, arrived from southern Ghana in the late 1990s. As its name suggests—a play on the international health organization—it specializes (and boasts considerable success) in healing. Over one hundred people were at a service I attended in June 2005 in a rustic stone edifice on the edge of town that had been built with funds raised from the weekly collection. (Their numbers had swelled to two hundred when I visited two years later.) Brightly dressed devotees filled the pews, clapping and dancing and praying for over two hours. (I am always struck by the vibrancy of these charismatic gatherings, with their colors and music and swaying bodies, a sharp contrast with the libidinally destitute services of my Anglo-Protestant upbringing.) The sermon was on sin and sacrifice—a thirty-minute lecture on the inherent sinfulness of humans, sin that could be removed, the pastor claimed, by accepting Christ as savior. "Come into the church," he instructed, "and your life will begin over. You will be freed from your sins, from those harms you have committed against others. Even sorcerers can be reformed, and we welcome them into the church. . . . In history's final sacrifice, Jesus died for our sins, and because of this sacrifice, we are saved." A message, it seemed to me, that resonated powerfully with local ideas about sacrifice and expiation, while also recasting them in nonlocal (Christian) ways. [3]

Toward the end of the service, a dozen attendees came forward to testify to often dramatic healings in their lives: many had suffered physical infirmities, others had experienced psychological problems, even madness, and all had been cured. After these testimonials, the pastor turned to me—a common practice with new attendees—and asked if I would address the congregation, telling what had brought me to church. I stepped to the front (nervously: what does a non-charismatic foreigner say in such a setting?) and explained that I was a "schoolteacher" who had been doing research in the area for many years and had recently become interested in the spread of the new churches. I told them I had heard about Croix Blanche from a man in Kuwdé who, after attending Sunday services for several months, had been cured of a crippling knee disease, a telling which produced loud applause from the congregation. I later heard that my presence was taken as a sign that good things were coming to the church.

It is worth pausing to speculate on the reasons for the greater success of this church, which has many times the converts of any of the other new churches in the area. It may be that the "prosperity gospel" of the churches in the cities—that focuses on and privileges the economic success of church and individual—does not sell as well in an area where there is virtually no possibility for economic growth, and that physical healing provides a more accessible and tangible benefit—and concrete proof of the efficacy of the Holy Spirit. A local observer of the new church scene in Farendé added that Croix Blanche's cachet also derives from its innovations: it introduced new elements into the liturgy and deploys candles during services, it was the first, and remains the only, of the new churches to build its own edifice, and it provides room and board (in a small mud structure near the church) for those who seek its healing powers.

An interesting feature of the set of new churches in Farendé, one first pointed out to me by friends in Kuwdé (for whom the churches have become an intense object of study), is that they all share similar beliefs while following different interdictions. Thus, Assemblies prohibits its members from drinking alcohol and mandates that women wear headscarves to church, while Croix Blanche proscribes its members from not only consuming alcohol but also going to the hospital and entering church with sandals or shoes. Church of the Pentecost, known for its loud music, bans "traditional" drums (whose heads are made from animal skins) from the church premises. And, of course, all the Christian churches differ from village religion in prohibiting animal sacrifice. The "totemic logic" of this system—of marking difference through behavior rather than belief, of distinguishing groups, according to Lévi-Strauss's famous thesis on totemism (Lévi-Strauss 1963, 1966), through differences in taboo (Group A prohibits the consumption of alligator, Group B of antelope, Group C of porcupine)—not only provides a shorthand for differentiating the various churches from one another, and the churches from village religion, but also permits the proliferation of that which is otherwise identical. Indeed, it also corresponds to a type of commodity logic (or perhaps better: the latter simulates totemic principles), through which the self-same—Pepsi and Coke (both brown liquids with similar tastes and the same narcotic effect), the two dozen shampoos lined up next to each other on the shelf at the grocery store—have to be rendered different (a feat accomplished through various sleights of hand, like branding and advertising) in order to be profitable. Pentecostal interdictions constitute, as it were, a totemic system for the new millennium.[4]

Of course, a few hundred devotees from among thousands of villagers does not a revolution make. But it would be a mistake to measure the impact of the new churches by numbers alone. Discussion of them fills the airwaves in the villages—in part because of their provocations (banning ceremonial participation, accusing the mission churches of pagan leanings) but also because they have become a lightning rod for much that is new and unsettling in the post-Cold War climate. Thus, these churches were immediately associated with the "changes" of the moment of "démocratie"—and indeed their appearance on the landscape was as responsible as anything for producing a concrete/visible sense that things had changed. As detailed below, they are also associated with the dramatic increase in witchcraft activity—of accusations and rumors, and a vastly expanded witchcraft imaginary—that has become synonymous with the contemporary moment.

## Holy Spirits

From their foothold in Farendé, the new churches have taken their charge into the villages of the northern massif. There, they have met with a stronger, more resistant, response than in Farendé. Thus, when Assemblies sought to hold Sunday services in the mountain community of Kuwdé, the village where I have conducted research over the past twenty-five years, the elders refused, saying that one church in the village (the Presbyterian Mission Evangélique, which sends a pastor from the plain each Sunday to hold a service in a mud brick house in the center of the community) was already enough. Undaunted, Assemblies pressed its case by insisting on substituting Christian for local funeral ceremonies—an intervention into the ritual life of the villages in many ways more direct and insidious than the holding of regular services. I begin exploring the back-and-forth between villagers and charismatics by describing these funeral interventions, interventions which are symptomatic of the current conjuncture.

Funeral ceremonies are unquestionably the most important of Kabre rituals, an importance that has only increased over the last century with the dispersal of northerners throughout the diaspora, for it is funerals (and initiation ceremonies) that serve to mediate long-distance relations among kin (Piot 1999:42, 166). It is not unusual, for instance, for the funeral of a respected community member to draw hundreds, sometimes thousands, back from the south. Funerals are also the place where local (non-Christian) conceptions are most recalcitrant, in part because death is a moment when important social work is accomplished (the redistribution of property and authority, the reaffirmation of ties among kin and friends) but also because death is an occasion for knowledge and study (rather than, say, emotion). What was the cause of death? Was foul play (witchcraft) involved? Did family and friends carry out their responsibilities in caring for the sick person? Was an out-married woman well treated by her husband's family? And, depending on the answers to these questions, how best to proceed with transforming the deceased into an ancestor? Kabre thus invest an enormous amount of ritual energy, performing up to eight ceremonies for the deceased over a five to ten year period. It is this sequence of ceremonies that charismatics have tried to short-circuit by substituting a single Christian service.

On the two such occasions I have witnessed—both involving the deaths of converts to the Assemblies of God—the church's pastor climbed the mountain on the day of the opening funeral ceremony and asked the community to assemble for a Christian service outside the homestead of the deceased. What was striking about both gatherings—the pastor standing at the homestead's entrance, family and community members huddled on rocks and wooden benches beneath the shade trees that front each homestead—was that the pastor spent only a few minutes memorializing the deceased (reading a passage from the Bible, then singing a hymn) before launching into a diatribe against local religion. On the first such occasion (in July 2003), the pastor piggybacked on local anxieties about a drought that was gripping the area (and had produced a series of divination sessions to uncover the reason for the rain's abeyance) to lecture villagers about what he regarded as their mistaken reading of the cause of the drought: "You think that if the rain doesn't come, it is because devils or witches are to blame. But that is wrong," he thundered. "God decides when it rains, not people. Witches can't stop the rain. You worship rocks and trees and think that they will help you. But these are idols, false gods. There's only one spirit in the world—the Holy Spirit. Accept Jesus into your life, and you will see that this power is greater than all of these other things."[5]

The second pastor's visit (in August 2004) followed a similar pattern. This man of the church spent only a few minutes addressing the life of the deceased before departing script and opening an attack on local religion: "After we are done with my benediction, you can return to your fields [to cultivate]. There is nothing more to be done for this sister. She is already next to God. Please just let her go. No more ceremonies are necessary. You need to leave your old ways behind, ways which only please the Devil. Stop sacrificing to these idols and follow Jesus Christ. Only then will you be saved."

Switching registers, from sermon to tutorial, the pastor then asked if there were any questions. After a long silence, a member of the deceased's family asked whether it was not important for families "to show others that a death had occurred." (One of the main purposes of Kabre funeral ceremony is to "announce" and make visible to a larger public the passing of a family member.) "This is no longer necessary," the pastor responded. "Once the deceased has been buried, and once a Christian service has been held, nothing remains to be done. And this was what the deceased wanted—a simple Christian service only." Since there were no other questions, the pastor gathered up his hymnal and Bible and departed the village.

Sitting through these two events, I found myself barely able to contain my irritation and was frankly astonished at the apparent acquiescence of locals in the face of these attacks on their beliefs. The second pastor's intervention seemed not only an extraordinary violation of etiquette—demeaning those who had welcomed him into their midst—but also a blatant example of those Othering discourses that had been so central to colonial and postcolonial interventions into the area for centuries. But this struck me as even worse, for here was one of their own, a compatriot missionary, telling them that their entire belief system was the work of the Devil.

The next day I asked Sandi ("San-dee")—a brazen defender of village tradition with a quicksilver tongue and laser mind, someone who could always be counted on to speak his mind—why people had not responded more vigorously to the pastor's assault on local value. He agreed that they should have, and said that he himself would have, but that it would have been inappropriate under the circumstances, for he was not a member of the family of the deceased and therefore had no right to speak in that setting. But he also added that speaking out would have made little difference. "Who was affected by the words of that pastor? Those who are already believers heard nothing that they hadn't heard before. And those of us who are not Christian have heard this message many times already and are unaffected by it. Besides, despite the pastor's warnings, the family did the sacrifices anyway." The true discussion of the pastor's visit, Sandi added, would occur in the workgroup drinking sessions during the coming days.

At these after-work séances—lively gossip sessions lubricated by the grainy sweet-and-sour taste of sorghum beer—there was indeed discussion of the Christian funeral service. Interestingly, people went after the pastor rather than his message. One man made a snide comment about how fatigued the pastor seemed after climbing the mountain, and about his fumbling attempts to properly greet people (a southerner, he was unfamiliar with northern etiquette and spoke the local language with difficulty). Another added that pastors are only in it for the money. A third asked whether the Assemblies of God might not be sending Christian funeral services to Kuwdé as retaliation for their having refused to allow Sunday services in their midst.

The session then turned lighter, with the recounting of humorous anecdotes about the hypocrisy of pastors: about one who preached to his congregation about the evils of animism but who sacrificed in private and, upon retirement, became a local diviner; about another who took his trousers to a tailor to be mended but who forgot to remove the magical objects he had put in one of his pockets and whose un-Christian predilections were thus revealed; about a third who preached the Christian message of turning the other cheek, but, when tested by a prankster who slapped him in the face after Sunday service, dropped his Bible and punched back; and—my favorite—about the pastor who preached the sin of adultery to his congregation while nevertheless carrying on his own secret liaisons. In visiting a female friend one day, he was forced to flee in haste when her husband returned home unexpectedly, and, in getting dressed, mistakenly grabbed his paramour's underwear, thinking it was his handkerchief. During his sermon the next day, the pastor began to perspire and took out his handkerchief, only to have his double life exposed before the entire congregation.

By 2006, criticism of the charismatic presence had become generalized and open and was voiced in almost every context. At a workgroup drinking session I attended in June of that year, a ritual leader informed those present that a mini-drought and food shortage in one of Kuwdé's satellite communities had been caused by a deceased man from that village who (due to a grudge against family members) had taken food into the grave with him. When the local interrer opened the tomb in question, he found it filled with food—"corn, yams, sorghum," this leader reported, before taking a swipe at those churches who urge their followers to stop participating in local ceremony: "So what would a Christian do in this case—allow this community to continue to suffer, or do the ritual that would return food to those in need?" At a ceremony in one of Kuwdé's sacred forests in June 2008, the ritual's doyen announced that he had had a dream the night before that "someone"—understood by all as a member of one of the new churches—had been trying to block the ceremony (with his/her mystical powers). This elder then warned about the perils of neglecting tradition.

What sort of cultural-ideological work is going on here? Are locals, through their snide comments and jokes about pastors, and their warnings about the risks of Christian affiliation, resisting the missionary message? And does the fact that they continue to perform the sacrifices—"in hiding," after the missionary's departure—indicate that they remain unaffected by this work? Or, as the Comaroffs (1991) have suggested in discussing mission work among Tswana of southern Africa, is there a subtle ("hegemonic") form of colonization at play in the back-and-forth between missionaries and villagers—that, despite villager rejection of mission ideology, nevertheless gradually subsumes the local? Namely, does the fact that locals find themselves in dialogue with pastors and church members around issues that were formerly uncontested—the origin of rain, the efficacy of local spirits, the power of witches—create an opening that not only normalizes the missionary presence and missionary interventions into the religious and cultural life of the community but also places them on the slippery slope of a "long conversation" (Comaroff and Comaroff 1991) that they are destined to lose?

Moreover, despite their resistance, locals have ceded ground in subtle ways. Thus, Christian hymns and references to the Holy Spirit have crept into funerary practice. In even the most traditional of homesteads, I have seen a head of family bless the food before beginning to eat. I have heard prayer in the name of Jesus offered at the start of community-wide reunions. And it is now routine in Farendé to include the pastors of the new churches in meetings with chiefs and rainmakers about the provenance of the rain. In yet another instance, a nurse midwife at the Case de Santé (birthing clinic) in Kuwdé stood opposed to an attempt to integrate indigenous medicine into its practice—because, he said, local medicine was "Satanic" (because indigenous medicines are said to be the property of local spirits).

An interesting moment—and another instance of the inexorable creep of charismatic influence—occurred in summer 2005 during Waah, the male age-grade ceremony that occurs every five years and is the high point of a young man's maturation into adulthood. In something of an exception to Christian practice—to the churches' stated opposition to allowing members to participate in local ritual—some of the new Christians decided to dance in the ceremonies. Like the other initiates, they donned the antelope horns of members of their class and joined their age-mates when they visited homesteads and danced in the market at Putikida. But they refused to enter the sacred forests where the spirits reside, instead peeling away from the larger group to dance at the entrance to one of the new churches. At the very least, the church is now part of the initiation landscape in a way that it was not a few years ago.

A response that is gaining ground among educated Kabre who are still partial to tradition—and one that I also witnessed in Ghana among Ashanti of the professional classes who remain attached to the funeral ceremonies of their ancestors—is to differentiate between "religion" and "culture." Kabre initiation (especially the dancing and wrestling that accompanies it), these defenders assert, is not "religion"; it is culture or "tradition." Thus some continue to perform the dances but not the sacrifices, while others do both but nevertheless gloss the latter as "non-religion." While this renominalizing move enables them to continue to participate in tradition, it does so at a price, for it reduces it to a type of play and renders it marginal alongside "real" religion (Christianity).

## Divining Interventions

Villagers have also generated a number of larger, more culturally robust responses to the charismatic presence and to the post-Cold War dispensation. Amidst a series of witch panics that have enveloped this area over the past ten years, they have repeatedly accused Christians of being responsible for what one man called an "epidemic of sorcery," and hence of seeking to harm or kill villagers.

Late spring (May/June) in the villages of the north is a moment of spiritual housecleaning. If the rain abates at this tender time of year (when the sorghum and corn have only just taken root), members of Kumberi, the house responsible for the rain, will visit a diviner to uncover the reasons for the rain's interruption—reasons that typically entail violations of ritual practice.

In May 1996, for instance, rain divination (to determine the reason why a mini-drought was choking the area) implicated the sons of a deceased elder from Kumberi for failing to perform ceremonies for their father that would have enshrined him as a house ancestor. Their refusal, the sons claimed, was due to the fact that their Christian father did not want non-Christian ceremonies performed on his behalf (although northern elders insisted it was rather the sons who did not want the traditional ceremonies).

In June 1998, the diviner summoned to assess the reasons for the rain's abeyance found that a community in the plain had inappropriately buried an elder from a ritually important house in his natal community rather than in his ancestral home in the mountains. He ordered the community to re-do the funeral, this time in the mountains, at which point the rains returned.

In May 2005, a diviner blamed the rain's tardy arrival on a canton chief who had banned funeral ceremonies for two months following President Eyadéma's February death, thus preventing the proper burial of an elder from Kumberi who had died during this time. The diviner asked them to perform the ceremonies in order to bring the rain.

As these examples illustrate, rain divination often becomes a cipher for issues beyond local concerns. These are often deeply politicized issues—of relations between Christian and non-Christian Kabre, between mountain and plain (or northern and southern) Kabre communities, or of loyalty to a deceased president and his political party—that are folded into local accounts of spiritual malfeasance. Not surprisingly, then, villagers' recent encounters with charismatic Christians have also made their way into rain divination narratives.

When the rain stopped in May 2001, divination identified as responsible party a woman in one of the new churches. A young man from Kumberi had died suddenly in early spring and the woman was fingered by the deceased's older brother. In a strange twist, this brother claimed that the woman had struck up a deal with him to kill his younger brother but that, when the latter died, he realized he might be next on her list and decided to come clean. At the same time, a local dog butcher came forward to claim that the woman had also confided her intentions to him.[6] This narrative—already circulating at the time of the rain divination—was invoked by the diviner, who added a few details (about collaborations with others in the village) and demanded retribution (the sacrifice of a white sheep) to bring back the rain.

The details of such divination narratives capture the imagination and get recounted and dissected in the days that follow: why was this "butcher" such a good friend? how did she manage to connive with one brother against the other? what problems were there between these two brothers? Similar narratives emerged in 2002 and 2003. Each time a member of one of the new churches was identified as responsible for the untimely deaths of community members. In all three cases, their identity as Christian was lightly coded, even unmentioned, within the divination narrative itself, but emerged full-blown in the recountings of the diviner's story in the days and weeks that followed.

Other strands of evidence were added to those from rain divination to produce an emerging consensus that the churches were witch havens. Thus, villagers point out that Christian converts not only stop engaging in local ritual but also no longer consult diviners. This latter is especially damning because it means that someone who is accused of witchcraft will forgo those procedures which detect evildoers—and which exonerate those who have been falsely accused. Then, too, villagers add, church members get up in the middle of the night—at precisely that moment when witches are up and about. (When I asked charismatic friends whether it was indeed the case that they arose in the dark of night, they acknowledged that they did—in order to pray against witch attacks. In a clever turn, then, villagers take believers' protective action as evidence that they themselves must be witches.)

Moreover, some of the new pastors light "fires" inside their churches—a reference to the candles that Croix Blanche lights during its services—fire being locally associated with witches' nighttime gatherings. A final piece of evidence that draws the connection tightly between Christians and witchcraft is the fact that the churches openly recruit those who have sinned, including self-proclaimed witches, in the hopes of reforming them—but villagers quickly add that attempts to remake a witch are always fraught, for, as one man put it, with a twinkle in his eye, "once having developed the taste for human flesh, it's hard to leave that behind."[7]

Significantly, the coding of charismatics as witches not only is a villager construction but also finds support in the churches themselves. Thus, a popular sermon in churches both north and south is the one that warns members to be on their guard—because the most dangerous witches are in the church itself, "perhaps sitting next to you," hiding behind the cover of being good Christians. Moreover, in a series of witchcraft cases heard by the Farendé canton chief over the past five years, members of the church have not shied away from claiming responsibility. In one instance, a series of untimely deaths in one of the villages led a diviner to identify a recent Assemblies of God convert as responsible. When confronted, this church member—as with the above cases involving the rain spirit, a woman[8]—admitted her complicity, while also identifying a dozen other (non-church) members as co-conspirators, many of whom were important elders in the mountain community of Farang, the seat of Kabre ritual. Needless to say, these elders denied their complicity and spent months in litigation attempting to exonerate themselves in local tribunals as well as in state court.

Another case involving church members produced initial denials but subsequent confessions. As recounted by the canton chief (at a public meeting on "development" in July 2006 at which he had been called on to speak to the ongoing witchcraft crisis [see chapter 5]), a young boy had stepped forward to tell of a recurring dream in which important members from two Farendé churches, including a pastor, had attempted to recruit him to join them in their nighttime escapades. When the chief confronted the accused, they denied involvement, but later confessed when he threatened to take them to a diviner (to discover whether or not they were telling the truth). One by one, the chief explained, they came to his homestead to admit their complicity. He concluded by saying that he was keeping a list of church members who were confessed witches, and that he had signed confessions from those who had admitted their involvement in this case.

But why would a church member step forward to claim identity as a witch (and thus accept responsibility for having killed another human)? Of course charismatic belief allows such, even encourages it, in that the human state is one of sinfulness, and no matter how depraved one's sin, confession and correct living hold out the promise of putting one on the path to salvation. Then, too, the new churches actively recruit those who have sinned, including witches. Moreover, while at first blush sociologically counterintuitive—because being labeled a witch can produce ignominy and ostracism—such confessions can also enhance social standing, for they bestow fear and power over others. I have known several who, when faced with accusations that they had killed a sibling or a child, chose not to deny them, presumably perceiving the tradeoff (loss of status/increase in power) as working in their favor.

Finally, and importantly, the effect of the accusations and rumors that swirl around northern witchcraft, and the panics that accompany them, especially when they pull important elders into the inferno, is often more damaging to the villages than to the church or to one of its members. It plays into church ideology (and southern representations) which cast the village and the north as cradle of witchcraft and Satanism. Then, too, they also do the reverse, fuelling villager fears of the churches and providing support for their own suspicions that they are witch factories. Such are the overdeterminations and contradictory outcomes of this cultural field (Geschiere 1997, 2006). (Indeed, it is important to keep in mind that witchcraft ideologies, like most of culture's inventions, are multivalent. It is precisely the flexible, shifting, empty nature of the figure of the witch that makes it such a potent signifier—and enables it to be put to sometimes opposed cultural-ideological ends.)

Of course such phenomena, and the spectacles and speculations that accompany them—the spectacles of accusation and counter-accusation, the rumors that circulate around certain named individuals, the adventures of witches recounted in precious detail, the debates that take place in court-yards and beer huts—fuel the imagination and lend credence to the sense of living in a moment of crisis. Indeed, it is no stretch to say that it is the buzz around sorcery cases like these that *produces* a sense of crisis as much as it reflects one whose source lies elsewhere. Recall a point I mentioned earlier in discussing witchcraft imaginaries within "Pentecostalite" public spheres in southern Togo and Ghana: that the charismatic churches themselves are responsible for—have themselves produced—an efflorescence of witchcraft imaginaries (and thus a certain traditionalism, an "African" religiosity) un-der the sign of the Pentecostal and the modern.

But the rhetorical invocation of "crisis," and the sense of living in crisis that such invocation produces, is internal to both village religion and char-ismatic Christianity. Villagers, like Pentecostals, are constantly proclaim-ing conditions of personal and collective sinfulness—sin/bad behavior that brings on calamity, whether personal or social/collective—but also behavior/ sin/crisis that can be resolved by appropriate human intervention (divination-sacrifice for the villager, confession-expiation for the charismatic). As sug-gested earlier, there is a circularity internal to prosperity gospel thinking, as well as to village religion, that produces the conditions of its success and its immunity from falsification.

## Hunting Pentecostals

The set of associations between Christianity and witchcraft has also opened out onto a broader field of meanings that are quick to associate the con-temporary moment with disorder. A particularly rich, culturally resonant instance is the way in which the local imagination seized upon the arrival of a baboon troop at the time of the 2000 harvest and appropriated it to the struggle with the churches. Appearing out of nowhere, and with no previ-ous history in the area, the monkeys descended on unguarded sorghum and yam fields and stripped them clean within hours. All attempts to kill or chase them away failed, including enlisting the help of soldiers with AK-47s from a nearby town. The monkeys had such exceptional vision that they could see people coming from far away and would quickly take flight. The threat to local livelihood was so serious that many who had spent their entire lives in the north spoke of leaving for the south.[9]

Seeking explanation for the monkeys' provenance, locals began floating theories. The first that gained traction was that they were Europeans, the same Europeans who had been menacing Togolese/Eyadéma/Kabre about "démocratie" and the "rights of man." In apparent confirmation, a hunter who killed two one night and called me to his homestead the next day to take his photo alongside his kill, asked, with a wry smile, whether the monkeys' faces didn't resemble those of "whites." While mulling (and secretly relishing) the thought of Euro-Americans as apes, and its play on metropolitan stereotypes of Africans, I acknowledged that I couldn't disagree. I also thought back to the time when a young boy sitting next to me in a homestead began touching the hair on my arm and said to his father, "he has body hair—just like animals."

By 2002, a different theory took hold, one that has held consensus into the present. Locals began asserting that the baboons were Kabre "revenants"—local witches who had died and "returned" as monkeys. Moreover, because of the churches' role in sheltering witches, they insisted, many were Pentecostals. The syllogism at work here: because of the new churches, there are so many witches on the loose; when they die and attempt to enter the world of the ancestors, they are cast out by the good ancestors; as a consequence, these "phantoms" take revenge by transforming themselves into monkeys and preying on the crops of those humans who nourish their better behaved colleagues—and further the work of the new churches by punishing those who are attached to local religion.

The monkeys' humanlike traits seem to provide support for the theory—and endless fodder for conversation. Beyond the similarity in facial and bodily features ("the only difference is that monkeys walk on all fours"), they have exceptional intelligence and always seem able to outwit and avoid humans. If surrounded on all sides, they will find the one escape route open to them—"as if they know our plans ahead of time." Their uncanny intelligence is also reflected in the fact that they sleep in different stands of trees every night (making it difficult to track them) and sleep one to a tree (making it harder to catch more than one at a time). Moreover, they attempt to deliberately divert hunters by heading toward one set of trees in the late afternoon and then switching to another at dusk. They even share features of human sociality: each band has a "chief" or "dirigeant," and they engage in humanlike wailing when one of their own dies ("they do funerals for the dead").

Early on, a local hunter confirmed the speculation that the apes were humans. He reported that he had pursued a large band one day and, when he "opened" his clairvoyance, saw that only one was a real monkey. All the rest were "revenants." As a consequence, he turned back, weak-kneed at the thought of killing people. While this humanist hunter had delivered

11. Hunting monkeys, hunting Pentecostals, Kuwdé 2008

important information—that the monkeys were indeed people—the moral of the story, as told today, is different: that, in order to succeed on the hunt, a hunter must "turn off" his clairvoyant power.

"But if the monkeys are human, when you consume them, aren't you . . . eating people?" I asked a hunter in June 2008. He had just killed nine in a single night—the local record—and was preparing them for the cooking pot. "No, when you kill them, they're just animals," he responded. "They have hair on their bodies, so you can eat them. It's the same with witches— it's why they turn their [human] victims into animals before consuming them, so that those who want to eat won't lose their nerve."

Despite the success of some hunters, and the discovery in 2005 of a strategy for protecting some of their fields from devastation—by planting their sorghum fields together (instead of dispersed, the usual practice), local farmers found that the baboons would only eat from those on the periphery, apparently fearing that the interior's dense forest, with its play of shadows, might conceal hunters—the monkeys remain undaunted and seem only to have grown in strength over the past five years. Moreover, because the sorcery epidemic has marched hand in hand with the plague of monkeys, local speculation connecting the two seems confirmed all over again.

## Witching Capital

After occupying a central place in mid-twentieth-century Africanist anthropology, witchcraft studies disappeared from the scholarly horizon for several decades. Their displacement was largely due to the fact that the earlier work on witchcraft had been strongly tethered to the study of village social dynamics (to seeing witchcraft as idiom for social tension within close-knit groups), and, as late-century anthropology moved to research locales beyond the village (cities/nation-states/diasporas), those topics which had been central to village studies lost salience. Recently, however, the ethnography of witchcraft in Africa has resurfaced with a vengeance—now, ironically, refigured to address global rather than local inequalities and antagonisms—and has provided scholars with fertile ground for exploring the intersection between global neoliberal/capitalist agendas and local African worlds.[10]

As should already be apparent, the Kabre sorcery archive is a luxuriant one. Drawing on the figure of the witch,[11] Kabre have generated a rich set of commentaries on recent shifts in their social world, shifts that are accompanied by significant changes in the technologies of witchcraft itself. Thus, they say that witchcraft today is in an expansive, innovative phase, one in which the entire logic of the phenomenon—its modes of accumulation and destruction, the identity of the witch and the witch-victim, the powers and technologies witches deploy, their methods of concealment—are undergoing rapid transformation. There has also been a shift of the phenomenon beyond the imaginary and borders of the village. Kabre witches today are prolific travelers, roaming far and wide during their nighttime odysseys—into the Kabre diaspora, to the capitals of West Africa, even to Europe. My argument will be that these transformations in the field of representation correspond to and index transformations in the political economy of the post-Cold War moment, and thus the transition to a logic of Empire and the thoroughgoing saturation of the Kabre social field with the logic of the commodity form. They stand as well as commentary on and critique of that form.

The history of Kabre ideas about witchcraft provides a neat periodization of changing local relations with the broader (colonial and postcolonial) capitalist economy. During the precolonial period, Kabre say, witches were few in number and didn't kill; they simply ate small holes in the arms or legs of their victims, leaving scars but little more. It was only during the colonial period, as Kabre ventured to the south of Togo and began working for money in European mines and plantations, that witches began to multiply and became deadly. It was also at this time that the idiom of the market metaphorized the language and imaginary of witchcraft: witches were said to convene in markets at night, where they exchanged their victims for money before consuming them with their compatriots.[12] During both of these earlier periods a witch's victims were always family members.

As the colonial and early postcolonial economy and its associated modes of production and exchange have been replaced by Empire's neoliberal logic/s of production and exchange, so too have Kabre witches mimicked—and, indeed, sought advantage from—this transformation. Thus witches today, even more than their colonial counterparts, are in search of money—and these traders in human flesh will forgo consuming their victims in order to put them into circuits of sale and resale. "Everyone's after money these days," Anawé, a local diviner-savant, told me in recounting stories of lavish witch markets in hyper-urban settings where African witches mingle with their European counterparts. "You might take your victim to market to consume with friends, but upon arriving you see what goods you can buy if you sold him instead. This seduces you to sell [instead of consume] but also to return again soon with another victim." As another put it: "Before, the night markets had sellers and butchers and consumers; today there are also those who buy and resell."

This new culture of accumulation—accumulation that has morphed from one based on the simple exchange of commodities, C-M-C, to one based on "expanded exchange," M-C-M or M-M$^1$ (Marx [1867] 1977)—is related to another shift in witchcraft's morphology. Today, unlike during the colonial period, witches often seek their prey beyond the family. "They kill indiscriminately (*yim*)," Anawé continued. "They go after anyone now." This depersonalization of witchly killing—also registering a switch from familial to nonfamilial modes of production—strikes those I know as a deep violation of their sense of right. This is not to say that a witch's killing was ever seen as morally positive, but rather that killing in the intimacy of the family has long been considered more legitimate than killing beyond it—not only because families produce enmity as well as amity (and thus create the conditions, sometimes justified, for revenge) but also because it is easier to detect (and undo) unjustified uses of sorcery within a familial setting. The contemporary shift to targeting victims beyond the family is unsettling precisely because, as one put it, "one never knows where death might come from and who is responsible," and because the mechanisms for redress (when unrelated individuals are involved) are not as ready to hand. Is this not also a way of signaling the depersonalized, indiscriminate, unknowable origins of power in today's world—of a (necro)political regime no longer tethered to the dictatorial state?

Consider, too, the way in which the occult has effloresced with the withering of the state, as if a remainder left by the end of sovereignty. If, as Agamben (1998) suggests, sovereignty and death are co-constitutive—if politics is always a necropolitics (Mbembe 2003) and there is an intimate association, indeed equivalence, between the sovereign and bare life, and between bare life and death (Agamben 1998:100–103), a truth always already written into African political imaginaries that link sovereignty with deadly power[13]—the remaindered witchcraft might be read as a type of haunting, a way in which the dictatorship continues to inhabit its afterlife. But witchcraft was also sovereignty's adversary during the 1970s and 1980s, with the Togolese state not only adjudicating cases of sorcery in the courts but also imagining subaltern trafficking in the occult as a threat to its ironfisted rule. This ambivalence—sovereignty and witchcraft as co-constituting, witchcraft as sovereignty's nemesis—is another instance of what Geschiere (1997, 2006) has described as the circularity of witchcraft discourse, helping account for its powerful grip on the political imagination.

Despite affinities between dictatorial power and stateless sorcery, between Cold War and post-Cold War sovereignties, there are also important differences. The sorts of citizen-subjects and the biopolitics produced by state and dictatorship are different in kind from those elicited by the field of a remaindered sorcery. The latter, indeterminate and open ended, is productive of a nomadic subjectivity that defies familial and chiefly authority systems and pursues its own sovereign accumulation—this by contrast with the vertically aligned sovereignties and subjectivities of the dictatorship complex and their deep commitment to relational personhood.

Contemporary witches, Kabre say, are also better at covering their tracks—a need produced by the infelicity of recent witchly killing—and stories abound about their new strategies of concealment. Thus, witches today hide their fires at night, fires that were formerly open to view. (By way of illustration, those I spoke to often used the on-again off-again luminescence of fireflies as metaphor for the diffuseness and unlocatability of witches' fires today, with one asking whether there wasn't an additional uncanny resemblance between the two: "Who has ever seen a firefly during the day? Just like witches, they're only visible at night!") Contemporary witches also use covert modes of transportation—traveling in "cars" beneath the earth (when they aren't flying in airplanes), a system of transport that one person described as like the Paris Metro. They have also now begun to use unsuspecting others, especially children, as a front—for instance, seducing a child with money or food into a friendship that indebts and eventually requires that the child offer up a family member—and hide behind new diseases like AIDs, a disease whose provenance Kabre say is not related to witchcraft but that, because of its elusive, multiform nature, allows a witch to conceal him/herself behind it.

Witches' use of subways for travel—a recent innovation, entering the popular imaginary only in 2004—is but one example of their avid appropriation of new technologies. Witches also use guns, have cameras and televisions for surveillance, and—their trademark—travel in airplanes. Computers have not yet entered the witchly lexicon of northern Kabre, though I have heard southern Togolese warn that witches can attack through the Internet and that one needs to be wary of email attachments that might contain witchcraft—a local version of the computer virus, although, significantly, one that does damage to the user rather than the machine. Cell phones can also be vehicles for witch attacks. A friend I called just after arriving in Lomé in December 2007 let her cell phone ring a dozen times before answering, later telling me that, despite recognizing my number, she was hesitant to pick up because she hadn't known I was returning then and was afraid that an evildoer might have borrowed my phone. "You have to be careful at the end of the year because debts people have with the Devil come due then and they're looking for new victims. My pastor told me not to answer the phone whenever I don't recognize the number or am not sure of the identity of the caller."

The giant antenna in Farendé for the cell phone company Togocel, installed in 2006, has also been appropriated by witchcraft discourse. The terrain beside it is rumored to be a favorite landing strip for witches' planes, especially those returning from the south, and, when in summer 2008, all the lights on the antenna burned out, locals suggested that night flyers were responsible—that they preferred dark to light and wanted to ensure that their aviation would go unnoticed. (Despite their attraction to technology generally, witches do not like lights. Indeed, as mentioned in the next chapter, one solution proposed by local residents at a conference on development to the current witchcraft epidemic was to bring electricity—light at night—to Farendé.)

When I asked Anawé about witches' fascination with and use of the latest technologies, he answered in rhetorical fashion: "What's surprising here? Powerful people need the latest [most powerful] things, and, since witches frequent the night markets, they have money to buy them." This laconic response not only associates powerful people with technologies of power—thus recognizing a potential class relation and a set of class markers within the sociology of witchcraft—but also suggests that such technologies generally might be acquired through illicit means, a point implied in the

12. Farendé Togocel antenna: witches' landing strip, 2008

statement of a man with whom I spoke who said that airplanes are made from human bones. Of course, such critical commentaries of those with power—and of witches—are always also tinged with jealousy and longing.

The nighttime escapades of witches are recounted in vivid and often alluring detail, details that are made public and then circulate, with commentary, when cases are litigated, as more and more are these days. When I stopped in at the canton chief's house in July 2003, he regaled a friend and me with the details of a case he had just finished hearing about the adventures of a local woman who had migrated south into the diaspora and there fallen in with a coven of witches. To gain acceptance, she had given up one of her own children (a child, in fact, who had recently died). She then fell in love with a young man in the group, and the two of them plotted the abduction and killing of her real-life husband. But the husband was clairvoyant and was waiting for them when their airplane came to abduct him. In accusing them, the husband said that if they themselves did not demand a hearing at the local chief's, he would. (Someone accused of witchcraft always has the right to a hearing—to defend his or her reputation against false accusation.) At the hearing, the wife denied the husband's accusation, but two of the other co-conspirators (the plane's "pilot" and the younger sister of the woman's lover) came forward as witnesses for the husband and testified in detail about the nighttime exploits of their "équipe" (team)—which involved journeys to northern Togo as well as to Lomé and Accra. The woman continued to deny the charge, and the case was remanded to the north—as are all unresolved cases of southern witchcraft—where the canton chief was asked to rule on it. He sent her to a diviner in Benin who administered a test—which involved putting a strong "medicine" in her eyes to see whether or not she cried, with crying indicating guilt. She was found guilty and finally confessed her complicity.[14]

This witchcraft narrative has all the features of the millennial potboiler: conspiracy and large-scale collaboration ("witches now work in 'teams'"), denial and eventual confession, a strong gendering of the witch, the use of airplanes, travel beyond local borders (and litigation that travels too), and—it came out later—the woman's alliance with members of one of the new churches. It is also filled with details not only about the persons involved and their plots but also about their specific roles in piloting airplanes. Indeed, there is an almost cinematic voyeurism in the telling and retelling of these cases (which, again, speaks to the "productivity" of the charismatic-demonic moment).

Such voyeurism was evident in a case that was making the rounds in Kuwdé in July 2004. It involved the escapades of an "équipe" of three adults and five children from Boua and Kuwdé who had raised money by selling witch-victims in the night markets in order to purchase an airplane. In those tellings I witnessed, people were especially intrigued with the roles played by each person in operating the plane: who had been the "pilot," who the "copilot," who the "ticket taker." One narrator identified a certain Kuwdé woman as the plane's "customs agent." But another disputed this detail. "She's not the customs agent on this airplane, she's the owner! I know this because she lives next to me and the plane is parked behind her house when she's not using it." (This assertion led to a humorous exchange about how the speaker would have known that an invisible airplane was parked beside her house—unless she too had clairvoyant powers [and thus might be involved in matters of the night]. "No. It's only what I've been told," she responded amidst peals of laughter.) She then proceeded to detail—according to what she had "heard"—who was the "pilot" (a young man from Boua), who the "copilot" (a friend of the man from Boua), who the "ticket taker," and who the "customs agent." This, again, was a witches' tale richly entwined with the landscape and technologies of the contemporary moment—an airplane with a "custom's agent," and thus one also accustomed to international travel.

A note on the social unit at the heart of contemporary sorcery discourse, the "équipe." It is a striking feature of witchcraft narratives today that unrelated individuals collaborate in groups of six to eight, this because, prior to the 1990s, it was unusual to hear of collaboration by more than two people or of collaboration among people who were not members of the same family. Such larger-scale cooperation—in collectives that bear the name of and are the same size as work or cultivation groups (*ekpare*)—would appear to be the result of two recent innovations in workgroup identity. Many of the new development initiatives, especially those involving microfinance, attempt to work through local *ekparena* (pl.), reorganizing them as income-generating groups and as mini-bureaucracies with elected officials (see chapter 5). Moreover, these workgroups have recently ("since the [1990s] moment of 'droits de l'homme' when our children began refusing to work for us, insisting that they too had rights and should be paid for their labor") been deployed by youth in the villages as moneymaking groups. They now charge up to CFAF 2,000 ($4) to cultivate someone's—even a parent's—field. It would appear that it is the pressure put on this form of traditional collective by neoliberalism's microfinance initiatives, and by money-seeking youth, that has commodified the *ekpare* and made it a prime target for appropriation by money-seeking witches—and by capitalist circuits of finance (Harvey 2005, 2007; Elyachar 2005).

Increasingly—another shift—Europeans are now beginning to appear in these stories, and this despite the fact that the long-dominant Farendé-Kuwdé narrative about Europeans has been that they do not engage in witchcraft. Europeans have special (mystical) powers, villagers assert, powers they use for good—to produce the technology for which they are known—while Africans, lacking the means to produce such things, use their power to kill. I initially read this as a false consciousness narrative—of locals having internalized a demonizing/neocolonial story about Africa. But when the canton chief repeated it in 2005, I understood it differently—as a vernacular theorization of African underdevelopment. Namely, it asserts that Africans, like Europeans, are endowed with strong powers but lack the means (infrastructure, money) to bring about their own development. Seen in this light, it is a story that bears resemblance to Euro-American scholarly critiques of global inequality—which connect wealth in Europe to its absence (cultures of death, necropolitics) in Africa—while nevertheless differing in its insistence on an agentive Africa, that, denied wealth creation, exercises its agency in the only way available to it.

In the mid-1990s, Europeans began appearing in witchcraft narratives, although still not as the bearers of deadly power. Here is a tale about one such European that made the rounds at that time: An unscheduled airplane—a witches' plane—landed one night at the airport at Niamtougou.[15] The European on duty went to inspect. When he entered the plane, he pulled out his notebook and began to record what he saw—"writing in his notebook" (or, in another account, "writing down numbers"). When he finished and tried to exit the plane, the door vanished ("he couldn't find the door"), preventing his departure. It was only after he voided his notes that the door opened and he was able to leave. (In some versions, the details change, while nevertheless preserving the larger point. Thus, in one account I heard, the man was American rather than European, and in another, he had a camera rather than a notebook—a camera whose pictures, when developed, were blank.)

The message, a defiant one, is that these Africans' "power" is stronger than that of the European/American. The European may have invented the airplane but he is unable to complete his record-keeping (here recognized—in a vernacular version of Foucault—as power/surveillance) because he is blocked by the witches' special/mystical powers.[16] Thus, by voiding his record of their arrival (in his notebook, with his camera), they render themselves invisible and beyond his control.

The view that Europeans do not themselves engage in witchcraft is today beginning to change. Although long journeys are risky ("if you're not home by dawn, you will fall from your plane"), witches travel to Europe and there encounter Europeans with power. In one telling, a father went to Paris in search of his son, but his plane was spotted by surveillance "televisions" located inside the plane of a European witch. A fight with guns ensued, during which the father realized that his son was on the side of the European. Eventually, he turned away empty-handed and returned home. I asked the narrator whether this was a tale of betrayal on the part of a child of the diaspora, or one of seduction/abduction by the European. "It is both," he answered. "Our children are forever neglecting us, but it is also because they are seduced by the goods and money of the European."

Still rare, such accounts of European sorcery are coterminous with the recent spread of Togolese into the overseas diaspora, and will no doubt increase as the diaspora continues to grow. But such should not be surprising, for one of the lessons of the study of witchcraft in this context is that it likes to ride the crest of the latest big thing.

---

These witchcraft stories rivet the imagination and come to define for Kabre much about their current predicament and power's operation in the contemporary world—its diffuseness and unlocatability, its lack of transparency, its conspiratorial nature, the inequalities it brings into being and oversees. They also betray important shifts at play in the world today—the blurring of old boundaries between family and beyond (and between familial and nonfamilial modes of production and exchange), between local and global, between specifically African powers and those of Europeans, between tradition and modernity. The world of the witch—arguably as "traditional" as any, filled as it is with mystical modes of causality and local conceptions of value—is nevertheless saturated with postmodern sensibilities and commodity logics and modes of exchange, deploying and indeed reveling in all the latest technologies and offering up protagonists who pursue money as much as the most committed capitalist. Here, too, is a blurring of the boundary between admiration and critique, for these witchcraft tales at once condemn a witch's means of wealth production while nevertheless condoning, if not celebrating, the desire for wealth itself.

But, too, for many Kabre, the world of witchcraft is a world of epidemic and moral panic (Weiss 2004b:16–19)—a world, preoccupied with death and the necropolitical, that is unraveling and out of control (cf. Geschiere 2006:223–26). As witchcraft account is stacked upon witchcraft account— and every week, it seems, there are new cases, cases that strike close to home, for they touch everyone or at least everyone's family at some point—the sense of living in a state of crisis is palpable.

## Orientalist Imaginings?

Of course, in writing about the witchcraft archive, the anthropologist runs the risk of re-orientalizing Africa, and thus of once again associating that continent with superstition and the occult (cf. Geschiere 2006:220–21). Would it not be better to ignore such beliefs—to write them off as glorified gossip—and simply focus on the "hard" realities of underdevelopment and politics? The answer should be apparent in the above. Witchcraft narratives are very much discourses about such hard realities—about unequal access and the failures of European development, about the il/legitimate constitution of political authority, about the temptations of illicit wealth production. They are concise, albeit allegorical, ways of trying to understand shifts in power's operation in today's world. Moreover, in that they are idioms through which many Togolese think and imagine the political (something akin to Christian End Times narratives, or neoliberal discourses about democracy and markets), by eliding them we silence and engage in violence against Togolese modes of self-representation. Better, I think, to fully engage them and try to understand them on their own terms. Moreover, by ignoring such discourses, we leave discussion of them to those (hack journalists, dime-store authors) who revel in orientalist (decontextualized) depictions of Africa.

## Afterthoughts

I have traced a sinuous path connecting the efflorescence of charismatic Christianity at the coast to its crusading offshoots in Farendé, to villagers' parrying with the churches and their fertile speculation about the secret lives (and afterlives) of its members, to the witch panics and imaginaries that have enveloped this northern region over the past ten years.

It should be clear that Pentecostal and villager religious imaginaries are mutually constitutive of, feed off, and indeed co-produce one another—and that charismatic incursions into this area are themselves responsible for the expanded witchcraft imaginaries and panics that have recently become routine. The charismatic needs the "other" of the witch and its putative home, the village, to prosecute its case—to offer evidence of Satan's existence, to produce a "lieu" of the Devil's habitation and a site for its eradication, to convince followers of the efficacy of the Holy Spirit. But it is precisely this preoccupation that villagers intuit and turn back on the churches, claiming it is church members rather than villagers who are the real sorcerers and sources of local malcontent.

In that charismatic and village religious imaginaries mirror and re-stage one another, it should not be surprising that they also come to resemble one another. Indeed, the extent to which Pentecostalism doubles as village religion is striking. Its "visions" and its Holy Spirit visitations remind of nothing so much as village divination and spirit possession. The efficacy and explanatory power it gives to the dream state and its scanning of the everyday for signs of the Devil (and the divine) bear clear semblance to village religion's similar preoccupations. Pentecostalism's obsession with witches and evil spirits bears affinity to the like concerns of those in the villages, and, just as village shrines protect against witchcraft, so too does charismatic Christianity present itself as something of an anti-witchcraft cult. Moreover, the role of sacrifice in correcting human error remains central to both (albeit figured differently through the body/blood of Christ than through the animal surrogate of the villages). Even Pentecostalism's zeal for money and prosperity finds its counterpart in village religion.[17]

And yet I hesitate to read this mutual imbrication, as postcolonial theory would, as simply another example of cultural appropriation—of the cannibalization and refiguration of Christianity by village religion, or of the local's "hybridizing" appropriation of charismatic Christianity. It certainly may be that, but it is also more[18]—and indeed ought to be read more along the lines suggested by Gates (1988), himself appropriating Derrida ([1972] 1982), in discussing processes of cultural mimesis in cultures of the African diaspora: that they entail "repetition [appropriation] with a difference." Not only is charismatic Christianity village religion with a new twist—a single historical sacrifice instead of ongoing sacrifices, a single spirit instead of multiple, a single pastor in place of a chorus of priests (and, needless to say, the same might be said of village religion's appropriation of the Pentecostal worldview)—but also, and more significantly, Pentecostals and villagers have both embraced a politico-religious imaginary that features prosperity thinking, celebrates information technologies, participates in the latest global imaginings, *and* believes in the immanence of divine intervention in the life of believer and community. Moreover, it is important to emphasize—lest we fall into the trap of reading all this as simply the reappearance of the neoliberal in the sphere of the religious—that this imaginary's enchantments are matched by its demons. Thus, its desire for the new and its cargo-cult-like rejection of the old is accompanied by moralizing judgments about the wealth of the avaricious money-seeker, the womanizing or duplicitous pastor, the deceitful neighbor or fellow church member.

It is especially the opening created by this new politico-religious imaginary that interests me—and the way in which both village religion and charismatic Christianity get ramped up through their encounter with one another and merge into something new and other. This is culture in crisis and in panic mode, a mode which, not incidentally, coincides with Pentecostal eschatological imaginings about radical rupture (Meyer 1998; van Dijk 1998; Robbins 2007) and the end of history (tradition) as we know it, engendering a temporality that is event-driven and punctuated, thus departing from the "time" of the ancestors and the Cold War political. The agency of the local here is visible precisely—and ironically—in its rejection of a past coded "African" and its appropriation of Euro-otherness, an otherness, however, that dresses up as locally authored or at least—is this not the point of the encounter at the Niamtougou airport between the European and local witches?—as locally dictated.

I want to refuse the position that sees such religious imaginaries as mere response to or reflection of a "crisis" that lies outside and beyond. These imaginaries themselves play a constitutive, generative role in the making of that crisis. But more, they *are* that crisis—not so much in the sense of having invented it, but rather as having taken it over and amplified it and spun it along lines of their own choosing. Thus, the "crisis" of the family, or the crisis of tradition, or the crisis of the churches is inexorably filtered and shaped *from the start* by local imaginaries and sociologies (imaginaries, as suggested above, that regard the notion of crisis itself as foundational). How else to think the fact that pastors are helping their congregants pray for witch-victims, or that in hunting baboons locals are consuming Christians, or that Sin might be responsible for the excess of death today? There is perhaps no better index of this point than the fact that when native sons and daughters returned from Lomé in July 2006 for a two-day conference on how to better "develop" their home region (see chapter 5), the main agenda item—occupying the entire first page of the two-page memo they distributed in advance—was not the area's lack of infrastructure, or its abandonment by the state, but "la crise de sorcellerie."

This chapter's story is also one of resistance *and* subsumption—a doubleness or ambivalence that seems emblematic of the contemporary moment (and of a crisis of the political as we know it). Yes, villagers may vigorously criticize the charismatic incursion, but they are also appropriated by it. Yes, witchcraft narratives are critical discourses, but people are also taken in by the desire for that which they criticize.

Two recent moments capture something of this doubleness—of the way in which refusal conjoins acquiescence—and thus something of the contradictory desires that characterize the current conjuncture.

When Farendé's middle school (Collège d'enseignement générale [C.E.G.]) director died of a stroke in February 2008, there was a heated battle over his body and over the ceremonies that would accompany him to the grave. The pastor of the church he attended in Farendé demanded that he be buried in that community with only a Christian service, while his natal village insisted on his return to the mountain for interment in the family's ancestral tomb accompanied by the full complement of ceremonies for the dead. After days of back-and-forth—while the body lay in a refrigerator in a town thirty-five kilometers away, awaiting the arrival of native sons and daughters from Lomé—both sides compromised. The body was returned to the mountain for burial (albeit in a coffin in a grave beside the family homestead rather than in one of the ancestral tombs) but the service was Christian, with the family agreeing to forgo its ceremonies. The concession was remarkable not only because it was the first time in Kuwdé's history that such ceremonies have been waived but also because the deceased was a beloved native son who had steadfastly demonstrated his respect for family and community. While both sides thus gave ground, this was clearly a compromise that favored Christianity, for, in granting ceremonial privilege to the church alone, it set a precedent that bespeaks a future beyond tradition.

The second moment occurred on a Sunday morning in June 2008. Sandi, the brazen defender of tradition and acid critic of the churches, slipped quietly into the rectangular mud hut in Kuwdé where the Église Évangélique service was being held and seated himself alongside the children in the front row. At the end of the sermon the pastor launched into an attack on tradition, asking who, if given the choice between the "old" (tradition) and the "new" (Christianity), would choose the new. Sandi was the first to thrust his hand in the air, and, when called on, boomed "the new." When I asked him later whether he was now a Christian, he laughed and said no—that he had just been caught up in the moment and later regretted that he had spoken at all. And yet consider: regretful or not, here was an arch-traditionalist attending church, sitting in the front row, hand in the air—"caught up in the moment"—voicing support for the words of a pastor who was calling for an end to tradition.

# FIVE

# Arrested Development

In the views of some observers, the third world in particular is being swept by a non-governmental, associational, or 'quiet' revolution that . . . may prove to be as significant to the latter twentieth century as the rise of the nation-state was to the nineteenth century.

—(Fisher 1997:440)

Today's democratico-capitalist project of eliminating the poor classes through development not only reproduces within itself the people of the excluded but also transforms the entire population of the Third World into bare life.

—(Agamben 1998:180)

## Signs of the Times

Drive through any town on the road to Togo's northern border—Notse, Atakpamé, Sokodé, Kara, Niamtougou, Mango, Dapaon—and you'll be greeted by a riot of signs announcing the work of development agencies (jostling for attention alongside those of the Pentecostal churches): AA, FED, PSI, CAPESP, AVOBETO, AVJADE.[1] This world of the acronym—this "alphabet soup of agencies" (Anderson 2006:63)—is the lingua franca of the neoliberal moment, a sign system that condenses and makes visible the NGO fervor that fills the West African landscape today.

In 2006, there were over five thousand NGOs and NGO-like Associations in Togo (FONGTO 2006), most created since the early 1990s.[2] Often little more than one- or two-person shell organizations, they appeared during the decade after the end of the Cold War—as if out of nowhere, like mushrooms after a spring rain—to capture international funding at a time

13. Signs of the times, Sokodé 2009

when state monies (salaries to civil servants, developmental aid to communities) had largely disappeared. Riding the tide of the times and quickly divining those projects favored by international donors (microfinance, education, AIDS, orphanages), an array of local actors (from de-salaried state employees to unemployed university students) opened offices to deliver social services to localities throughout the country—and to access scarce personal resources.

Alongside these smaller organizations, a new breed of international mega-NGO also crowded the development field, introducing ambitious countrywide projects, many focused on health and education. One such organization, BØRNEfonden, a Danish child sponsorship agency whose aim was to increase school attendance through broad interventions into family life, initiated projects in twenty-seven locales throughout the country. Another, an American NGO with a Foucauldian name, Population Services International (PSI), launched high-visibility projects focusing on HIV, teen pregnancy, and malaria. Known for its creative approach, PSI paid motorcycle-taxi drivers to educate clients about the risks of AIDS, held seminars with truck drivers and soldiers about condom use, purchased television ads and giant billboards urging parents to keep their daughters away from older men, and distributed insecticide-treated bed nets (to ward off malarial mosquitoes) to over half a million Togolese families.[3]

In filling the gap left by the state when it withdrew from the development field in the 1990s, these new organizations are reconstituting the terrain of the biopolitical. It is they more than the state who are now organizing the production of life (who and what is valued, who will be supported and who left behind) (Rose 2001, 2007; Redfield 2005, 2009; Comaroff 2007; Fassin 2007; Bornstein and Redfield forthcoming). It is also they who are redefining the political (mandating and monitoring elections, encouraging political decentralization, urging that chiefs be replaced by mayors). In thus assuming responsibility for the organization and production of material and political life, it is these new international organizations that have become the new sovereign—but a sovereign that is driven by distant international agendas. It is also a sovereign—or a set of sovereignties—that is decentralized, unregulated, and often anarchic and haphazard.

This NGO revolution—this revolution in the biopolitical—has produced a significant, if still emergent, reshuffling of local groups and categories. "Village," "workgroup," "chief," "tradition"—categories and social forms in place since the early colonial period—are all being unsettled and refigured, and, in the case of chiefs, swept aside. Such displacement of figures and forms associated with the past of course marches hand in hand with, and constitutes a secular version of, the Pentecostal attack on and jettisoning of tradition.

In this chapter, I examine those development projects and practices that appeared in Farendé-Kuwdé at the turn of the millennium. I am interested especially in those new modes of subject-making these projects implemented, and in the way they came to inhabit and transform peoples' everyday lives. I am also interested in the effects of these projects' failures (for the projects creating the most stir only a few years ago have now abandoned the area). In the end, while producing sometimes dramatic change in local self-understandings and in the organization of everyday life, they left the material development of the region largely unaffected. Moreover, they have produced a surprising set of local discourses about the causes of such abandonment.

I also look at efforts by departed native sons—mostly civil servants in Lomé—to "develop" their home region. These elites return annually to engage in dialogue with kin and villagers about local development and to counsel them on strategies for raising money and attracting NGOs. Not surprisingly perhaps, and proving the expansive nature of what counts as "development," their discussions in July 2006 and 2007 focused as much on witchcraft—on those accusations and counter-accusations filling the local airwaves—and its effect on the development of the region as on material development per se. Development would be impossible, they intimated, unless the jealousy that turns friend and family member into foe—crystallized in the witchcraft accusation—was first set aside. This sentiment was echoed in advice I had recently received from a friend who suggested that the money I had contributed to a local development fund would all be for naught unless I sought out a ritual specialist to banish a witches' market that convened each evening atop a large tree outside a community homestead—a tree whose capacious umbrella canopy indeed seemed to invite such imaginings. At the time, I dismissed his comment as a product of his ripe imagination and of the fact that he seemed easily seduced by occult logic, but I now read it as also indexing the intimate connection locals see between development's success and the settling of longstanding jealousies, for discussion about witches is always one about enmity among humans as well (cf. Smith 2008).

## Developing Farendé

There is a long history of development practice in the Farendé-Kuwdé area. In the 1950s, the Presbyterian Eglise Evangélique, under the guiding hand of French missionary Jacques Delord, built the first school and health clinic—and, in so doing, conjoined religion and development in the local imaginary. Delord—whose name seems scripted from missionary legend, and whose pioneering evangelizing and development efforts in the area have made him into a local hero—not only inaugurated the area's first education and health projects but also modeled Protestant enterprise for the local population. A short, wiry man of indefatigable energy (whom I met in France in the 1980s—when he was in his eighties and still full of vigor), Delord not only established the first school and clinic but also turned his home into a small business enterprise. Built on a hillside with a fetching view of the verdant plain between the two Kabre massifs, the missionary's house was surrounded by terraced gardens filled with luxuriant and exotic produce—lettuce, tomatoes, cucumbers, flowers of European origin—and fed by an ingenious system of irrigation. Delord invited the best students (and committed churchgoers) to work there on Saturdays, reimbursing them with pocket change. While small in scale and materially insubstantial, this practice was nevertheless rich in symbolism—providing a condensed image, even spectacle, of wage-earning and Christian ingenuity—and gestured toward a larger and different future.[4] It also rewarded and shaped a small vanguard of Christian schoolboys who would go on to become salaried pastors, teachers, and civil servants in the independent nation-state.

A side story here, but one that intersects with and nuances the larger story about the Togolese postcolony I have been telling. The future dictator, Eyadéma, attended Delord's school in the 1950s when the missionary took him in after he had been exiled from his home community for ensorcelling his parents. Eyadéma was never a strong student and dropped out after a few years to enlist in the French colonial army, but he remained forever indebted to Delord for saving him and initiating his lifelong relationship with the French. He even flew the retired missionary-linguist back to Togo in the 1970s to celebrate the publication of his doctoral dissertation, an esoteric analysis of a Kabiyé verb form (Delord 1976). But if Eyadéma remembered the missionary with fondness, he felt less kindly toward many of his classmates and acknowledged little debt to the Farendé-Kuwdé area more generally. One classmate who attended Lumumba University in Moscow—Cold War Soviet counterpart to the US Fulbright program—returned home to occupy a post in Togo's Ministry of Agriculture, only to be imprisoned when he criticized a Eyadéma agricultural initiative. Another, who went to Germany for an apprenticeship in electronics, opened a successful television store and repair shop in Lomé, a store that was pillaged by soldiers and emptied of its merchandise during the troubles of the 1990s—an act which could never have occurred without the dictator's authorization. A third former classmate, a Delord favorite who went to France to study linguistics (and served as a native "informant" in the famous Griaule-Dieterlen anthropology seminar on African "mentalités"), was de-salaried and prevented from ever publishing the results of his research when, upon his return from Paris with a typewriter keyed to the International Phonetic Alphabet (IPA), he was accused by the dictator of trying to impose Farendé's dialect on the national project of "alphabetization."[5] A fourth Eyadéma classmate, an invalid school teacher confined to a wheel chair, and someone whose support of several generations of schoolchildren has made him a venerated figure in Farendé, was exiled at the start of his career by the dictator to a school in a mountain community whose rocky paths made circulating in his wheel chair nearly impossible.

While these disciplining tactics were trademark Eyadéma and thus in many ways unexceptional, the consistency with which they were carried out on classmates from Delord's school suggests another motivation as well: that the dictator used them to get back at classmates who had mocked him in the schoolyard for being a poor student. Moreover, locals contend that something similar, reprisal for past slights, has left Farendé-Kuwdé off the beaten track and underdeveloped to the present day. And another likelihood: that local attachments to new forms of sovereignty today are at least in part motivated by sovereignty's failures—and Eyadéma's reprisals—during the dictatorship era.

Delord's and the Presbyterian Church's monopoly over local development ended during the 1970s and 1980s. During these Cold War years, European and American development agencies entered the field, funding a series of small-scale projects—latrines, wells, more efficient cooking hearths, fertilizers, higher-yielding crops—and the US Agency for International Development (USAID) introduced an Animal Traction program throughout northern Togo that touched the Farendé area. "AnTrak," as it was known among those Peace Corps volunteers responsible for its local implementation—volunteers, tellingly, whose prior experience with farming largely consisted in gardening in their parents' suburban backyards—aimed to revolutionize local farming with cattle-pulled plows. The best-funded development initiative of the era, AnTrak nevertheless resolutely failed to impact local farming practice. None of the farmers who were entrusted with cattle seriously took up the charge, and those who managed to avoid repossession (by repaying the money advanced them toward acquisition of the animal) typically used them for chores other than cultivating, such as hauling products to market. A sad, albeit all-too-typical, example of the failure of development during this moment.[6]

But the work of these Euro-American development agencies during the Cold War years was overshadowed by that of the state-run Affaires Sociales. Established when Eyadéma came to power in 1967, and with a secure funding stream and a broad reach, Affaires Sociales occupied a central place in the development field—and in the local imagination about development—throughout this period. With a mandate to promote "cultural modernization"—to bring rural areas into the orbit of the modern nation state by creating a literate/healthy/prosperous citizenry (cf. Mitchell 1988; Ferguson 1994, 1999; Escobar 1995), Affaires Sociales–Farendé launched a range of projects: working with local schools to teach adults to read, running seminars on contraception and malaria prevention, providing small loans for farmers to purchase fertilizer, helping families in times of harvest failure/fire/inundation. The small but dedicated staff benefited from the fact that they were native to the region, enabling them to better integrate their work into the life of the community than any other initiative of its time. By the mid-1990s, however, Affaires Sociales' money had run out and its staff was reduced to a single person, who continued to show up at work without pay for ten years until he retired in 2004. Today, Affaires Sociales exists only as memory.

It is against this backdrop—of longstanding albeit sporadic encounters with Euro-American development projects and of a more sustained but now abrogated engagement with the state-run Affaires Sociales—that a new round of NGOs arrived in Farendé in the 1990s. These were NGOs attuned to the times, enacting a development version of neoliberalism's political philosophy. They aimed to bypass the "corrupt" state and go straight to the "grass roots" (cf. Ferguson 2001), promising responsiveness to local needs and insisting upon local participation. Again reflecting the zeitgeist of these neoliberal times, they were against "handouts," expecting locals to match any gift of aid with their own contribution of money or labor.

---

The largest, most ambitious project of the decade after the National Conference—and a project that continues to fill the developmental imagination in the area six years after its departure—was the Danish child sponsorship program BØRNEfonden ("foundation for children"). Believing, as one of its promotional flyers states, that "the development of the community depends on the development of the individual" (BØRNEfonden 2005), BØRNEfonden seeks to address Africa's development crisis by focusing on the education of children—and does so by setting up personalized relations between Scandinavian families and individual children in West African villages. For each sponsored child in one of its target communities, a donor family pays school fees, purchases school uniforms and books, contributes food to the child's family, and subsidizes regular health checkups. BØRNEfonden today runs over a hundred village-based projects in four francophone West African countries. It had twenty-seven in Togo alone during the 1990s.

When BØRNEfonden arrived in Farendé-Kuwdé in 1992, locals immediately took to the program—though, it seemed, less out of a strong desire to see their children educated than to capture scarce resources in a time of crisis. Families flocked to BØRNEfonden's center in Farendé to put their names on the list, and, because the project stipulated that it would support only one child per family, some attempted to game the system by sending children to live with childless uncles or grandparents—a play on identity not unlike that engaged in by winners of the green card lottery in Lomé. Kabre in the south also sent children back to the north to live with siblings, so that they might partake in the spoils. In the mid-1990s, hundreds of families in the communities of Farendé, Kuwdé, and Tchi-Kawa had children in the program, with school enrollments swelling to new highs.

The quid pro quo was not only that children had to go to school and remain in good standing but also that parents had to write letters to the child's sponsor in northern Europe several times a year. These letters thanked the donor—often a donor couple—for their aid and detailed the progress of "their" child. One such note:

> I write to inquire about your health and that of your family. My wife and I, and your daughter Essowé, are in good health. Your financial aid has enabled us to change our lives and rise above what we had before. Thanks to the money you sent, I have started a garden and my wife is selling kerosene in the market. With our earnings we can better feed Essowé.
>
> Essowé has just begun the new school year and feels fortunate to have this opportunity. Her school day begins at 6:30, when she is already in the school yard. . . . Her favorite subject is arithmetic, though she also finds it difficult and spends many hours studying after she comes home at night. . . .
>
> May God Bless you for your help and support you in your work.

The return letter described where this Danish couple lived—in a small town two hours from Copenhagen—and said that the man worked for an automobile company. They complimented Essowé for her hard work at school and encouraged the parents in their newfound work initiatives. The letter closed by promising continued support if Essowé continued to perform at school.

This process of letter-writing was the vexed talk of the airwaves when I was in Kuwdé in the late 1990s. For most parents, the writing itself was an excruciating process. Penned in French by someone whose speaking and writing ability was typically little more than elementary-school level, the letter was submitted to a staff member in Farendé who subjected it to often withering critique of its spelling/grammar/content, after which the parent was sent home to start over. In some cases the parent of the sponsored child trudged up and down the mountain for weeks, ninety minutes each way, writing and rewriting, before the letter was accepted. It was then sent to Lomé, where it was translated into English by a member of BØRNEfonden's team of translators—nine full-time employees rendering letters from French to English for Togo's twenty-seven projects—and sent to the sponsoring family in Scandinavia, a process that reversed itself when the family wrote back.

I want to pause for a moment on this letter-writing, which I see as the

14. BØRNEfonden headquarters, Farendé 2008

symbolic heart of BØRNEfonden's project. It is the letter which makes the aid flow, for the letter conveys a sense of direct contact between "child" and sponsoring "parent" (despite the presence of multiple intermediaries—the real parent who actually penned the letter, those who critiqued/edited/ translated it, the sprawling apparatus of the international organization). This is the "affect" that child sponsorship programs call on and nurture: inciting, indeed hailing, Europeans not only to invest in the life of an African child—"their" child—and thus in Africa's future, but also enabling this European couple to have a personal relationship with that child. The letter speaks from the heart—from one heart to another—expressing both need and gratitude ("your financial help has enabled us to change our lives and rise above the standard we had before. Thanks to the money you sent, . . ."). Thus, too, it reinscribes the African subject as aid-dependent, as (always) saved by the European—and the African parent as always inadequate and incomplete/impotent (cf. Bornstein and Redfield forthcoming). Notice that the African parent here has gone the way of the African sovereign, both replaced by new international agencies—new sovereignties—agencies disguised as parents, and would-be parents as agencies. Notice, too, what is never expressed but always implied: that this is a case of virtual adoption, with a

Danish couple becoming "parent" to an African child ("*your* daughter Essowé"), a child who nevertheless has parents, but ones who are unable to provide for their children.

But the letter-writing also struck me, whether intentional or not, as very much about the "disciplining" and humiliation of the peasant. Picture this stream of farmers from mountain villages making their way down rocky paths to Farendé, letters stuffed in the pockets of their tattered overcoats, presenting themselves at the BØRNEfonden office where they are made to wait—often for hours, sometimes all day—before their letter is covered in red ink and they are instructed to return home and start over. The message conveyed through the letter-writing process is about the role of education and the superiority of "l'homme du papier" (the person who knows writing)—the staff member who knows the conventions and protocols of letter-writing and who thus commands the magic that makes the money flow. If this were not about discipline, about conveying the inferiority of the peasant, why make him rewrite again and again when a translator in Lomé will rework and sanitize it for the Danish couple? Moreover, the threads extend outward from a practice like this into the larger social field, a field in which "tradition" and (nonliterate) chiefs are on the way out, being replaced by modernity and (literate) mayors.

Another effect of this project and sign of the times: A parent of a sponsored child told me that he was in more frequent contact with the European couple who supported his child than with kin in southern Togo—that, because of the ongoing economic crisis, the latter no longer sent remittances back home and only infrequently made their annual trips to the north as before, and that he was now more reliant on the European couple for his survival. Again, a shift away from local to translocal dependencies/sovereignties/ governmentalities, with a Danish development agency standing in for family and state—teaching rural peasants how to be proper citizen-subjects.

In 2002, after ten years in Farendé, and needing to cut nine of its twenty-seven Togo projects, BØRNEfonden closed its doors and moved on, citing staff misconduct and excessive bickering and jealousy among villagers. The office in Farendé and BØRNEfonden's headquarters in Lomé had been flooded with complaints from families who had not been chosen—and with revelations about the gaming and scamming that others were engaged in. The village of Tchi-Kawa complained that it was discriminated against by those from Farendé and had been denied promised resources. And, the last straw, the local head of staff in Farendé was accused of building his own bar-boutique with project monies. As a result, BØRNEfonden decided to withdraw from what it saw as a hornet's nest of local infighting and invest elsewhere.

And yet, despite this sudden abandonment, and despite the ordeal and humiliation of the letter-writing, people in Farendé and Kuwdé today see BØRNEfonden as the high point of recent development efforts in the area. It brought money and resources to the north, it brought the offspring of diasporics back home, it filled the schools with children, and more generally it animated the region. Moreover, remarkably to me when I first heard it, locals blame themselves for BØRNEfonden's departure. "It is because of our jealousy, because we couldn't get along with one another, that they left," is a refrain I heard again and again. This seems a secular version of the Pentecostal "blame tradition" narrative—"we blame ourselves for our backwardness"—and, as in that instance, it seems an attempt to resist victimizing narratives that vacate local agency, locating responsibility beyond local control.

---

Compare BØRNEfonden for a moment—in order to draw out the commonalities between this particular project and a continent-wide phenomenon—to Oprah's much publicized South African Leadership Academy for Girls. The latter is certainly more extravagant in every way—with its $40 million spent on a single school to educate a few hundred teenage girls—but the goal of the project, and the means used to achieve it, bear striking similarities to BØRNEfonden's. Not only do both projects promote education as the solution to Africa's development impasse but also both attempt to create a direct relationship between donor and recipient, in this case between Oprah—who herself was involved in the selection process—and the girls chosen. The affective dimension of this form of development aid—the personalized, seemingly unmediated, nature of the relationship between donor and recipient—was strikingly embodied in the hour-long TV special that aired in the US in spring 2007.[7] There, the resplendent Oprah was shown having face-to-face interviews with each girl, listening to and sharing in the sadness of their life stories—often-tragic stories of parents and siblings lost to AIDS or violent crime, and ones that paralleled Oprah's own hardscrabble childhood in rural Mississippi. The tears and hugs that ensued literally embodied and gave concrete visibility to the personal nature of the relationship. Moreover, there was no question: these were now Oprah's children, and children she would save—from Africa.[8]

BØRNEfonden's letter-writing does not share the same degree of intimacy, but it is not far removed—and its aim is the same.[9] I see both as symptomatic of the moment, as embodying the ethos of a thousand contemporary child sponsorship projects across the continent that imagine a European dropping from the sky to save an African child.[10] Is this not the secular equivalent of Pentecostalism's immanence of global affect—of something like a direct, unmediated, deeply personalized, visitation by the Holy Spirit?

---

The people of Farendé and Kuwdé were quick to adapt to the development landscape of the new millennium, acquiring a sophisticated understanding—and developing a vernacular ethnography—of the contrasts between various NGOs.[11] They also developed complex strategies for attracting NGOs to their communities. The most interesting (and apparently effective) involved—borrowing a page from Eyadéma's book—a type of performance. Thus, to gain the attention of an NGO that has just moved into the area, a community would invite its representatives to a meeting, serve them food and beer, call out the musicians—and outline their needs. Moreover, in a departure from anything I saw in the 1980s—where chiefs and elders always represented the community to the outside world—this staging of "need" and "gratitude" was usually directed by young, educated men and women from the community. The entire event thus cleverly presented to the typically European or American NGO representatives a seductive image of, on the one hand, an Africa committed to preserving the best of its "traditions" (sociality, etiquette, musicality), while, on the other, an Africa embracing the modern (through its educated youth). When such events are successful, Kabre boastfully claim that they have "captured" an NGO, a term resonant with the performative seductions of initiate-fiancés—but also an instance of what Bayart (1989, 2000) has referred to as "extraversion," that dynamic (at the heart of African socio-political process broadly) whereby livelihoods and rents are appropriated from an outside. Moreover, as with Eyadéma, one has the sense that the mere act of "capturing," of staging the successful performance, is as much the point as accessing whatever (usually insignificant) material returns find their way to the individual or community. Such performances also of course bear affinities to the praise-singing—"animation"—for Eyadéma during the Cold War years, praise-singing now directed toward a new sovereign.

---

A second development project that parachuted into the Farendé-Kuwdé area during this time was the Association Villageoise des Jeunes en Activité pour le Développement et l'Épanouissement (Village Association of Youth Working for Development and Progress). AVJADE was founded by a Farendé man living in southern Togo, a civil servant whose salary disappeared during the cutbacks of the 1990s and who, like many in the political class at the time, went in search of new ways of making money.[12] He created AVJADE as an Association and then an NGO, found a German sponsor to finance its start-up, and opened an office in Farendé.

AVJADE drew inspiration from the wave of microfinance schemes that were all the rage during the 1990s and that constituted a sort of poor man's/ global south version of capital's liquidity during this boom time, capital whose very availability, it was imagined, would produce its own increase (Yunus 2003; Elyachar 2005:191–212). Providing small loans for group (six-eight person) projects, AVJADE aimed to stimulate entrepreneurial activity and its companion cycle of investment and savings, and to do so, in step with these populist times, by engaging local need and initiative. After issuing a call for proposals for projects in need of start-up capital, AVJADE's director selected ten groups each from Farendé and Kuwdé, with projects ranging from animal husbandry, to rice cultivation, to vegetable gardening, to beer making. Each group was given a loan of CFAF 60,000 ($120), to be repaid a year later with 10 percent interest.

A particular feature of AVJADE, and again one in concert with the times, was its focus on youth (cf. Elyachar 2005:25–26), with older and middle-aged men and women discouraged from participating. This commitment to youth, AVJADE's project manager told me in June 2005, was an attempt not only to bring this project into line with a recent NGO priority across the subregion but also to empower young entrepreneurs in the hopes that they would begin to unsettle rural gerontocracies and production regimes (seen by civil servants, and the urban middle class, as resistant to change).

Another special feature of AVJADE was its mandate that groups constitute themselves as mini-corporations ("bureaus")—electing officers (president, vice-president, secretary, treasurer) and acquiring papers of incorporation at the local préfecture. This mimesis of the bureaucratic was seen by AVJADE, and by civil servant supporters, as a modernizing move—not only better positioning locals to capture external sources of funding but also disrupting peasant modes of organization.

This practice has today become generalized, spreading beyond AVJADE to workgroups throughout the area. When I was in Kuwdé in summer 2004, a small group of cultivators from a neighboring village came to visit me, seeking support for a poultry project they were launching. They showed me their papers—typed, stamped, signed by the préfet—and asked if I might help finance a project to raise a special breed of disease-resistant chicken ("poules de race"), a chicken recently introduced into Togo by a German NGO. To demonstrate their seriousness, they showed me a chicken coop they had just finished building, equipped with door and lock, and said they were now waiting on an investor to help with the purchase of the chickens. To this end, they had recently written a Chinese NGO for help, but were also soliciting other sources of aid.

In contrast to when I was in the area in the 1980s and 1990s, such solicitations have now become commonplace. Whenever I return to the north, I am routinely visited by small groups of locals—groups that bear acronyms like ASV (Association pour la Santé du Village), UDE (Union des Élèves), JJF (Jeunes Joueurs de Football) and that have elected officials and papers signed by the préfet—who come to ask for help in funding a health clinic, aiding a farming cooperative to buy fertilizer, supporting the local soccer team. Moreover, when back in the States, I routinely receive email messages from northern acquaintances asking for help in a project they are launching. I would insist, nevertheless, that my taking on NGO-like qualities is more an index of these times than of any shift in status (from student to salaried professor)—and that this mimesis of the bureaucratic is as performative (as sign of the modern) as it is instrumental.

Such microfinance efforts are also notable instances of what Harvey (2005, 2007) has referred to as "accumulation by dispossession" (see also Elyachar 2005), a privatization of the commons (Marx [1867] 1977; Thompson 1966; Hardt and Negri 2005), whereby formerly inalienable social networks or common resources are made available to and appropriated by financialized modes of accumulation. Note, moreover, that such efforts have succeeded where colonial- and postcolonial-era attempts to alienate—create a market in—land failed. "Privatize labor and don't worry about the land" would seem to be capital's lesson of the moment, with all irony noted, for microfinance advertises itself as helping the poor, as being the latest solution to global poverty (Yunus 2003).

Eight years after its inception, AVJADE still exists—the project manager goes to his office every day and some of the original workgroups still function in its name—but its German funding source has dried up and few of the loans have ever been repaid. When I visited the local project head in 2005—an energetic young man who, despite having drawn little salary for the previous two years, remained upbeat and committed to the project—he admitted that the workgroup idea had been a failure. Few of the projects had achieved their ends, and most groups had simply divided the money among members of the group to spend on personal consumption. He remained committed to the idea of microfinance, however, and said that if more money became available, he would initiate a program of loaning money to families. Families, unlike workgroups, he said, have clear lines of authority—a senior male can command labor and hold others responsible—and, if need be, can be "shamed" into repaying the loans.

## Disposable Elders, Youthful Futures

Consider the types of projects that fill the development horizon today: child sponsorship, school enrollment, microfinance, orphanages, child trafficking, AIDS, malaria. No longer focusing, as during the 1970s and 1980s, on material inputs—investment in infrastructure (roads, bridges, hospitals, schools) or rural production (fertilizer, ploughs, irrigation)—those projects with traction today are more concerned with youth and human development (cf. Elyachar 2005:25–26). "Let's eliminate disease and educate the continent's children," these projects seem to be saying, "and in this way attempt to secure Africa's future."

While commendable—who would stand against the education of children?—such a uniform set of commitments is not without its blind spots. For one, this investment in human potential—in an emergent future—is striking for its vagueness and lack of specificity. Oprah's school aims simply to train future leaders, BØRNEfonden's child sponsorship program does little more than send children to school—with both hoping that investing in education and human development might be the answer to Africa's problems. But what use is human potential without the means or resources to put into practice that potential?[13]

Moreover, why is so much expended on getting children into the schools and so little on the schools themselves—schools that are appallingly ill equipped for the task of education? Those schools I know are not only resource-starved but also staffed by teachers dispirited by the fact that they receive paychecks only intermittently. To compensate, but only making matters worse, they put the students to work in their fields—a practice that has grown from one afternoon a week five years ago to two full days a week now. Add in the high rate of failure—only 10–15 percent of Togolese pass the baccalaureate each year—and it is little wonder that students quickly lose heart and drop out.

The corollary of this commitment to a youthful future (Weiss 2004b) is an implicit abandonment of Africa's past and its over-thirty generation. There are echoes here of the Pentecostal insistence on a radical break with the past, and also complicity with the "death of a continent" discourse that circulates in the international arena today about Africa (O'Reilly 2000). As the head of the Togolese branch of BØRNEfonden told me in summer 2005: "We have to start thinking long-term, ten to twenty years from now. When we support a child in school, we have to focus on what that child's contribution will be when he or she is twenty." By this he meant not only that expectations needed to be lowered for the short term but also that Africa's future is its salvation.

There are also gendered implications of the new dispensation. In focusing on women and girls—girls' (not boys') education, women's (explicitly not men's) participation in microfinance schemes—the new projects bypass men, cutting them out of the spoils of the new order. The African male, like the African dictator, seems here consigned to the dustbin of history. While I am all for supporting undervalued groups, especially women—and, indeed, moving women more into the mainstream will certainly have a salutary effect on the political life of African nations—those in development ought also to worry about the emasculating effects of their projects' singular focus (cf. Weiss 2004b:14). Indeed, might not the new initiatives also be partly responsible for the recent dramatic increase in domestic violence across the continent (Oyekani 2000; Morris 2006:84; Mbembe 2006:326–27) or the gendered atrocities that have accompanied its recent civil wars?

## Traffic in Children?

As a friend and I descended the mountain from Kuwdé into the plain one morning in summer 2006, a teenage boy on a shiny motorcycle climbed past us and disappeared into a cornfield. "Nigeria," my companion said. "He's just back from Nigeria, where he worked for a year and received this motorcycle as his prize."

Among young and old alike, this fifteen-year-old was the talk of the town—as was another boy in a southern community I visited a few weeks later who had also gone to Nigeria and returned with a sleek chrome machine that he drove endlessly around the mud pathways of his village. All—elders and children alike—were envious of these motorcycle children while nevertheless also criticizing a practice that pulled able bodies away from the village. They also worried about the conditions under which their children labored in Nigeria and about what would happen were they to get sick—with "no family to care for them."

As the sound of the motorcycle receded, I realized these were precisely the children whom dozens of international NGOs were focusing on in a massive child trafficking campaign in West Africa—a campaign that streamed across US and European newspapers in 2006 with articles on "The New Slavery" and "Slavery Is Not History." Sparked by the discovery in 2004 of a Gulf of Guinea boat bound for Gabon filled with Togolese children packed in like sardines—evoking nothing so much as Middle Passage slave ships—Amnesty International and Human Rights Watch had taken up the cause and successfully brought West African "child trafficking" to the attention of NGOs working on human rights issues. By 2006, a score of international agencies in Togo were devoting money to the cause and the Peace Corps had assigned a dozen volunteers to work on it in Togo's rural north—an area which the ongoing crisis had made a prime recruiting ground for middlemen trying to lure children to Nigeria, Ghana, Cote d'Ivoire, and Gabon. Even Oprah joined the cause—after reading an October 2006 article in the *New York Times* on child labor in Ghana—and created a website devoted to child trafficking in West Africa.[14]

When I was in Togo in 2007 and 2008, it was hard to read the success of the international initiative. On the one hand, it was notable how the information campaign spearheaded by the NGOs had spread into local schools and villages, where teachers and parents had been quickly won over by arguments that their children were being lured into conditions of exploitation beyond their control—and by those (Nigerians) who many Togolese believe can never be trusted. Teachers discussed the issue in school-wide meetings, and fathers brought it up when drinking with the workgroup after village farming sessions. Moreover, teachers were instructed to inform parents of children in their classes about unauthorized absences in an attempt to quickly identify those who might be thinking of leaving. And, yet, when I asked whether any children had been discouraged from leaving, the question was met with skepticism. In Kuwdé and its satellite villages alone, ten children had gone to Nigeria and returned with motorcycles, and even parents who openly criticized the practice seemed beguiled. They were also disarmed by the response of the child-migrants themselves: that no matter how hard they worked in Kuwdé, they could never purchase a motorcycle, and that they are young and do not mind working hard for a few years. "Who can really blame them?" one parent said. "It's our poverty—the fact that we can't offer them anything better—that is at the root of all this."

For me, the violation is not only that a child's labor is exploited, with middlemen and Nigerian landowners enriching themselves on the backs of Togolese children's sixteen-hour days—and, even more, that some children disappear altogether—but also that Kabre households lose the labor and heft of their most able workers. Those in their mid to late teens—the demographic drawn away to work in the fields and sex hostels of Nigeria—are

15. Trafficked teen with Nigerian prize, Kuwdé 2008

precisely those who typically provide the lion's share of labor in a family's fields and kitchens. The departure of children to Nigeria thus further impoverishes an area long struggling to cope with the crisis of the last fifteen years.

A new wrinkle in the anti-trafficking campaign appeared in 2007, with potentially dramatic consequences for local labor and parenting practices. Some of the NGOs working on child trafficking began suggesting that longstanding Togolese child labor-exchange arrangements—which send children from the north to work for family or friends in the south during the holidays (and sometimes longer)—also fall under the umbrella of the new laws against child trafficking. In the Kabre case, children leave the north to spend up to three months with family in the cities and on the farms of southern Togo to help with work in fields and kitchens, in return for pocket change and money to buy school uniforms and pay school fees. These are intra- and inter-familial fostering practices that have been at the heart of local cultures and their diasporas since at least the early colonial period, addressing needs on both sides of the north/south divide.

To be sure, these long-distance relations can be exploitative, with northern children sometimes treated like stepchildren and made to work long hours for southern kin, kin who are enriched by their labor. But these relationships can also be, and often are, warm and affectionate and may be no more exploitative than those at home. They also provide children with benefits—schooling, travel, and the expanded horizon that travel offers, and, most alluring to the children themselves, the opportunity to participate in southern youth culture—to which they would otherwise be denied.

Intra-familial fostering arrangements shade into others that also now fall under the new anti-trafficking statute. In summer 2007, a Kuwdé friend was asked by a schoolteacher who lived in a nearby town whether one of his daughters would come work for the teacher and his childless wife for the summer holidays to help with cooking and chores around the house. In return, they would put the girl up and introduce her to life in the city. The risk for this ten-year-old was that the couple would work her from sunup to sundown, but the potential gain, according to the father, was that living with the teacher and spending time in town would expand his daughter's horizon and convince her to take school more seriously. It would also, he added, subtract one mouth from his already stretched family budget.

These are not easy calls either way, and my point is not so much to decide the pros and cons of intervening in arrangements like these—although at the very least it should be acknowledged that such interventions will be enormously disruptive of longstanding social practice while also denying poor northerners an opportunity for advancement. Rather, I wish to draw attention to the way in which local practice is now swept up in—marked, commented on, policed by—the new international order and its jurisdictions, in the process calling into question and potentially refiguring vernacular meanings of childhood, family, work, exploitation. Note, moreover, the irony that the most recent development in the trafficking initiative—the focus on local rather than cross-border circulation of children—was not the practice for which the new laws were intended, and witness the genealogy, the sinuous pathways and "frictions" (Tsing 2004), by which global-local articulations are operating in this case. What began as a story in the *New York Times* about cross-border trafficking (with evocative Middle Passage imagery) in turn played to the sensibilities of a recently reinvigorated global human rights community and of NGOs in search of a new cause, then made its way into the assemblies of national legislators, who were won over by the mere mention of the always-suspect "Nigeria," and finally morphed into a blanket indictment of often unrelated child labor practices (which most of the ratifying legislators also engage in). And the concern with child trafficking was ferried along these conduits by those functionaries of the new international order: journalists, human rights workers, an African bourgeoisie.

## Development/Modernization 2006–2008

In July 2006, Farendé-Kuwdé's departed sons—members of the Lomé "Ami-cale" (Association of Friends)—returned to the north to convene kin and villagers to discuss how to further "develop" their home region. For two days, several dozen expatriates met with a few hundred villagers in the yard of a local school. Discussion ranged from development of infrastructure, to reforestation, to schooling, to democratization, to the local witchcraft epidemic. For northerners and southerners alike, the latter was the most important agenda item and was originally scheduled for discussion at the top of the first day but was put off to the second because, as one participant put it, "if we start with witchcraft, the discussion will never finish and all other issues will be pushed to the side." An important subtext of the two-day event was an attempt by expatriates and youthful northerners to initiate a process of replacing the local canton chief with a mayor. This chief, a large imposing man in his mid-fifties, is unlettered (and therefore looked down upon by many in the younger generation) and also surprisingly maladroit at local protocol and jurisprudence (and had thus alienated many Farendé elders). He is thus perceived as ill equipped to oversee the area's further development.

The infrastructure agenda struck me as starry-eyed in the extreme. Here were members of a small out-of-the-way community, with a single dirt road through the town's center, dreaming big and proposing to bring electricity to the area, to pave the town's main road, to build feeder roads from outlying farms, and to invest in a project that would bring tourists to the area. In order to fund these projects, those present committed themselves to a money-raising scheme that, true to the spirit of the times, would use local investment of money and labor to induce contributions from NGOs. Passing the hat—with northern cultivators donating CFAF 200 ($.40) and southern civil servants CFAF 5,000 ($11)—they netted $1,500 by year's end and sent a delegation to the local préfet to solicit his help in finding NGO support. They also proposed sending a party to the new president of the republic, Eyadéma's son Faure, to seek his support—although that mission never materialized. Two years later, they remain well shy of their fundrais-ing goals—the electricity project alone was assessed at $170,000—and none of their agenda items has been implemented, and yet people remain com-mitted and hopeful, a hopefulness that, given development's history in the area, I find breathtaking.

Those gathered also committed themselves to a reforestation project, overseen by a departed son who works as an associate director for the Peace

Corps. This native son spoke eloquently during a half-hour presentation about the benefits of "reboisement"—one of the subregion's pet projects of the moment—and urged members of the three villages to take up the cause. (This was no easy sell, however, for preserving non-fruit-bearing trees flies in the face of local practice, where high population densities put pressure on firewood and where fields are annually set ablaze to clear them for planting.) To underscore his own commitment, he had brought several hundred saplings from the south to distribute to the three villages and organized a planting session on the morning of the second day of the reunion. (Notice how global agendas—here, "reforestation" as development mantra of the moment, a project with cachet in European capitals and their development wings in the former colonies—are conveyed and insinuated into the local community by a salaried native son, albeit operating now as private citizen.)

The discussion about the schools, led by the director of the local middle school (C.E.G.), began with an announcement that the Lomé Amicale would continue to supplement teacher salaries—a practice begun during the 1990s when state monies dried up and salaries were paid only intermittently. After this welcome start, however, the conversation quickly soured. A teacher complained about how much time his students spent at all-night dances—causing them to doze through much of the next day—and about how demoralizing he found the overall learning environment. Parents complained about philandering teachers, especially one who had impregnated a local daughter with no intention to marry her. And all complained about the high incidence of witchcraft in the schools—of students witching teachers in retaliation for poor grades, of teachers witching recalcitrant students, of students witching other students. A particularly troubling instance of the latter was recounted by the father of a girl who became despondent after a classmate told her that he and his father had ensorcelled her (after she had refused the boy's advances) and that they had already consumed 80 percent of her body—"all but the head."

This colloquy on schools was followed by a lively, at times riveting, discussion of "democratization," which also opened the door to criticism of the local chief. The Peace Corps associate director took the floor to correct what he saw as villager misconceptions of democracy. Democracy, he asserted, did not mean that everything was in "disorder." (This was a widely embraced reading of the events of the 1990s: that "démocratie" opened the prison doors and allowed convicted criminals to walk free [because Eyadéma was forced by the human rights organizations to free political prisoners] and that it disrupted those hierarchies that render family life orderly [because "rights of man" discourse enabled women and children to assert their autonomy].) Democracy, this civil servant continued, developing an analogy that could have been lifted from Agamben (though with a more positive spin than the Italian theorist's on life under surveillance), is not all that different from dictatorship, with the law now taking the place of chiefs and sovereigns. By way of example, he cited a recent Peace Corps rule that sends volunteers home if they violate a ban on riding motorcycles (because of several recent volunteer deaths), and supplemented this with an account of surveillance cameras in the US capturing those who commit traffic violations—violators who are then notified by mail. "In democracy," he concluded, "laws make people orderly."

The discussion then turned to the recent (2005) presidential election, and criticized "those" who had interfered with the electoral process. All knew, though he was never named as such, that the reference was to the canton chief, who had barred political parties other than Eyadéma's RPT from campaigning in Farendé and had reported the names of political dissidents to the president's vengeful sons. Choosing a pragmatic approach, critics of the chief suggested that those from the Farendé area who would vote for the opposition were so few in number that their votes would make no difference. "Don't worry about them. Just let them vote," one said. "Besides, the debate between different parties makes the campaign more interesting." His point, and that of the other civil servants who spoke up, was not so much to be a shill for democracy as to unsettle local attachments to a dictatorship politics that turned elections into orchestrated charade—and that were responsible for blocking the return of development money to Togo.

My own interest in this discussion was not only in the way it linked local experience and political theory but also with the fact that the conversation itself—and indeed much of what I witnessed throughout the two days—seemed a textbook instance of democracy in practice: of frank and open debate about difficult issues, including the critique of political authority, with any and all having their say. But such a characterization meets irony at every turn: not only was the conversation staged as auto-critique ("we aren't democratic"), but also it is precisely communities like this that representatives of international agencies see as authoritarian and repressive, as the Other to "democracy."

A handful of expatriates, in alliance with the director of the C.E.G., worked persistently throughout the two days—albeit with finesse and notable restraint—to convince locals and the canton chief himself that electing a mayor and becoming a "commune" was in everyone's interest. They not only pointed out that the chief would still have his say in the domains of ritual and witchcraft adjudication while working alongside a mayor charged with animating the area's economic development but also suggested that this would relieve him of duties that he found stressful and beyond his expertise.

What was significant about the attempt to sideline the chief was the way in which it dovetailed with post-Cold War state decentralization projects. Beginning in 2005, the Togolese state began encouraging towns to follow the French model of becoming largely autonomous mayor-run "communes." Under this arrangement, traditional chiefs would remain (at least for the time being), but their powers would be curtailed—limited to overseeing local ritual and adjudicating cases of witchcraft—while mayors would manage the administration of the commune and oversee its economic development—attempting to attract NGOs and private companies to the area. As such, the commune and the mayor would operate independently of the state, not only relieving the latter of its financial obligations to the locality but also effectively rendering the locality beyond state control, potentially turning the nation-state into a series of fiefdoms. This arrangement, with its bifurcated administrative apparatus, also of course represents a further attack on "tradition" and drives another wedge between tradition and modernity.

A related conversation, one that initially arose at the 2006 meeting but was treated more fully in 2007, concerned a call by the canton chief to create several new villages in Farendé, by subdividing those that already existed. This proposal was in part motivated by local politics—the chief was in a power struggle with the *chef du village* and hoped that by adding two or three more chiefs, he could marginalize his enemy—but it was also fueled by the larger climate of political and economic restructuring. Having more villages, a supporter of the chief argued, would enable locals to make the case for more economic aid and for greater representation in regional and national politics. But consider: the boundaries of these villages were drawn over one hundred years ago, during the early colonial period, and have resisted modification right up to the present—despite significant changes in local demography and political authority along the way. Their reworking today provides another index of the unusual nature of the contemporary moment.

It became clear to me during the two days—and throughout similar conferences in July and December 2007, and July 2008—how much control the Lomé expatriates now exert over life in the villages. All of the conference's agenda items were decided upon in the Lomé Amicale, and most of the money raised for projects came from the pockets of its members. Moreover, it was they who were calling many of the shots in the struggles over chiefship and the formation of new villages, and they who insisted upon the discussion about witchcraft. Indeed, these expatriates refer to themselves—though not in the presence of northern kin—as "les intellectuels" (the brains or managers) of life in the northern villages.

To be sure, the dependency of locals on departed sons and daughters who are salaried and educated, and who send remittances back home, is a longstanding feature of life in Farendé-Kuwdé and throughout the broader subregion. But the nature and extent of this dependency seems different today. In the past, expatriates sent their money home and returned for ceremonies, and these actions often gave them an important voice within their families. However, they usually kept their distance from village and chieftaincy politics. Such is no longer the case.[15]

But these civil servants' more sustained involvement in the life of the village ramifies in other ways as well, both facilitating and supplementing the work of the NGOs in transforming the organization of life and politics in this area. And, ironically, in that many are civil servants of the state, they are responsible for hastening the dissolution of the strong relationship between state and locality that was at the heart of the dictatorship complex.

The reason that witchcraft was the two-day conference's centerpiece was not only because of the rash of accusations/confessions that recent years have witnessed—and the fear, preoccupation, and excessive spending that have resulted therefrom—but also because the jealousies that lie at the heart of witchcraft accusations are those that tear apart the social fabric of the community and interfere with any imaginable future. Moreover, in that many of the most spectacular recent cases of witchcraft in Farendé-Kuwdé stretch across the Christian/animist divide, they elicit and speak to the major social tension in the community today. In so doing, and in attending to expatriate demands that such tensions be addressed, the people of Farendé are saying that development qua development cannot proceed without the resolution of local conflict and the setting aside of debilitating, even deadly, enmity.[16]

Much of the discussion about witchcraft on the conference's second day entailed the canton chief's blow-by-blow recounting of a series of cases he had heard in recent months—a telling that represented a response to his critics, for he aimed to show that he, and he alone, was up to the task of checking this epidemic and of fulfilling chiefly responsibility in this dangerous domain. He filled the schoolyard with vivid accounts of night riders, of landing strips in the north where witch planes touched down (most notably next to the recently installed antenna for Togocel), of north-south liaisons, of elaborate conspiracies. At one point, he said he thought that God had put Africans on earth to kill one another, a remark that brought tears to the eyes of a schoolteacher friend—because of, he said, its sad truthfulness. The chief's voyeuristic telling of detail upon detail from those cases brought before him—the responsible parties and their victims, the nature of the plots and the nighttime activities of the protagonists, the vehicles deployed—was but a prelude to his recounting of how the cases themselves had unfolded: of the ways in which accusations of wrongdoing were followed by denials, and of how he had ferreted out the truth by outwitting naysayers or taking them to diviners (who administer tests to determine truth-telling). Again and again, the moral was that there were deadly forces afoot and that the chief was rooting them out—thus, that he was fully competent in adjudicating such cases and that chiefship was playing an indispensable role in addressing the larger problem of witchcraft's proliferation.

Unsurprisingly, perhaps, the chief's boastful recitation of his abilities as a witch-finder elicited further critique. He was reprimanded—albeit indirectly, with speakers referring to the practices "of chiefs"—for profiting excessively from witchcraft trials. A case sent to the chief from the south, for instance, might net him up to CFAF 50,000 ($100)—and this simply for hearing the case, before sending it on to a diviner for further adjudication (where an additional hefty sum will be added). The director of the C.E.G. even suggested—in private, off the record—that it was in the chief's interest to feed the frenzy around such cases in order to keep them coming, for this was one of his only sources of income during the contemporary (post-Cold War) moment. This director added that he felt that only one or two out of ten cases brought before the chief were legitimately about witchcraft (with the rest involving people who had sicknesses that could be quickly dispatched with medicine—"if only they went to the hospital") but that the chief insisted on taking them all.

There is a complicated dance going on here between sovereignty and witchcraft, with occult inflation clearly something more than just a penniless chief's invention. If, as suggested in the last chapter, we also see the increase in witchcraft as something remaindered by the end of dictatorship sovereignty, as the return of the necropolitical—of a dictatorial politics of death—then the canton chief, a type of remaindered sovereign, would appear to be an odd policeman of sorcery's excess. But just as Eyadéma exploited the Janus-faced relationship between sovereignty and witchcraft—policing sorcery while also claiming it as source—so too does the canton chief attempt to adjudicate and contain witch panic while hinting at his own familiarity with the dark arts—for how else could he so fearlessly operate in such deadly waters? Moreover, in proclaiming witchcraft's ubiquity to-day—of a state of emergency become norm—the canton chief is attempting to reassert his sovereign status as one who presides over exceptional states (Schmitt [1922] 2007, [1927] 2006; Agamben 1998, 2005)—which many read, however, as the desperate last gasp of a waning sovereignty.

An interesting moment occurred for me when a young man sitting next to me leaned over and said he felt uncomfortable discussing "sorcellerie" in my presence. This was an embarrassing side of African history, he said, and, since Europeans do not practice witchcraft, he worried about the implications of others finding out that Farendé was a haven for witches. I responded by saying that there is jealousy everywhere, as much, if not more so, in Europe and America as in Africa—and that he should not let Europeans off the hook so easily. I added that it was little wonder that, with so little wealth and such few means at their disposal, some in Farendé resorted to the occult to enhance their wealth. He shot back immediately, correcting me for thinking that witchcraft could add to someone's worldly wealth—"what you get at night can't be transferred to the day," he said—and chiding me for equating witchcraft with jealousy. "Witches are real. You may have plenty of jealousy in Europe, but you don't have witches. And witches kill. But I am not so interested in what is going on in Europe as in what Europeans will think of us if they know we have these powers and these problems."

I found this intervention arresting. It was not only the clear-headedness of this Said-ian critique bubbling up in the most unlikely of settings—on a school bench, under a shade tree, in a remote West African community—but also the certainty of my interlocutor's refusal of the anthropological view that metaphorizing witchcraft (as just another idiom for talking about jealousy) made it intelligible and defensible to a non-African audience. In rendering witchcraft as proxy for something like "emotion" or "conflict"—as the anthropological archive suggests—I was, he insisted, well wide of the mark in coming to terms with the local view of things (cf. West 2007).

But, to return to the question posed at the end of the last chapter, where does such critique leave the anthropologist? I find myself unable to embrace either extreme: fully accepting/representing the local view—that witches really exist and are destroying Farendé—or remaining silent altogether. The former would provide further grist for the orientalist mill, and the latter, as previously mentioned, would leave the field of witchcraft studies to those (journalists and development workers—and Pentecostals) who have made a history of demonizing Africans and village religion. My own preference is to continue to point out the socio-rationality of the belief in witches—by embedding it in a dense field of fraught political and social relations—while nevertheless acknowledging my interlocutor's critique: that the field of sorcery is one of excess grounded in an ontology that may forever escape my own understanding.

The chief's long soliloquy on witchcraft ended with a set of prescriptive suggestions. One visitor from Lomé proposed that each village call out its witches—identifying them publicly, thus shaming them, and then exhorting them to stop their nefarious activity. Another tendered the idea that they be exiled to witch villages near the northern border. "They are criminals, murderers," she suggested, "and they ought to be sent away." Another suggested that bringing electricity to the area would ameliorate the situation, since witches have an antipathy to light (for fear of detection). In the end, it was proposed and agreed upon that a "commission" be set up to study the phenomenon—a committee consisting of local diviners, ritual leaders, pastors, chiefs, and the school director. This bureaucratic solution to the problem of the occult—with the schoolteacher presiding—struck me as utterly consistent with the spirit of these neoliberal times.[17]

## Locating Agency and Sovereignty

Notice the differences between international development agendas and the more local ones discussed at the conference in Farendé. While the former focus on schooling and health—on "human potential"—the latter focus largely on infrastructure—on roads and electricity—as well as on the social relations that structure or impede development practice. Not only do international donors seem little interested in infrastructure anymore, but also it is hard to imagine a similar conference run by members of the international community discussing witchcraft or chiefship. This story of ships passing in the night is an old one when it comes to development in Africa.

But it also puts the lie to the famous populism of the new NGOs. The current development moment is widely advertised as more attentive to the local and more democratic than what came before. Thus, its proponents claim that, unlike earlier top-down initiatives, development today has been scaled down and localized. It goes directly to the "grass roots"—to villages in rural areas where it attempts to decipher local need and stimulate local agency. And yet development's large agendas and preoccupations—its focus on youth and condoms and mosquito nets and schools, on African potential and futures—are all vetted and decided elsewhere, beyond the continent in the boardrooms of the international agencies and NGOs that fund development today.[18] Ironically, it was the era of top-down development policy—when Affaires Sociales, the dictatorial state's development agency, had the run of Farendé—that development was more sensitive to local need.

Farendé-Kuwdé's experience illustrates another sober truth: that despite ongoing development efforts over the last twenty years, changes to the material life of Kabre have been negligible. At best, BØRNEfonden's aid to schoolchildren supplemented family diets for a short period, and AVJADE's loans to workgroups put some money into the pockets of group members, money that was quickly dissipated on family budgets. But this is stopgap charity work, not development that raises the living standard and advances the material life of communities.

If standard of living has remained stagnant, however, the same cannot be said of the biopolitical life of these communities. Dramatic shifts are underway in how "population" and life itself is produced (Redfield 2005; Comaroff 2007)—in how social and political life is conceived and organized, and in how persons imagine their capacities and relationships with one another—in what Nikolas Rose (2007:22–27), following Foucault, has called processes of "subjectification." It is only in the last few years, and largely as a result of BØRNEfonden's child sponsorship program, AVJADE's microfinance initiative, the campaign against child trafficking, the Pentecostal assault on village religion, and those other small projects and campaigns that have swept through these communities in the wake of state collapse, that longstanding categories of persons and groups have begun to be reshuffled. Youth as opposed to elders, and girls rather than boys (and men), are being hailed by all the latest projects. Workgroups, long the prototype of non-alienated collectivized labor, are being reconfigured as income-generating mini-corporations, thus also opening the "commons" to new modes of accumulation (Harvey 2005, 2007; Elyachar 2005). The labor of children is being recalibrated, and longstanding fostering and domestic work arrangements are being unsettled (at the same time that laboring for exploitative middlemen and wealthy landowners in Nigeria is valued over labor to family). Chiefs are being thrust aside in favor of fundraising mayors, and chiefs' major sphere of jurisdiction (village religion, "tradition") is under assault, calling into question the nature of authority and the political itself. And village boundaries that have been in place for at least one hundred years are being redrawn to accommodate post-Cold War electoral and financial politics.

Moreover, much of the emphasis of development today, from microfinance to schooling, is on individual responsibility and initiative (Englund 2006; Bornstein and Redfield forthcoming)—with the onus on individuals to discipline themselves and manage their own affairs both in school and in their work (Moore 2005; Ong 2006), this by contrast with the commitment to relational dependency that has long been at the center of Kabre work and familial cultures (Piot 1999). Providing another push in this process of re-subjectification, the NGO itself is neither place-based nor place-reifying. Not only does it disrupt and destabilize existing hierarchies and the places those hierarchies organize, but just as importantly, while certain projects are "community-based," most are not. They target specific individuals and draw them out of the community—to their clinics and training sessions and schools—or enter the community to address a particularized need before withdrawing again.

In thus extracting "individuals" from groups—in stripping away local culture, enacting an enclosure of the cultural commons—development is creating a type of "bare life" (Agamben 1998) and remaking citizen-subjects for a new, albeit unknown, order. This seems an instance of what Agamben (1998:6) imagined when he suggested that what is distinctive about the contemporary moment is "the zone of indistinction (or, at least, the point of intersection) at which techniques of individualization and totalizing procedures converge."

But at the same time, this process of extracting individuals from local attachments is supplemented by new dependency relations, away from those on southern kin (who, due to the current conjuncture, no longer have money to return to the north) toward Euro-American aid agencies, and, in BØRNEfonden's case, European individuals. Put otherwise, this shift from local to translocal dependency relations involves the substitution of one set of dependencies and affective attachments for another, replacing those that are known and face-to-face by those that are virtual, distant, and unknown.

These processes of surrogation and individualization that accompany the dismantling of the dictatorship complex—and of the strong attachment to locality and dependent personhood on which that complex thrived—are thus not so much an exodus from sovereignty as a submission to new forms of sovereignty. Sovereignty is here displaced from dictator to agency, from chief to mayor and schoolteacher, from cult of the ancestors to church, from group to self-disciplining individual.

To say as much—to suggest that the terrain of the biopolitical and the production of life is being dramatically reworked by the new agents and agencies of the post-Cold War moment—is not to suggest that that there is no opposition to these initiatives. The pluses and minuses of the new projects are endlessly debated, and, despite the efforts of the international agencies to hail subjects in new ways, old habits and subjectivities live on.

But it is also the case that locals embraced BØRNEfonden and blamed themselves when it abandoned them, and that they willingly, even enthusiastically, created workgroup "bureaus" and staged performances for NGOs. In short, they seem positively captured by the new moment and willing to risk much for an unknown future. To be sure, their engagement with these initiatives was also, and in some cases primarily, motivated by the need for money and resources, but it was also driven by their desire for the new.

As with charismatics and their appropriation of Christian imaginaries, I want to read these performances agentively and acknowledge that locals might be asserting their agency through immersion in Euro-otherness. Like Pentecostals, they are tired of the old and welcome the new. They are upbeat about and have a nostalgia for the future. They are saying, in effect, that they *want* to submit themselves to modern/postmodern forms of disciplinary power because this is their point of entry into the modern and the global. I thus see these local efforts to engage with rather than run from the strictures and structures—and hegemonies and novel subjectifications—of the new moment as a desperate plea for acknowledgement and inclusion/membership in the new global order (Ferguson 2002, 2006), as a protest against their expulsion from humanity, and against those who would see them as merely disposable.

# SIX

# The Death of a Culture

Eyadéma's death, or at least the story told on the streets about his death, is spectacularly overdetermined. Not only a tale about the literal death of the dictator and the decomposition of his body, it also reads as symptomatic of the death of the dictatorship and the era it defined. But it condenses other histories as well, most notably that of the death of culture or "tradition," now rotting away in the villages, an end-of-tradition embodied in the uninterred corpses that litter the landscape today—those not given proper treatment because of the charismatic interdiction on local ceremony. Eyadéma's death also concretized the demise of those authority relations that sanctioned and nurtured the ceremonial complex, relations that radiated out from the village all the way to the metropole. With Eyadéma's passing, as it were, an entire cultural system, and the political culture that patronized it, entered history's dustbin.

Today in the northern villages, young schoolteachers, many of them Pentecostal, are replacing animist chiefs as local authorities, and they never miss an opportunity to criticize tradition and proselytize the "rights of man." They walk arm in arm with the NGOs and the churches, pushing the new humanitarian agendas and deciding who to support and who not to support. Bizarrely, all this stirring of the pot, this new biopolitics, is carried out on a resource-starved terrain that last saw inputs to infrastructure over twenty years ago. Equally puzzling, the new agendas are largely immaterial, targeting youth and gesturing towards an unknown future, content on developing human potential, whatever that might mean.

I am especially interested in the way temporality and spatiality get reconfigured by the new dispensation (cf. Weiss 2004b). Today, the linear time of the dictatorship (with its modernist teleologies and steady sources of income) and the continuous time of the ancestors is being replaced by a noncontinuous temporality, one that is "punctuated" (Guyer 2007) and event-driven, and one that anticipates a future while closing its eyes to the past.[1] This is not only the temporality of the Pentecostal, of "event" and radical rupture (and End Times futurity), but also that of the NGO, the new sovereign who appears and disappears, hopping in and out, slithering snake-like before disappearing into its black hole (its eyes fixed on a distant future). "We used to be able to count on things, knowing that if you did this you would get that," a Farendé resident said at the Lomé Amicale's December 2007 development conference. "But today everything is in disorder. You never know when it will be your time, when you might get lucky and when not."

The re-temporalizations of the new dispensation are matched by a rescaling of the spatial. The distant is now proximate in ways that it never was before, and the proximate seems distant. Thus, at the same time that kin in southern Togo have disappeared from the horizon, a family in Europe parachutes in to provide financial and affective support. At the same time that ancestral shrines and mission churches are losing their importance in mediating access to the divine, the Holy Spirit descends from some distant realm to save a soul. At a moment when local ceremony no longer provides entertainment, satellite TV and the Internet connect to distant elsewheres and to other spectacles. And, where a chain of human connections used to mediate communication between far-flung friends and kin, with word passing from person to person and village to village, cell phones now leapfrog those webs of connection and incite direct, instantaneous contact. This evacuation of the proximate, this disconnection from village and neighborhood and nation—manifest in its most extreme form in the sprint to enlist in the green card lottery, and to depart the space of the local altogether—works by substitution, slotting in imaginary and distant objects for those that are close at hand.

An entire spatiotemporal system and cosmology—of time moving teleologically from past to present to future (the time of the dictatorship and the time of the ancestors) and of spaces connected as dots on a map (a village to the city to the metropole)—is thus rescaled by the post-Cold War moment, with implications not only for the lives of those undergoing these changes but also for theory. Much of the theory to which we are accustomed, and I would not exclude postcolonial theory here, relies on notions of temporality and spatiality that are continuous: of pasts that produce (and "haunt") a present, of proximate spaces that influence/colonize/appropriate one another—billiard ball conceptions of history and cultural influence.

How, though, to come to terms with the new temporalities and spatialities of the present, with the immanence and simultaneity of the global, with a moment in which all outsides have been banished (Hardt and Negri 2001) and cultural production itself is reconfigured as at once, or simultaneously, globally and locally authored, with a biopolitical which seems both produced from above and below? Thus, how to think culture and culture-studies today without remaining trapped by epistemologies generated by earlier colonial and postcolonial knowledge formations, and, more broadly, how to make the current moment as "productive" for scholarship as it has been for cultural production itself?

---

Eyadéma's naked body—unmasked, disrobed, vulnerable—might also be read as a stand-in for the bare or naked life (Agamben 2000) produced by the post-Cold War moment. Stripped of citizenship rights—of access to development, to free water—by the retreat of the state, and of culture and tradition by the churches and NGOs, those in the villages have been reduced to naked life. With their ceremonial system in ruins, they no longer command the respect of southern diasporics (whom they ruled like royalty as recently as ten years ago). With village and family authority systems in disarray, the conviviality that was these social units' trademark is now a thing of the past. With witches everywhere, raw nerves and necropolitics are the stuff of everyday life. This once-proud aristocracy does little anymore other than scratch a living out of rocky soils.

Oddly, they blame themselves as much as others for their abandonment and disposability. When southerners no longer return to the north for ceremonies, they invoke their own bad faith. "It is our neglect of tradition that has produced the disorder that now reigns." When their children leave to work as would-be slaves in Nigeria, they shrug their shoulders. "It is our poverty that drives them away." When an NGO departs the area, they claim it was their fault. "We couldn't get along with each other. It was our jealousy that made them leave."

There may be something culturally dictated here—a reflex to look inward first, to not accuse others when one knows that he or she is also to blame. This has long been the impulse at the heart of witchcraft discourse: evil in the world derives from the local not the beyond; the witch who is trying to kill you is always close to home, often in your own family. But I think there is something more going on as well. To claim responsibility for one's "abandonment" is not only to fall in line with local norms of conduct (and, implicit within such ownership of responsibility, to retain agency and the power to change things for the better) but also to seek acknowledgment or recognition by international humanitarian groups. "This self-criticism makes us stronger for the future and will help impress the next NGO," the director of the middle school in Farendé responded when I asked him about this instance of self-blame. He followed this up with a disquisition on how destitution is what the NGOs are seeking. "The village they like is one that is like an orphaned child, one that has nothing but also one that will be grateful to be saved," he concluded.

In the same way that Eyadéma invented states of emergency and Pentecostals produce an ongoing state of crisis, the northern villages are "producing" their own abandonment, producing themselves as disposable naked life—in order to be recognized.[2] Moreover, is not this self-willed encampment related to the Pentecostal desire to jettison the past and start anew? Both gestures are aimed at recognition and seem motivated by the desire to be acknowledged as full members of the twenty-first century.

To put this in Fergusonian (1999, 2002, 2006) terms, Togolese, like others across the continent, are acutely aware of their position in the world today, of their "abjection" or expulsion from (or persistent non-inclusion in) European modernity—a modernity they see every night on the TV screen but cannot touch, a modernity they hear spoken but may never inhabit (cf. Weiss 2009). In the same way that Ferguson reads mimesis of the modern and emulation of European style among Zambians as a type of global plea, as an attempt to stake a claim to the "rights of full membership in a wider society" (Ferguson 2006:161), I see something similar at work in Togolese appropriations of charismatic Christianity and in villagers' invocation of the rhetoric of "abandonment." Both are passionate pleas to establish their rights to inclusion in global society.

This same desire is what motivated those lottery winners who were denied visas to sit in at the US Embassy in Lomé throughout the spring and summer of 2008. Despite the serendipity of the selection process, those who were chosen had an abiding sense of entitlement. "We were picked for visas, then denied them on arbitrary grounds, and we are here to claim what is rightfully ours," the organizer of the sit-in said when I met him in June 2008. Behind him, the group of 300 strong, all dressed in red ("to show our wounds"), united in prayer to the Holy Spirit, one of their thrice-daily pleas for divine intercession. With a persistence that strained credibility—they showed up every day for five months, from eight o'clock in the morning to five in the evening, through blistering sun and driving rain, until forcibly

16. Embassy protestors demanding global inclusion, Lomé 2008

removed in early October by Togolese security forces—they were pleading for global access.

---

Jean and John Comaroff (2000, 2004) have recently suggested (see also Weiss 2004a, 2004b, 2009) that a signature feature of the neoliberal moment in Africa and beyond is the delinking of the domains of production and reproduction, engendering a crisis within the domain of social reproduction. The Togolese material from the post-Cold War moment would appear to provide a particularly cogent example of social reproduction's travails at this moment, but also of the novelties and desires that such a crisis can produce. Witness the array of new kin-related practices that have drifted through previous chapters—from the way in which Pentecostalism substitutes a new spiritual community for family and neighborhood, to the arranged marriages and adoptions that define the pursuit of visas, to the "adoption" practices of BØRNEfonden, to the "child trafficking" panic in the northern villages, to the manner in which authority structures within families are being undone by children who invoke the "droits de l'homme."

Moreover, what does it mean for social reproduction that NGOs and distant European families are becoming surrogate parents for children in remote villages or that siblings are shuffled between homesteads to qualify for NGO aid? What does it mean that kinship and marriage are being rein-vented and refigured by visa practices that conjoin unknown partners and generate debts across an ocean? And what does it mean for social reproduc-tion that the traffic in children to Nigeria generates resources for the local marriage market while at the same time removing labor from families and workgroups? Finally, what does it mean when such instrumental practices become binding or even desired? Some of the more touching visa lottery stories are those in which partners of convenience became lovers and even spouses. And some of the BØRNEfonden-inspired shuffling of children be-tween houses lead to permanent realignments, with children staying on beyond the departure of the NGO.

Again, I remain compelled by the privations of the current moment and sympathetic to the ways in which the death of tradition, the end of chief-ship, and the dissolution of the dictatorship complex have disrupted those frames that are responsible for reproducing the conditions by which life is lived. And I read the rumors that circulate in Togo today of missing human organs, often reproductive organs, as symptomatic of the very real crisis of social reproduction that the collapse of these structures has engendered. But I also want to remain open to those new possibilities that are emerging out of the current moment, especially because the old structures were so closely tied up with power hierarchies that benefited the few and rendered submissive the many.

---

But what of the "political" in a moment of wholesale rejection of the past and embrace of Euro-otherness, at a time when an entire nation (region? continent?) has a single desire—to go into exile and evacuate the space they call home—and in an era when the only form of protest is that being staged at the US Embassy, as if being denied a visa to leave was the only grievance worth fighting for? And what of the political in an era of diffuse power when it is difficult to locate the source of one's discontent and to know what might be an appropriate and effective response?[3] And what of the political when it is hard to know on what side of power any actor lies? Does the Pentecostal's identification with Christianity and middle-class desire, and their disavowal of African tradition, place them on the side of power, or does their opposition to the culture and authority relations associated with the dictatorship complex and Cold War geopolitical interests position them against power? Does the peasant's embrace of tradition place him in bed with the chief- and dictator-ship system, or does his marginal economic status position him—always and forever—on the other side of power? Needless to say, politics here can no longer be located in any of the standard gestures or in any of the usual places.

I am compelled by recent calls to resist the romance of resistance (Abu-Lughod 1990; Mbembe 1992a, 1992b, 2001; Ortner 1996) and to fight the impulse to make theory adequate to political desire. Political aspirations certainly need to be tempered by experience, by the times in which we, and those about whom we write, live. But the question of the political is begged by the material itself, by the way in which old systems of authority (within nation, village, and family) are being refused, by the numbers of those who sign up for the visa lottery and the persistence of the protestors at the gates of the embassy, by the mass conversions of West Africans to charismatic Christianity, by the way in which witchcraft imaginaries shadow global capital. For all the shifts of the post-Cold War moment, political agency seems far from evacuated.

Moreover, the Derridean gesture represented in the desire to deconstruct old forms of authority and the cultures that attend them, to wipe the slate clean, to return to naked life, strikes me as in and of itself a form of political aspiration. In taking apart old authority structures, not only local but also geopolitical, this cultural revolution bespeaks an opposition to power and the status quo, and an openness to new forms of sociality and the political—to be sure, forms unknown and desires still inchoate, but an openness nonetheless. Furthermore, there seems a recognition that remaining incarcerated by tradition and the local, by Togolese-ness or African-ness, leads away from rather than toward global inclusion and a better life. Is there not here a nascent post-national, even global, conception of citizenship?

But wither anthropology in the face of culture's sacrifice? A discipline that feasted on those cultures that nested within the colonial and the Cold War state apparatuses, it has long made its living celebrating the local (its complexity, its nuance, its alternative rationalities and subjectivities), and, in anthropology's reincarnation as postcolonial studies, valorizing the local's encounter with its others (its ways of appropriating, domesticating, and hybridizing the state and the global). However, both theoretical moments—moments I was keyed into and remain compelled by—are past, and the cultural formations that accompanied them are dead or dying.[4] In their place are those futurities and immanences, those rescaled temporalities and spatialities, those commodified imaginaries and desires, those global aspirations that Togolese and many West Africans are today embrac-

ing with such zeal—in short, much that the old paradigms figured as politically suspect and lacking in cultural thickness and authenticity. And, yet,
if our interlocutors are tired of being incarcerated by local categories and
cultures, and long for the new horizons of global citizenship, it behooves us
to do what we have always done best and follow their lead, even if it means
giving up all for an unknown future.

# NOTES

INTRODUCTION

1. Since it was Cold War geopolitics that was responsible for the political culture that dominated Togo from the 1960s through the 1990s, this is the term that seems most apt in describing this period—and "post-Cold War" its aftermath.

2. "Tradition" in this area has long been pluralist and hybrid, mixing local and global style, northern and southern (Togolese) cuisine, spirit worship and Christianity. The new moment—politically liberal and charismatically Christian—is less tolerant of difference and more committed to religious and cultural purity.

3. While Mbembe's early work (1992a, 1992b, 2001) is arguably "postcolonial," his more recent essays on sovereignty (2003, 2005, 2006) owe more to Agamben (1998) and Schmitt ([1922] 2007, [1927] 2006), as well as to the recent scholarly turn to political theology, than to postcolonial theory.

4. In a similar vein, Saskia Sassen (1996:1–30) suggests that sovereignty today is being "unbundled" from the nation-state and redistributed to supranational agencies and institutions. For similar arguments in the African context, see Comaroff and Comaroff (2000, 2006a), Ferguson (2001, 2006), Mbembe (2005, 2006), and Moore (2005).

5. If Mbembe's (2003) deployment of the term "necropower" is intended to remind scholars that sovereignty and biopower forever work through violence and terror, he also suggestively outlines a particular ("late modern colonial") regime of sovereignty-violence which has relevance for my own work (and which complements Hardt and Negri's account of the way in which power and the biopolitical operate in a time of Empire). Such a regime, whose prototype is the occupied territories of the West Bank, deploys a system of surveillance and control that is three-dimensional and multiple rather than encircling and spatially divided, horizontal rather than vertical, simultaneously above and below, doubled back on itself, fully immanent, blurring the lines and collapsing the antinomies that defined the modernist biopolitics of the colony or concentration camp.

6. As useful and politically salient as I find Agamben's (1998, 2000) notion of bare or naked life, its theorization often remains Euro- and state-centric, measuring subjectivity through a liberal humanist, top-down view of the person. Thus, someone who has lost all rights and protections granted by the state, and has been reduced to bare life (in, for example, a concentration or refugee camp), is imagined to be socially dead

and stripped of culture and agency. As Jean Comaroff (2007) has pointed out in discussing AIDS victims in South Africa, this is a thin, anthropologically naïve account of subjectivity and political agency. It fails to recognize that despite state erasure, AIDS sufferers might nevertheless "assert a stubborn connection to socially meaningful existence" that not only makes possible their everyday survival but also produces new subjectivities and sources of political mobilization (Comaroff 2007:209–11; see also Fassin 2007:509). The Togolese case presents a further challenge to bare-life theory: how to think bare life and subaltern subjectivity when abandonment is only partially state-authored and thought also to be of one's own doing (see chapter 5)?

7. The suggestion that there is something politically reactionary in assuming that things have changed (because such a position mimics global capitalism's own ideology) or that by focusing on the new means one will forget or ignore older ongoing structures of oppression, ignores the truism that the relationship between theory and politics is indeterminate—that there might be multiple political commitments within any theoretical position—and that all of the global theorists mentioned above are to the left of the political spectrum. Conversely, remaining tied to earlier theory—and to the view that the more things change, the more they stay the same—may also blind one to exploring power's new configurations.

8. I am not claiming that cultural hybridity *per se* has vanished, here or elsewhere. Rather, I am suggesting that the hybridizing of Euro-modernity with African tradition—that cultural formation specific to West African colonial and postcolonial periods, especially that of the dictatorship moment—is no longer desired and is on its way out.

9. Despite my insistence that a moment of crisis in West Africa has produced a set of interconnected changes and dictated a series of substitutions—slotting in parastatal for state sovereignties, Pentecostalism for tradition, fantasies of exile for identification with the nation, individual for group, commodity for gift—it is important to keep in mind that there is diversity in the way different individuals and localities have responded to the crisis, that processes of substitution are never complete, that every response carries its own excess, and that outcomes are forever indeterminate and unknown.

10. Also contributing to an emerging pan-regional culture are those relays that occur across national borders—among Togolese, Nigerian, and Ivoirean Pentecostalisms; between visa lottery in Togo and Nigerian 419 and Cameroonian feymania; in development practice; in strategies for dealing with state cutback.

11. Given the convergence of story and postcolonial experience, it is perhaps no accident that West Africa has produced ethnographers who are remarkably agile, even virtuoso, storytellers—John Chernoff (1979, 2003, 2005), Michael Jackson (1982, 1989, 1995, 2004, 2005), Paul Stoller (1987, 1989, 1995, 1997), among others.

CHAPTER ONE

1. Toulabour's 1986 book, *Le Togo sous Eyadéma*, is an underappreciated masterpiece of political anthropology that brilliantly decodes the cultural politics of the Cold War dictator. His more recent work on the militarization of the Togolese state during the post-Cold War period (Toulabour 2005) is equally insightful. I also draw inspiration from the work of Schatzberg (1988, 2001), Bayart (1989, 2000), Mamdani (1996), Werbner and Ranger (1996), Bayart, Ellis, and Hibou (1999), Hibou (1999, 2004), Roitman (1999, 2005), Ferguson (2001, 2006), Moore (2005), and Comaroff and Comaroff (2006a, 2006b).

2. Agamben (1998:101): "The king's body must also and above all represent the very excess of the emperor's sacred life."

3. There are multiple recitations of how the killing occurred. Eyadéma's version during the Cold War years—that he killed Olympio on the embassy steps—is not supported by Foccart (1965–67:697), who maintains that Eyadéma told de Gaulle in a meeting at the Elysée in 1967 that he dragged Olympio from his hiding place beneath a car parked in the yard of a residence next to the embassy and there shot him to death. Many Togolese maintain that it was not Eyadéma but rather a French soldier who shot Olympio—a view implicitly endorsed by Eyadéma himself in the late 1990s when he began publicly denying that he had killed Olympio.

4. Perhaps "resistance" here is too strong a term, for her and her husband's attempts to conceal her from the dictator produced her near-seclusion. Still, it is told on the street as a resistance story, for she effectively evaded Eyadéma's grasp.

5. Togolese "animation"—the performance of praises sung to the dictator—had its origins in two unlikely sources: Zairean praise-singing of Mobutu, itself an imitation of Chinese praise-singing of Mao (witnessed by Mobutu on a visit to East Asia in the 1970s), and French military music (admired by Eyadéma during his time in the colonial army). This type of mimesis and appropriation is a common feature of postcolonial West African political cultures.

6. Eyadéma supporters point out that it was Olympio who engineered this conjunction, and thus Olympio, not Eyadéma, who set precedent for the merging of national and presidential biographies.

7. These chiefs preside over administrative units that were first created during the colonial period. "Prefectures" were divided into "cantons," and cantons into "villages" and "quartiers." Each quartier, village, and canton had/has a chief, with the chief of the smallest unit, the quartier, reporting to village-level chiefs, who report to a canton chief. The canton chief in turn reports to a préfet, who is an employee of the Togolese state. Quartiers typically contain between three and five hundred inhabitants, and villages between two and five thousand, though some villages are larger. I rely on these administrative designations throughout the text, though in places I follow lay/anthropological usage in referring to the quartier as a village.

8. After independence, francophone African countries, unlike their British counterparts, shared a single currency whose rate of exchange was directly tied to the French franc. Given the franc zone's relative strength and stability on the world market (in contrast with the inflationary currencies of many of the former British colonies), this was a largely beneficial relationship—until 1994, when, with a single blow, the value of the CFA franc was cut in half.

9. During the "démocratie" moment of the early-mid 1990s, for example, northerners were harassed and chased from farming communities throughout the south despite the fact that they had lived cheek-by-jowl with their southern landlords for years, often generations, and "Kabiyés" (northerners) were routinely referred to on the streets of Lomé by the Ewe near-homonym "Kabileto"—monkeys. In another instance of ethnic stereotyping, an acquaintance from the south told me in 2005 that whenever he meets a northerner his emotions betray his intellect—that despite knowing that northerners are not all the same and that many do not support the regime, his anger over the fact that he can never feel safe on the streets of his own country at night, because of harassment from northern soldiers, is so intense that he has a visceral dislike of all northerners. Yet again, a friend told me in 2006 that the northern president of the private security firm that employed her had just sacked two secretaries

of southern origin (who were fully competent and had labored long overtime hours for their boss) and was in search of a replacement from the north, because he feared that a southerner might betray his company's "secrets." Such instances of a Togolese "tribalist" imaginary could be multiplied endlessly.

10. I mean "class" here in Bourdieu's (1984) sense—as a group that sets itself apart and marks its "distinction" from others through practices of accumulation and consumption, practices here made possible through proximity to the patrimonial state.

11. To wit, the desire for revenge led Olympio's exiled son Gilchrist to orchestrate a series of coup attempts from neighboring Ghana in the 1970s and 1980s, which in turn prompted Eyadéma to declare states of emergency, and, over the longer term, to increasingly militarize everyday life—and incited Eyadéma's sons to try to assassinate Gilchrist when he returned to Togo in 1993. Gilchrist also organized and financed Togo's major opposition party, the Union des Forces de Changement, causing Eyadéma to put in place electoral laws that would bar his exiled rival from running for office at home. Such incessant parrying and provocation between the two families, it is suggested, is largely responsible for Togo's forty-year political gridlock.

12. A Eyadéma story indexes the way in which the IT revolution during the 1990s not only showed the dictator out of step with the latest tech developments but also presented new challenges to the regime—making it impossible to police information flows and the nation's borders as before. At one point, an exiled dissident sent a scathing email message to a Togo listserv, detailing government corruption at the highest levels. When the posting was reported to Eyadéma, he asked if they had a copy of the letter and, when told yes, asked them to destroy it—so as to prevent its wider circulation. He was then given a lesson in the ways of the Internet and told that the letter had already circulated, via the push of a button, to thousands all over the world, and that policing this domain would require a whole new set of strategies. In the end, the regime decided that controlling the flow of guns was more important than limiting cyber-access and the flow of information, and focused more on intelligence and border control.

13. Among "Ernest's" more notorious tortures were "la piscine" (the swimming pool), a urine- and feces-filled waterhole in which victims were made to swim; "la salle d'attente" (the waiting room), a room where subjects were whipped until they bled; "café matinal" (morning coffee), a regime that required victims to stare into the sun while holding rocks in their outstretched arms; and—"the hardest and most painful"—the "Boulevard 13 janvier" (the Lomé street named after the day of Eyadéma's first and second coups), a 100-meter hallway of razor blades and sharp rocks that victims walked on their knees, before hot peppers were rubbed in their open wounds (Soussou 2002:5).

14. One of the abiding enigmas of the country's politics during the Eyadéma years was that Togolese never engaged in armed revolt against the regime. Several coup attempts were organized, but always beyond Togo's borders and by deploying non-Togolese mercenaries. (Thanks to Tabea Haeberlein for drawing my attention to this point.) Any answer must attend not only to the state's monopolization of the means of coercion/violence but also to the way in which Eyadéma spectacularly produced himself and monopolized the airwaves on the street.

15. Moreover, despite its probably invented nature, the event lived on in state discourse—referred to years later by members of the regime as "the August 16 terrorist act"—as if naming it made it real and rendered its meaning transparent.

16. I hasten to add that such qualities and tactics of rule are not the exclusive domain of

African postcolonial states but are shared by regimes the world over (cf. Comaroff and Comaroff 2006a:36–42).

17. Kourouma lived in Lomé between 1983 and 1993, thus observing/experiencing Eyadéma up close during the volatile years between the end of the Cold War and the national conference (Kourouma 2001:260).

18. In recognition of the increasing political importance of the diaspora, the government's website remained up and running during the hours immediately after Eyadéma's death, posting hourly updates on the state of things in Lomé, and attempting to assure that calm was prevailing. At the same time, opposition websites in Paris and Toronto claimed the opposite—that people in Lomé had taken to the streets.

19. As mentioned above, Gilchrist Olympio was barred from running by a law—designed explicitly to exclude him—mandating that anyone running for office had to be resident in-country for twelve months prior to an election. Gilchrist had barely escaped an ambush (orchestrated by Eyadéma's son Ernest) during an earlier presidential campaign and has remained in exile in Paris ever since.

20. Among other reasons, their "friendship" was due to the fact that Eyadéma, like Zaire's Mobutu and Cote d'Ivoire's Houphouët-Boigny, had contributed large sums to the election campaigns of French presidents, including Chirac (Foccart 1973–74:81).

21. There are two other accounts I have heard of why the body was not shown at the funeral. According to the first, Eyadéma told one of his sons that when he died he might resuscitate—and that they should refrain from immediately burying him. The sons waited several days, during which time the scalded body putrefied, making it impossible to display. According to the second, Eyadéma told a son that when he died they should bury him in one of the traditional tombs in his natal village—and do so quickly so that he would be "reborn." (Kabiyé reincarnation beliefs encourage the quick burial of cadavers, maintaining that a still-"wet" (limber) body stands a better chance of rebirth than a stiff one.) The narrator of this second account added that Eyadéma was sighted by a soldier in 2008 at a nightspot in the northern city of Kara, near his natal community. Notice that both narratives are variations on the same "return of the dictator" theme, albeit one failed, the other triumphal.

CHAPTER TWO

1. While most of my work on the new churches has been in Togo, I spent the summers of 2001 and 2004 in Accra and there visited churches and interviewed devotees. Despite differences of language and political context (Ghana is West Africa's neoliberal poster-child, and Togo its enfant terrible), the Ghanaian material complements, and remains broadly consistent with, that from Togo, illustrating the presence of a vast field of Pentecostal/charismatic worship that crosses national boundaries throughout the subregion, especially along the Nigeria-Benin-Togo-Ghana-Cote d'Ivoire coastal corridor.

2. There is a rich, rapidly growing literature on Pentecostalism in Africa. I have been especially influenced by the work of Gifford (1998, 2004), Meyer (1998, 1999a, 1999b, 2002, 2003, 2004a), and van Dijk (1997, 2001a, 2001b) on Ghana and its diaspora, as well as that of Maxwell (1998, 2000, 2008), Marshall (1991, 1995), Marshall-Fratini (2001), Englund (2003, 2007), Engelke (2004, 2007), Shaw (2007), and Comaroff (forthcoming) on its spread across the continent.

3. I hasten to add that there is a more progressive, indeed feminist, side to such surveillance practices and prohibitions, for they afford young women protection in resisting the sexual advances of male superiors in the workplace. Several professional women

in their mid-twenties told me, for instance, that without their faith they would have had to accede to such advances, and that the popularity of the new churches had made their refusals acceptable—in ways impossible only a few years ago.

4. Note, however, as Meyer (2004b) and Comaroff (forthcoming) point out, that while today's Pentecostals share with Weber's Puritans the conviction that profit is proof of compliance with divine design, they are more assertively this-worldly and prosperity-oriented than their Puritan forebears.

5. The "middle class" in West Africa is famously difficult to define. With most personal incomes untaxed and off the books, it is nearly impossible to obtain income hierarchies, and, as Barber (1997) points out, families have complex constellations that make them hard to class-categorize—stretching across rural/urban divides, income levels, and family type. My own use of the term refers to the broad group of people in Lomé and Accra below the monied political class but above those who subsist on the informal economy (barely making ends meet and unable to own land or a house). For this middle class, literacy and professional standing are paramount, as is the display of class markers—through dress and property ownership. It is those who occupy this middle tier who flock to the charismatic churches today in Accra and Lomé.

6. Especially in the large churches, translating is something of an art form, demanding skills not only linguistic but also choreographic. Thus, translators follow pastors around the stage as they preach, doubling their movements and gestures—sideways, forward, backward, pausing when the other pauses, raising left hand in the air as the other raises the right—and mimicking the pastor's voice cadence—speeding up and slowing down, now more excited, now toned down, back-and-forth, call-and-response. The translations themselves are closely followed by the congregants, who offer on-the-spot corrections of poor renderings. On one occasion I witnessed, a translator was made to sit down mid-sermon for a series of minor translation errors and was replaced by another.

The figure of the translator/interpreter has deep cultural and historical resonance throughout the subregion. Not only are vernacular religious traditions replete with modes of indirection/translation—diviners, for instance, become ventriloquists for the deities, interpreting their demands and desires for humans—but also local colonial and postcolonial political cultures were/are shot through with modes of linguistic mediation and indirection. Thus, chiefs in the south of Ghana and Togo speak to their subjects through "linguists" (who render chiefly language into the vernacular), and colonial authorities deployed a vast network of local translators in managing colonial subjects.

7. It is ironic that critics are making this charge of ritual excess in the villages, for the older ceremonies were much sparer than those of today, as are those present-day ones from which southerners are absent. The extravagance of contemporary ceremonies is modernity's creation, for it is the upwardly mobile civil servant sons and daughters of those in the villages who return home to stage lavish funeral ceremonies, attempting to outdo their peers and civil servant colleagues in the south. Indeed, the ceremony to which the schoolteacher alluded was sponsored by a functionary from Lomé.

8. In a fine overview article of the global spread of contemporary Pentecostal/charismatic religion, Joel Robbins (2004b) suggests that a major reason for its success—for Pentecostalism's ability to travel—is that the charismatic message is at once universal and particular, offering an unchanging Christian salvational message while also accommodating cultural specificity by preserving local spiritual ontologies. In Ghana

and Togo, for example, charismatic Christians at once hew to the universal Christian story while also carrying out their work against witches and spirits, in the process both reproducing and deviating from local categories.

9. In another articulation between global necropolitical regimes and the Pentecostal churches, the US State Department recently sponsored a conference on West African Pentecostalism to explore whether its churches might be effective agents in the "war on terror"—as checks on Islamic fundamentalism in a resource-starved area. Invitees included not only government officials but also academics working on Pentecostalism.

10. I hasten to add that End Times thinking and capitalist culture coexist not only in West Africa but also in the White House, at least during the reign of Bush, and thus that there is perhaps something in the contemporary moment that insists upon this convergence. For two recent theorizations of this conjunction, see Guyer (2007) who argues that there are striking similarities between Christian evangelical thought and contemporary macro-economic theory, and Comaroff and Comaroff (2000) who suggest that millennialism is at the heart of contemporary capitalism.

11. The phrase "end of history" has a long genealogy in Euro-American thought—present in the works of Hegel ([1807] 1979), Marx ([1848] 2005), and Kojève ([1948] 1980), among others, and given wide currency in the 1990s through the popularity of a book by Francis Fukuyama (1992) celebrating the fall of communism and the triumph of neoliberal capitalism. I use the expression here to refer to a West African Pentecostal imaginary that at once draws on the optimism of the current global moment—to break with authoritarian rule and stultifying tradition, thus also with those teleologies that accompanied them—while also aspiring to a more radical, transcendent End of History as we know it.

12. There are of course important differences between Ghana and Togo in the contemporary moment, with the former a neoliberal success story and the latter a clear failure. How, it is important to ask, does the same ideology work in both places? In fact, the similarities between the two contexts are in many ways far greater than the differences. Ghana is still struggling to free itself from decades of authoritarian rule and sixty years of colonial humiliation. And Togo, despite the ongoing presence of an authoritarian state, is nevertheless flush with the spirit of the neoliberal moment, with its liberalisms (of press, politics, and religion) and privatizations, and with the retreat of the state from the social field. In both places, then, Pentecostalism speaks powerfully to desires for liberation from oppressive pasts and to the embrace of those liberties promised by a post-Cold War present.

13. Note however that there is diversity on, even critique of, this issue within the charismatic community itself. A friend who attends an Assemblies of God church in Lomé claimed—in offering commentary on a sermon in another charismatic church we were visiting—that her church differed from the "Ministries" (Action Faith and Praise Chapel and Winner's Chapel, for example—all with origins in Nigeria) in emphasizing the sincerity and purity of one's relationship to God rather than one's this-worldly/economic prosperity.

14. Notice here the same epistemology as that found among non-Christians in the northern villages: when the rains fail and divination turns up a cause, and amends are made but the drought continues, locals visit the diviner again to ask what "other" problems there might be that prevented the rains from coming (rather than questioning the underlying assumptions of the system of belief itself). And so on, until the rains return—and the "right" cause is found. There is an old anthropological

truism here: that systems of belief are empirically nonfalsifiable—that potential disconfirmation is taken as human fallibility rather than as flawed systemic logic (Evans-Pritchard 1937).

15. In an essay on the African Anglican church's antigay stance, Hoad (2004:75–76) suggests that that church's preoccupation with the heterosexual nuclear family is linked to the crisis of the family and social reproduction under neoliberalism, a reading that might also account for the tenacity of similar commitments among West African charismatics.

16. See Blunt (2004) for an insightful essay about Kenyan Pentecostal interpretations of the predatory behavior of the state in a neoliberal moment, interpretations that constitute a charismatic reading of history and contemporary politics.

17. It should be kept in mind, however, that Pentecostalism's appeal also derives from the way it folds in local specificity (Robbins 2004a, 2004b), and that it cannot be grasped from a distance or simply read off from Empire's global script. In demonizing spirits of the village, in espousing a messianic eschatology, in proffering an antipolitics politics, the charismatic deflects global designs in locally meaningful and ever unpredictable ways.

CHAPTER THREE

1. The Diversity Visa (DV) Lottery is the global lottery system that annually awards up to 50,000 permanent US work visas to those from countries with low rates of immigration to the US, especially those in the global south. Applicants apply online and are randomly selected by lottery (in Williamsburg, Kentucky), before submitting themselves to a lengthy process of medical exams and embassy interviews in their home countries. If they successfully jump through all these hoops, they receive a green card (and, five years later, are eligible to apply for US citizenship).

2. For instance, in DV-2005, 2,857 Togolese were selected while only 233 Beninois were chosen—numbers that reflect the size of the applicant pool. In the same year, 53 were chosen from Niger, 76 from Burkina Faso, 321 from Cote d'Ivoire, 1,540 from Cameroon, 3,618 from Kenya, and 3,974 from Ghana (http://www.state.gov/r/pa/prs/ps/2004/34602.htm). In DV-2006, 2,138 Togolese were selected, while 328 were chosen from Benin, 164 from Burkina Faso, 374 from Cote d'Ivoire, 1,639 from Cameroon, 2,867 from Kenya, and 3,880 from Ghana (http://travel.state.gov/visa/immigrants/types/types_2646.html#). In DV-2007, 1,592 Togolese were chosen, and 218 were selected from Benin, 95 from Burkina Faso, 308 from Cote d'Ivoire, 1,461 from Cameroon, 2,337 from Kenya, and 3,088 from Ghana (http://www.state.gov/r/pa/prs/ps/2006/69146.htm). NB. The lottery drawing takes place six to eight months after the completion of online registration in early December, with the embassy interview up to sixteen months after the drawing. Thus, those in the DV-2007 pool applied in fall 2005, were chosen by lottery in late spring 2006, and went for the embassy interview in 2007.

3. Of course, this is true everywhere today. My daughter in the US recently purchased a North Face jacket on eBay which she soon discovered—after taking it to a North Face store to inquire about a flaw in its design—was a knock-off. My university's president, on a recent trip to China, received a brand-name tie as a gift from a state official, a tie which he discovered—when he tried to exchange it at the airport for another more suitable to his taste—was a fake.

4. Such entrepreneurs help others apply for the lottery and assist selectees in preparing their dossiers for the embassy interview.

5. I also draw on conversations and interviews I have had with dozens of Togolese lottery applicants and winners on both sides of the Atlantic, as well as with three consular officials at the US Embassy in Lomé who are responsible for interviewing winners before they are granted visas. Given the sensitive, semi- and extralegal nature of the material presented, I have used pseudonyms throughout the text to protect the anonymity of all individuals.

6. The low incidence of winners who actually go for the embassy interview—only 1,500 out of 3,000—is largely due to the high cost of the interview fee, the medical exam, and the plane ticket. If a winner is unable to draw on family or friends in the diaspora for help, it is unlikely that he or she will be able to afford these finances alone. As well, those winners who fail the medical exam—because they have AIDS or some other extreme medical condition—are barred from obtaining a visa (and thus from going for the embassy interview).

7. It is widely thought that methodical preparation alone during the application and interview process is not enough—that luck, divine intercession, and/or the assistance of local deities/spirits is indispensable to visa lottery success.

8. While the State Department notifies up to 100,000 people worldwide that their names have been drawn, it only has 50,000 visas to give out each year and proceeds down the list of those selected from top (low case number) to bottom (high case number) until their quota has been filled. Typically, they tap no more than 40–50,000 for the interview.

MISE EN SCÈNE

1. The region's sacred landscape is characterized by innovation/hybridization as well. One small example: the ancestral tombs in Kuwdé are located on top of that community's highest ridge, a ridge that was renamed "Canada" during the 1980s—this because the chief's son, a whiz in school who won a scholarship to business school in Montreal, failed to maintain contact with family throughout the years he was abroad. Like the dead in the tombs, local opinion had it, this wayward son disappeared without a word and without sending any money back home. But renaming a sacred space after a distant global locale, one associated with frustrated hopes, also serves to transform the meaning of that space.

CHAPTER FOUR

1. Of course some "villagers" have converted to Pentecostal Christianity. But I retain this term not only because the number of village converts is small but also because those leaders and pastors in the churches, most of whom hail from the south and identify as non-village and educated, draw the lines in precisely this way.

2. Both Catholic priests and Presbyterian pastors were famously tolerant of local religious practice, turning a blind eye when followers engaged in ancestor or spirit worship, and, according to charismatics, were morally lax in disciplining non-Christian behavior like drinking, adultery, and polygyny.

3. The local ritual system is preoccupied with correcting human error—with chastising those who have neglected duties to spirits and ancestors, with reforming witches—and deploys sacrifice to that end.

4. For a related theorization about kinship and gender relations in Melanesia, see Roy Wagner (1977) and Marilyn Strathern (1988), who argue that kin groups, and the categories "male" and "female," are seen as analogues of one another and require differentiation (through ritual) for social life to proceed. I have suggested (Piot 1999)

that something similar is true of Kabre kinship and gender domains—and am here proposing that they use a similar logic in parsing the churches.

5. His sermon was filled with mistaken conceptions of local religion. Thus, Kabre do not think witches are responsible for stopping the rain's arrival, nor do they worship rocks or trees. The spirits to whom they pay obeisance inhabit groves of trees that are metonymically associated with the spirits but are never confused with the trees themselves. And, needless to say, the pastor's rendering of the local term for spirit (*iluku*) as "devil," a practice inherited from European missionaries, further distorts and demonizes local conceptions.

6. Butchers' clairvoyance, and their association with those animals that witches use to guard their human victims before taking them to market, make them privy to much that goes on in the night world.

7. The evidence associating the churches with witchcraft keeps snowballing. In summer 2007, a rumor circulating in Lomé held that certain charismatic churches reclaimed the bodies of deceased members so that they could sell prized body parts (hearts, kidneys, genitals) in the local fetish markets or in the international organ trade. In June 2008, a former churchgoer from Kuwdé claimed that the pastor in the church she had attended helped members pray for witch victims. It seems that the charismatic preoccupation with money-making and prosperity is easily trans-coded as witchly desire, for witches are also in the business of searching for economic prosperity—especially of exchanging humans for money.

8. While much of the reason for the contemporary gendering of the witch as female—a recent identification only, for until the 1990s Kabre witches were more often male than female—has to do with the fact that more women than men join the churches, it may also be tied to the backlash unleashed by development's focus on women and girls to the exclusion of men and boys (see chapter 5).

9. This event has generated a first novel by a talented young author, the son of the director of the Farendé Middle School (Kpatch 2008).

10. Among others, Geschiere (1995, 1997, 2006), Ciekawy (1998), Ciekawy and Geschiere (1998), the Comaroffs (1999, 2000), White (2000), Ashforth (2001, 2005), Moore and Sanders (2001), de Boeck and Plissart (2005), and West (2007) have contributed important recent studies about witchcraft and the occult in postcolonial Africa.

11. I flout longstanding anthropological protocol in using the terms "witch" and "sorcerer" (or "witchcraft" and "sorcery") interchangeably, this because the technicalities of definition in the literature—that "witch" refers to an evil-doer with innate powers whereas "sorcerer" identifies one who works with "medicines" or magical implements—are confounded in the Kabre case, and because the French terms sorcier/sorcière/sorcellerie have seeped into Kabre everyday discourse.

12. In Marxian terms (Marx [1857] 1973, Gregory 1982), these transformations correspond to the shift from an economy of "consumptive production" dominated by the gift form to one of "productive consumption" dominated by the commodity form. Under the former, social life and economy are oriented toward the production of persons and relationships (with things seen as producing persons), while under the latter, all of life is oriented toward the production of commodity-things (with persons themselves being consumed, and subsumed, by the production process, thus reversing the thing-person relationship of the gift form).

13. Eyadéma not only inaugurated his rule through bloody coup but also is said to have

killed his political rivals (and his parents) with occult powers, narratives that are commonplace throughout the political cultures of Cold War West Africa.

14. Such "confessions" are sometimes induced by the sheer expense of continued litigation. Thus, if a person does not have the money, she might choose to rest the case, accepting a guilty verdict, rather than return to another chiefly court and pay yet again to defend herself, especially if public opinion—and likely chiefly opinion as well—has already turned against her.

15. Located close to the Kabre homeland in northern Togo, the Niamtougou airport is reputed to be a favorite landing strip for witches from the Losso ethnic group. Indeed, a civil servant friend whose charge it was to oversee the budget for the airport said that, after several commercial planes had crashed while trying to land there, it was determined that they had been interfered with by Losso witch planes. This civil servant then approved a state budget line for a runway ceremony to prevent Losso witches from landing their airplanes there in the future.

16. The book has long stood as metonym for the power of Europeans in this area. Thus, "l'homme du papier" ("the person of the book")—during the colonial era, the missionary and the colonial officer, today, the schoolteacher—has long been a figure of prestige. Today, in the "bureaus" that proliferate in the villages—introduced by neoliberal NGOs in the 1990s (see chapter 5)—it is the "secrétaire," the one who keeps minutes, who "writes," not the president or the treasurer, who is the leader and most important member of the group.

17. For the reverse, the ways in which the Pentecostal has penetrated and transformed the local religious landscape, see pp. 111–12 above.

18. One problem with this postcolonial theory move is that it too readily, if inadvertently, reinscribes the notion of the bounded culture, which, when confronted with an other, translates and refigures that other into the (categories of) the self. Such a view, while not entirely wrong, reproduces a static view of culture history.

CHAPTER FIVE

1. AA is the acronym for Aide et Action, FED for Fonds Européens pour le Développement, PSI for Population Services International, CAPESP for Cercle d'Action pour la Protection de l'Environnement et de la Salubrité Publique, AVOBETO for Association des Volontaires et Bénévoles du Togo, and AVJADE for Association Villageoise des Jeunes en Activité pour le Développement et l'Épanouissement.

2. The only difference between an Association and an NGO is that the latter is state-licensed—a small irony of the Togolese neoliberal moment. One of the advantages of state recognition (and official NGO status)—which, however, can take several years ("unless you know someone at the ministry and are willing to pay them; then you can get your license overnight," the Togolese head of an NGO watchdog organization told me in summer 2005)—is that import taxes on all materials entering through the port are much lower. Thus, while the Togolese state is no longer able to skim money from projects as it did during the 1970s and 1980s, nor to control the direction of the project after it has been licensed, it nevertheless retains significant power in deciding which projects/NGOs will be approved. "It is unlikely," my interlocutor continued, "that an Association tracking human rights or electoral violations will be approved, or one that is headed by a member of the political opposition. All development projects in this country remain political."

3. PSI is a prototype of the new transnational NGO on the development scene today.

Combining welfare with market principles—its website refers to it as the "leading non-profit social marketing organization in the world" (www.psi.org)—PSI eschews strict handouts and insists on local buy-in, selling (albeit at submarket prices) bed nets and HIV medication to locals, rather than simply giving them away. It also insists on measurable returns on its investment—a numerical decrease in cases of malaria or HIV—before reissuing support for specific initiatives.

4. See Comaroff and Comaroff (1991:200–213) for a parallel set of examples of missionary spectacle among the Tswana of Southern Africa during the nineteenth century, spectacle, the Comaroffs suggest, that subtly contributed to the colonizing of Tswana consciousness during the early missionary encounter.

5. Linguists from Eyadéma's home village mischievously told the dictator that the typewriter keys were those of the Farendé dialect, an accusation that was patently false, for the symbols of the IPA are neutral signifiers of (all) the world's phonemes.

    Alphabetization—not only in Togo but across the continent during the 1970s—was the attempt to render into written form, to "alphabetize," Africa's unwritten languages (using the IPA). The project was necessarily selective—in Togo's case, only two out of forty languages were chosen as "national" languages (to be taught in the schools and given a page in the state's daily newspaper)—producing fierce competition and a sometimes vicious politics of selection among those from different ethnic groups—and, in this case, among those speaking different dialects within the same ethnic group.

6. Why such failure when there was so much apparent good will and such generous commitment of resources? As with many similar programs during this time period, AnTrak's designers conceived of development largely as a "technical" rather than a sociological problem. Thus, they imagined that the apparent benefits of the technology alone—the fact that a farmer could cultivate three times as much land with a cattle-pulled plow as by hand—would lead to its ready adoption. In fact, however, there were enormous nontechnical obstacles to integrating such a novelty into the local production system. How, for instance, to siphon labor from other areas to meet the crucial task of weeding, which still had to be carried out by hand? How to draw women into a labor regime (to satisfy the need for weeding) from which they had long been excluded, while avoiding the adverse effects of such a shift on their domestic and commercial commitments? How to manage the burden of a system of debt that ran counter to local ideas about debt reimbursement? How to square the individualistic orientation of AnTrak—whose Cold War American designers were opposed to anything resembling socialism—with longstanding commitments to group labor? It was the failure to adequately address these sociocultural factors—and their articulation with the novelties of plow agriculture—that posed insurmountable obstacles and led to the project's eventual failure.

7. Thanks to Jean Comaroff for pointing out another striking contemporary instance of direct, embodied development aid: through the International Breast Milk Project, American women are now sending breast milk to AIDS mothers in South Africa (http://www.breastmilkproject.org/press_world_aids_day.php).

8. Not surprisingly, there has been enormous controversy around Oprah's project. Many African-Americans wonder why Oprah is spending so extravagantly so far from home. Many in the development community wonder why so much money was being spent on a single school with a small number of students. But even more troubling have been reports that the school has been enveloped by jealousy among the girls, by reports of abuse, and by restrictive rules and policies that have prevented some

from remaining connected to their families (http://www.iol.co.za/index.php?art_id=vn20071027083625354C957334).

9. I asked the head of BØRNEfonden-Togo in June 2005 whether donor couples were allowed to visit the children they sponsored. He said they discouraged such visits because of the uncertain political situation in Togo.

10. It is important to emphasize that theorists of the global (Deleuze and Guattari 1983, 1988; Hardt and Negri 2001, 2005; Clough and Halley 2007) do not see the resurgence of "affect" in the contemporary moment as a throwback to, or survival from, an earlier phase of capitalist/precapitalist development, of a time when intimate relations had not yet been replaced by an impersonal market. Rather, they see it as an aspect of the very latest phase of capitalist development, a time when immaterial/affective labor has become dominant and integral to capitalist reproduction.

11. I was repeatedly told, for example, about the differences between American NGOs (which they found less to their liking because they tended to set more conditions on the individual or community, to require specific forms of entrepreneurial/profit-generating activity, and to mandate the need for measurable returns) and European ones, and within Europe, about the differences between Scandinavian NGOs (their favorites) and those from southern Europe.

12. The head of FONGTO said that over a tenth of the new NGOs and Associations—600 out of 5,000—had been started by civil servants, some retired, others still in the employ of the state.

13. Is it not the case that resource deprivation, rather than subject formation, has always been Africa's problem? People on the continent have never been short on entrepreneurial spirit and hustle, nor on flexibility when it comes to labor markets. Indeed, the African citizen/laboring subject that is the target of development discourse today has always—at least since the time of the Atlantic slave trade—been Africa's supreme already finished product. What the continent has always lacked are the means and infrastructural resources to enable it to compete on the global market.

14. A note on the larger social context here. Those Kabre children who are "trafficked" are in their mid-teens, mostly boys willing to exchange their labor on Nigerian farms for room and board and a year-end prize: a motorcycle, a mill for grinding grain, tin for a roof. Some girls go too—to work as domestics or in the sex trade. Coming from villages where they would otherwise be farming for parents, these teens are easily seduced by the lure of wealth abroad. Moreover, they are recruited by locals who have already made the trip to Nigeria and returned with a motorcycle or mill—teens who work for Nigerian middlemen and have been promised additional riches in return for new recruits. In Nigeria, these migrant children live together in isolated compounds, often far from towns and cities, and work from sunup to sundown cultivating root crops and cereals. Needless to say, the field owners and middlemen are making spectacular profits off the labor of these Togolese teens.

15. The seizing control of the villages by southern civil servants is true on a broader scale as well. In the much-hyped legislative elections of October 2007, all those elected from the northern regions were civil servant inhabitants of Lomé—who now have an important say in the management of local affairs in their home districts.

16. In a fine analysis of a community in rural Kenya, James Smith (2008) similarly suggests that development and witchcraft co-constitute one another.

17. A year later, at the July 2007 meeting, the committee reported its findings, suggesting that the surge in witchcraft was due to the neglect of local shrines, especially anti-witchcraft shrines; to the fact that church members had been going into sacred forests

to cut firewood—in violation of forest rules; to the larger conflict between charismatic Christians and "animists"; and to the lack of strong local diviners (who might quickly identify witches). Not only did these findings take the side of village religion in its struggle with the new churches—though the committee's recommendations were less pro-"tradition" than anti- anti-tradition—but also they implicitly drew the connection once again between "démocratie" (here: pluralism of the churches) and the "disorder" of the contemporary moment.

18. These agencies also remain unregulated and beyond critique, this not only because they are "charitable" organizations (making it hard to be anything but thankful for their gifts of aid) but also because, with the retreat of the state, there is no regulatory body to monitor them.

CHAPTER SIX

1. Jane Guyer (2007), in a thought-provoking essay that explores notions of temporality in recent macro-economic theorizing and evangelical Christian thought (and finds striking similarities between the two), suggests that we inhabit today a bipolar temporal regime of extreme presentism and distant futurism, in which the middle ground of the "near future" (where linear reason developed its mid-range projects) has disappeared. She credits her research in Nigeria with inspiration for this set of ideas, though does not explore that context in this article.

2. There is an emerging literature (Ferme and Hoffman 2004; Hoffman 2004; Keen 1998, 2005) that discusses the ways in which groups targeted by the international humanitarian community play to the categories and biases of aid givers, even switching identities—from perpetrators to victims of violence—to garner support.

3. Arguably, the one exception is villager certainty that charismatic Christians are the source of their current malcontent. Is this not, however, an example of misplaced concreteness—and further evidence of the confusing nature of the current moment? While charismatic attacks on tradition are an understandable sore spot with villagers, they are only one of a series of contemporary sources of affliction, including the withdrawal of state entitlements, the replacement of the sovereign by evanescent agencies that favor some and not others, general abandonment and abjection by the global. Is villagers' blaming of charismatics not a form of scapegoating or compensation for their inability to identify diffuse power's source and their need to find an object upon which to channel frustration and discontent?

4. When I speak of the sacrifice or death of culture, I am referring to the end of a specific cultural formation—that of the West African village during the colonial and Cold War eras—not to generic culture. While the changes of the last ten years are replacing "traditional" culture in the villages, they remain cultural in the most full-bodied anthropological sense of that term.

Abu-Lughod, Lila. 1990. "The Romance of Resistance: Tracing Transformations of Power Through Bedouin Women." *American Ethnologist* 17 (1): 41–55.

Agamben, Giorgio. 1998. *Homo Sacer: Sovereign Power and Bare Life*. Stanford: Stanford University Press.

———. 2000. *Means without End: Notes on Politics*. Minneapolis: University of Minnesota Press.

———. 2005. *State of Exception*. Chicago: University of Chicago Press.

Allison, Anne. 2001. "Cyborg Violence: Bursting Bodies and Borders with Queer Machines." *Cultural Anthropology* 16 (2): 237–65.

Anderson, Jon Lee. 2006. "After the Warlords." *New Yorker*, March 27.

Appadurai, Arjun. 1990. "Disjuncture and Difference in the Global Cultural Economy." *Public Culture* 2 (2): 1–24.

———. 1991. "Global Ethnoscapes: Notes and Queries for a Transnational Anthropology." In *Recapturing Anthropology: Working in the Present*, edited by Richard Fox. Santa Fe, N.M.: School of American Research Press.

———. 1997. *Modernity At Large: Cultural Dimensions of Globalization*. Minneapolis: University of Minnesota Press.

Appiah, Anthony. 1991. "Is the Post in Postmodernism the Post in Postcolonial?" *Critical Inquiry* 17 (2): 336–51.

———. 1992. *In My Father's House: Africa in the Philosophy of Culture*. New York: Oxford University Press.

Apter, Andrew. 1999. "IBB = 419: Nigerian Democracy and the Politics of Illusion." In *Civil Society and the Political Imagination in Africa*, edited by John Comaroff and Jean Comaroff. Chicago: University of Chicago Press.

———. 2005. *The Pan-African Nation: Oil and the Spectacle of Culture in Nigeria*. Chicago: University of Chicago Press.

Arendt, Hannah. 1951. *Origins of Totalitarianism*. New York: Harcourt Brace.

Asad, Talal. 1973. *Anthropology and the Colonial Encounter*. Atlantic Highlands, N.J.: Humanities Press.

Ashforth, Adam. 2001. *Madumo: A Man Bewitched*. Chicago: University of Chicago Press.

———. 2005. *Witchcraft, Violence and Democracy in South Africa*. Chicago: University of Chicago Press.

Balibar, Etienne. 2003. *We, the People of Europe? Reflections on Transnational Citizenship.* Princeton: Princeton University Press.

——. 2009. "Strangers as Enemies. Further Reflections on the Aporias of Transnational Citizenship." Paper presented at Duke University, April 2009.

Banque de France. 2003. Rapport Zone Franc. http://www.banque-france.fr/fr/instit/telechar/discours/rapzf03.pdf.

Barber, Karin. 1997. *Readings in African Popular Culture.* Bloomington: Indiana University Press.

Bataille, Georges. 1985. *Visions of Excess: Selected Writings, 1927–1939.* Minneapolis: University of Minnesota Press.

——. 1993. *The Accursed Share,* vols. 2 and 3: *The History of Eroticism and Sovereignty.* New York: Zone Books.

Baucom, Ian. 2005. *Specters of the Atlantic: Finance Capital, Slavery and the Philosophy of History.* Durham, N.C.: Duke University Press.

Baudrillard, Jean. 1996. *The System of Objects.* London: Verso.

Bayart, Jean-François. 1989. *L'État en Afrique: La politique du ventre.* Paris: Fayard.

——. 2000. "Africa in the World: A History of Extraversion." *African Affairs* 99: 217–67.

——. 2008. *Global Subjects: A Political Critique of Globalization.* Cambridge: Polity Press.

Bayart, Jean-François, Stephen Ellis, and Béatrice Hibou. 1999. *The Criminalization of the State in Africa.* Bloomington: Indiana University Press.

Benjamin, Walter. [1936] 1969a. "The Story-Teller: Reflections on the Works of Nikolai Leskov." In *Illuminations: Essays and Reflections.* New York: Schocken Books.

——. [1939] 1969b. "Theses on the Philosophy of History." In *Illuminations: Essays and Reflections.* New York: Schocken Books.

Bhabha, Homi. 1994. *The Location of Culture.* New York: Routledge.

Blunt, Robert. 2004. "'Satan Is An Imitator': Kenya's Recent Cosmology of Corruption." In *Producing African Futures: Ritual and Reproduction in a Neoliberal Age,* edited by Brad Weiss. Leiden: Brill Publishers.

Bordo, Susan. 1993. *Unbearable Weight: Feminism, Western Culture, and the Body.* Berkeley and Los Angeles: University of California Press.

BØRNEfonden Organizational Flyer. 2005.

Bornstein, Erica. 2003. *The Spirit of Development: Protestant NGOs, Morality and Economics in Zimbabwe.* New York: Routledge.

Bornstein, Erica, and Peter Redfield. Forthcoming. "Genealogies of Suffering and the Gift of Care: A Working Paper on the Anthropology of Religion, Secularism, and Humanitarianism." In *Forces of Compassion: Humanitarianism Between Ethics and Politics,* edited by Erica Bornstein and Peter Redfield. Santa Fe: School for Advanced Research Press.

Bourdieu, Pierre. 1984. *Distinction: A Social Critique of the Judgment of Taste.* Cambridge, Mass.: Harvard University Press.

Buggenhagen, Beth, Stephen Jackson, and Anne-Maria Makulu, eds. 2010. *Hard Work, Hard Times: Ethnographies of Volatility and African Being-in-the-World.* Berkeley and Los Angeles: University of California Press.

Butler, Judith. 1993. *Bodies That Matter: On the Discursive Limits of Sex.* New York: Routledge.

——. 2006. *Precarious Life: The Power of Mourning and Violence.* London: Verso.

Castells, Manuel. 1996. *The Rise of Network Society.* Malden, Mass.: Basil Blackwell.

——. 1997. *The Power of Identity.* Malden, Mass.: Basil Blackwell.

——. 1998. *End of Millennium.* Malden, Mass.: Basil Blackwell.

Chakrabarty, Dipesh. 2000. *Provincializing Europe: Postcolonial Thought and Historical Difference*. Princeton: Princeton University Press.

Chatterjee, Partha. 1993. *The Nation and Its Fragments: Colonial and Postcolonial Histories*. Princeton: Princeton University Press.

Chernoff, John. 1979. *African Rhythm and African Sensibility: Aesthetics and Social Action in African Musical Idioms*. Chicago: University of Chicago Press.

———. 2003. *Hustling Is Not Stealing*. Chicago: University of Chicago Press.

———. 2005. *Exchange Is Not Robbery: More Stories of an African Bar Girl*. Chicago: University of Chicago Press.

Ciekawy, Diane. 1998. "Witchcraft in Statecraft: Five Technologies of Power in Colonial and Postcolonial Coastal Kenya." *African Studies Review* 41 (3): 119–41.

Ciekawy, Diane, and Peter Geschiere, eds. 1998. Containing Witchcraft: Conflicting Scenarios in Postcolonial Africa. Special issue of *African Studies Review* 41 (3).

Clough, Michael. 1992. *Free At Last? U.S. Policy Toward Africa and the End of the Cold War*. New York: Council on Foreign Relations Press.

Clough, Patricia, and Jean Halley, eds. 2007. *The Affective Turn: Theorizing the Social*. Durham, N.C.: Duke University Press.

Cole, Jennifer. 2001. *Forget Colonialism? Sacrifice and the Art of Memory in Madagascar*. Berkeley and Los Angeles: University of California Press.

Comaroff, Jean. 2007. "Beyond Bare Life: AIDS, (Bio)Politics and the Neoliberal Order." *Public Culture* 19 (1): 197–219.

———. forthcoming. "The Politics of Conviction: Faith on the Neoliberal Frontier." In *Vital Matters: Religious Movements, Emergent Socialities and the Post-Nation*, edited by Bruce Kapferer.

Comaroff, Jean, and John L. Comaroff. 1991. *Of Revelation and Revolution*, vol. 1: *Christianity, Colonialism and Consciousness in South Africa*. Chicago: University of Chicago Press.

———. 1997. *Of Revelation and Revolution*, vol. 2: *The Dialectics of Modernity on a South African Frontier*. Chicago: University of Chicago Press.

———. 1999. "Occult Economies and the Violence of Abstraction: Notes from the South African Postcolony." *American Ethnologist* 26 (2): 279–303.

———. 2000. "Millennial Capitalism: First Thoughts on a Second Coming." *Public Culture* 12 (2): 291–34.

———. 2004. "Notes on Afromodernity and the Neo World Order: An Afterword." In *Producing African Futures: Ritual and Reproduction in a Neoliberal Age*, edited by Brad Weiss. Leiden: Brill Publishers.

———. 2006a. "Law and Disorder in the Postcolony: An Introduction." In *Law and Disorder in the Postcolony*, edited by Jean Comaroff and John Comaroff. Chicago: University of Chicago Press.

———. 2006b. "Criminal Obsessions, after Foucault: Postcoloniality, Policing, and the Metaphysics of Disorder." In *Law and Disorder in the Postcolony*, edited by Jean Comaroff and John Comaroff. Chicago: University of Chicago Press.

Connerton, Paul. 1989. *How Societies Remember*. Cambridge: Cambridge University Press.

Cooper, Frederick. 2001. "What Is the Concept of Globalization Good For? An African Historian's Perspective." *African Affairs* 100:189–213.

de Boeck, Filip. 1996. "Beyond the Grave: History, Memory and Death in Postcolonial Congo/Zaire." In *Memory and the Postcolony: African Anthropology and the Critique of Power*, edited by Richard Werbner. London: Zed Books.

de Boeck, Filip, and Marie-Francoise Plissart. 2005. *Kinshasa: Tales of the Invisible City.* Brussels: Ludion.

De Genova, Nicholas, and Nathalie Peutz, eds. 2009. *The Deportation Regime.* Durham, N.C.: Duke University Press.

Deleuze, Gilles. 1995. "Postscript on Control Societies." In *Negotiations: 1972–1990.* New York: Columbia University Press.

Deleuze, Gilles, and Félix Guattari. 1983. *Anti-Oedipus: Capitalism and Schizophrenia.* Minneapolis: University of Minnesota Press.

——. 1988. *A Thousand Plateaus: Capitalism and Schizophrenia.* Minneapolis: University of Minnesota Press.

Delord, Jacques. 1976. *Le Kabiyé.* Lomé: Institut National de la Recherche Scientifique.

Denning, Michael. 2004. *Culture in the Age of Three Worlds.* London: Verso.

Derrida, Jacques. [1972] 1982. "Différance." In *Margins of Philosophy.* Chicago: University of Chicago Press.

Ellis, Stephen. 1993. "Rumour and Power in Togo." *Africa* 63 (4): 462–76.

Elyachar, Julia. 2005. *Markets of Dispossession: NGOs, Economic Development, and the State in Cairo.* Durham, N.C.: Duke University Press.

Engelke, Matt. 2004. "Discontinuity and the Discourse of Conversion." *Journal of Religion in Africa* 34 (1–2): 82–109.

——. 2007. *A Problem of Presence: Beyond Scripture in an African Church.* Berkeley and Los Angeles: University of California Press.

Englund, Harri. 2003. "Christian Independency and Global Membership: Pentecostal Extraversions in Malawi." *Journal of Religion in Africa* 33 (1): 83–111.

——. 2006. *Prisoners of Freedom: Human Rights and the African Poor.* Berkeley and Los Angeles: University of California Press.

——. 2007. "Pentecostalism Beyond Belief: Trust and Democracy in a Malawian Township." *Africa* 77 (4): 477–99.

Eni, Emmanuel. 1988. *Delivered from the Powers of Darkness.* Ibadan: Scripture (Nigeria) Union Press and Books.

Escobar, Arturo. 1995. *Encountering Development: The Making and Unmaking of the Third World.* Princeton: Princeton University Press.

Evans-Pritchard. E. E. 1937. *Witchcraft, Oracles and Magic among the Azande.* Oxford: Clarendon Press.

Fassin, Didier. 2007. "Humanitarianism as a Politics of Life." *Public Culture* 19 (3): 499–520.

Ferguson, James. 1994. *The Anti-Politics Machine: "Development," Depoliticization, and Bureaucratic Power in Lesotho.* Minneapolis: University of Minnesota Press.

——. 1999. *Expectations of Modernity: Myths and Meanings of Urban Life on the Zambian Copperbelt.* Berkeley and Los Angeles: University of California Press.

——. 2001. "Transnational Togographies of Power: Beyond the State and Civil Society in the Study of African Politics." In *The Study of African Politics,* edited by Joan Vincent and David Nugent. Cambridge, Mass.: Basil Blackwell.

——. 2002. "Of Mimicry and Membership: Africans and the 'New World Society.'" *Cultural Anthropology* 17 (4): 551–69.

——. 2006. *Global Shadows: Africa in the Neoliberal Order.* Durham, N.C.: Duke University Press.

Ferme, Mariane, and Danny Hoffman. 2004. "Hunter Militias and the International Human Rights Discourse in Sierra Leone and Beyond." *Africa Today* 50 (4): 73–95.

Fischer, Michael. 2004. *Emergent Forms of Life and the Anthropological Voice.* Durham, N.C.: Duke University Press.

Fisher, William. 1997. "Doing Good? The Politics and Antipolitics of NGO Practices." *Annual Review of Anthropology* 26: 439–64. Palo Alto, Calif.: Annual Reviews, Inc.

Foccart, Jacques. 1965–67. "Tous les soirs avec de Gaulle." *Journal de l'Élysée* 1:697.

———. 1973–74. "La fin du Gaullisme." *Journal de l'Élysée* 5:81.

FONGTO (Fédération des Organisations Non Gouvernementales Togolais) Publication. 2006. Lomé.

Fortes, Meyer, and E. E. Evans-Pritchard, eds. 1940. *African Political Systems.* London: Oxford University Press.

Foucault, Michel. 1980. *Power/Knowledge: Selected Interviews and Other Writings, 1972–1977,* edited by C. Gordon. New York: Pantheon

———. [1978] 1990. *The History of Sexuality. Volume I: An Introduction.* New York: Vintage Books.

Frank, Andre Gunder. 1971. *Capitalism and Underdevelopment in Latin America.* New York: Penguin Books.

Fukuyama, Francis. 1992. *The End of History and the Last Man.* New York: Free Press.

Gates, Henry Louis. 1988. *The Signifying Monkey: A Theory of African-American Literary Criticism.* New York: Oxford University Press.

Geschiere, Peter. 1995. *Sorcellerie et politique en Afrique: La viande des autres.* Paris: Karthala.

———. 1997. *The Modernity of Witchcraft: Politics and the Occult in Postcolonial Africa.* Charlottesville: University Press of Virginia.

———. 2006. "Witchcraft and the Limits of the Law: Cameroon and South Africa." In *Law and Disorder in the Postcolony,* edited by Jean Comaroff and John Comaroff. Chicago: University of Chicago Press.

Geschiere, Peter, and Francis Nyamnjoh. 2000. "Capitalism and Autochthony: The Seesaw of Mobility and Belonging." *Public Culture* 12 (2): 423–52.

Gifford, Paul. 1998. *African Christianity: Its Public Role.* London: Hurst.

———. 2004. *Ghana's New Christianity: Pentecostalism in a Globalising African Economy.* Bloomington: Indiana University Press.

Gilroy, Paul. 1993. *The Black Atlantic: Modernity and Double Consciousness.* Cambridge, Mass.: Harvard University Press.

Glaser, Antoine, and Stephen Smith. 2005. *Comment la France a perdu l'Afrique.* Paris: Calmann-Lévy.

Gordon, Avery. 1996. *Ghostly Matters: Haunting and the Sociological Imagination.* Minneapolis: University of Minnesota Press.

Gregory, Christopher. 1982. *Gifts and Commodities.* New York: Academic Press.

Grosz, Elizabeth. 1994. *Volatile Bodies: Toward a Corporeal Feminism.* Bloomington: Indiana University Press.

Guyer, Jane. 2004. *Marginal Gains: Monetary Transactions in Atlantic Africa.* Chicago: University of Chicago Press.

———. 2007. "Prophecy and the Near Future: Thoughts on Macroeconomic, Evangelical, and Punctuated Time." *American Ethnologist* 34 (3): 409–21.

Hansen, Thomas Blom, and Finn Stepputat. 2005. "Introduction." In *Sovereign Bodies: Citizens, Migrants, and States in the Postcolonial World,* edited by Thomas Hansen and Finne Stepputat. Princeton: Princeton University Press.

Hardt, Michael. 1993. *Gilles Deleuze: An Apprenticeship in Philosophy.* Minneapolis: University of Minnesota Press.

———. 2007. "Foreword: What Affects Are Good For." In *The Affective Turn: Theorizing the Social,* edited by Patricia Clough and Jean Halley. Durham, N.C.: Duke University Press.

Hardt, Michael, and Antonio Negri. 2001. *Empire*. Cambridge, Mass.: Harvard University Press.

————. 2005. *Multitude: War and Democracy in the Age of Empire*. New York: Penguin.

Harvey, David. 1989. *The Condition of Postmodernity: An Enquiry into the Origins of Cultural Change*. Cambridge, Mass.: Basil Blackwell.

————. 2005. *The New Imperialism*. New York: Oxford University Press.

————. 2007. *A Brief History of Neoliberalism*. New York: Oxford University Press.

Hegel, Georg Wilhelm Friedrich. [1807] 1979. *Phenomenology of Spirit*. Translated by A. V. Miller. Oxford: Oxford University Press.

Hibou, Béatrice. 1999. "The 'Social Capital' of the State as an Agent of Deception, or the Ruses of Economic Intelligence." In *The Criminalization of the State in Africa*, edited by Jean-Francois Bayart, Stephen Ellis, and Béatrice Hibou. Bloomington: Indiana University Press.

————, ed. 2004. *Privatising the State*. New York: Columbia University Press.

Hirst, Paul, and Grahame Thompson. 1999. *Globalization in Question: The International Economy and the Possibilities of Governance*. Cambridge: Polity Press.

Hoad, Neville. 2004. "Neoliberalism, Homosexuality, Africa, the Anglican Church: The World Conference of Anglican Bishops at Lambeth, July 18–August 9, 1998." In *Producing African Futures: Ritual and Reproduction in a Neoliberal Age*, edited by Brad Weiss. Leiden: Brill Publishers.

Hobsbawm, Eric, and Terence Ranger, eds. 1983. *The Invention of Tradition*. Cambridge: Cambridge University Press.

Hoffman, Danny. 2004. "The Civilian Target in Sierra Leone and Liberia: Political Power, Military Strategy, and Humanitarian Intervention." *African Affairs* 103:211–26.

————. 2007a. "The City as Barracks: Freetown, Monrovia, and the Organization of Violence in Postcolonial African Cities." *Cultural Anthropology* 22 (3): 400–28.

————. 2007b. "The Meaning of a Militia: Understanding the Civil Defense Forces of Sierra Leone." *African Affairs* 106/425:639–62.

————. nd. "Building The Barracks." Unpublished book manuscript.

Holland, Eugene. 2002. *Deleuze and Guattari's Anti-Oedipus*. New York: Taylor and Francis.

Jackson, Michael. 1982. *Allegories of the Wilderness: Ethics and Ambiguity in Kuranko Narratives*. Bloomington: Indiana University Press.

————. 1989. *Paths Toward a Clearing: Radical Empiricism and Ethnographic Inquiry*. Bloomington: Indiana University Press.

————. 1995. *At Home in the World*. Durham, N.C.: Duke University Press.

————. 2004. *In Sierra Leone*. Durham, N.C.: Duke University Press.

————. 2005. *Existential Anthropology: Events, Exigencies and Effects*. New York: Berghahn Books.

Jameson, Frederic. 1985. "Postmodernism; or, The Cultural Logic of Late Capitalism." *New Left Review* 146:53–92.

————. 1991. *Postmodernism; or, The Cultural Logic of Late Capitalism*. Durham, N.C.: Duke University Press.

————. 2003. "The End of Temporality." *Critical Inquiry* 29:695–718.

Jenkins, Philip. 2002. "The Next Christianity." *The Atlantic Monthly*, October.

————. 2007. *The Next Christendom: The Coming of Global Christianity*. New York: Oxford University Press.

Kaplan, Robert. 2005. "America's African Rifles." *Atlantic Monthly*, April. http://www.theatlantic.com/doc/200504/Kaplan.

Katch, Patrick. 2008. *Les singes de Dèkoukou*. www.Thebookedition.com/les-singes-de-dekoukou-de-katch-patrcik-p-4947.html.

Keen, David. 1998. "Aid and Violence with Special Reference to Sierra Leone." *Disasters* 22 (4): 318–27.

———. 2005. *Conflict and Collusion in Sierra Leone*. New York: Palgrave.

Kojève, Alexandre. [1948] 1980. *Introduction to the Reading of Hegel: Lectures on the Phenomenology of Spirit*. Ithaca: Cornell University Press.

Kourouma, Ahmadou. 1998. *En attendant le vote des bêtes sauvages*. Paris: Le Seuil.

———. 2001. *Waiting for the Wild Beasts to Vote*. English translation by Carrol F. Coates of *En Attendant le Vote des Bêtes Sauvages*. Charlottesville: University of Virginia Press.

Labarthe, Gilles. 2005. *Le Togo, de l'esclavage au libéralisme mafieux*. Marseille: Editions Agone.

Lévi-Strauss, Claude. 1963. *Totemism*. New York: Beacon.

———. 1966. *The Savage Mind*. Chicago: University of Chicago Press.

Malaquais, Dominique. 2001. "Arts de feyre au Cameroun: Figures de la réussite et imaginaires politiques." *Politique Africaine* 82:101–18.

Mamdani, Mahmood. 1996. *Citizen and Subject: Contemporary Africa and the Legacy of Late Colonialism*. Princeton: Princeton University Press.

———. 2002. *When Victims Become Killers: Colonialism, Nativism and the Genocide in Rwanda*. Princeton: Princeton University Press.

———. 2009. *Saviors and Survivors: Darfur, Politics, and the War on Terror*. New York: Pantheon Books.

Marshall, Ruth. 1991. "Power in the Name of Jesus." Review of African Political Economy 52:21-38.

———. 1995. "'God is not a Democrat': Pentecostalism and Democratisation in Nigeria." In *The Christian Churches and the Democratisation of Africa*, edited by Paul Gifford. New York: Brill.

Marshall-Fratini, Ruth. 2001. "Mediating the Global and Local in Nigerian Pentecostalism." In *Between Babel and Pentecost: Transnational Pentecostalism in Africa and Latin America*, edited by Andre Corten and Ruth Marshall-Fratini. Bloomington: Indiana University Press.

Maurer, Bill. 2005. "Introduction: Ethnographic Emergences." *American Anthropologist* 107 (2): 1–4.

Marx, Karl. [1848] 2005. *The Communist Manifesto*. Public Domain Books.

———. [1857] 1973. *Grundrisse: Introduction to the Critique of Political Economy*. New York: Vintage Books.

———. [1867] 1977. *Capital*, vol. 1. New York: Vintage Books.

Maxwell, David. 1998. "Delivered from the Spirit of Poverty?: Pentecostalism, Prosperity and Modernity in Zimbabwe." *Journal of Religion in Africa* 28 (3): 350–73.

———. 2000. "'Catch the Cockerel Before Dawn': Pentecostalism and Politics in Postcolonial Zimbabwe." *Africa* 70 (2): 247–77.

———. 2008. "African Gift of the Spirit: Pentecostalism and the Rise of a Zimbabwean Transnational Religious Movement." *Africa Today* 55 (1): 138–41.

Mbembe, Achille. 1992a. "Provisional Notes on the Postcolony." *Africa* 62 (1): 3–37.

———. 1992b. "Prosaics of Servitude and Authoritarian Civilities." *Public Culture* 5 (1): 123–45.

———. 2001. *On the Postcolony*. Berkeley and Los Angeles: University of California Press.

———. 2003. "Necropolitics." *Public Culture* 15 (1): 11–40.

———. 2005. "Sovereignty as a Form of Expenditure." In *Sovereign Bodies: Citizens, Migrants, and States in the Postcolonial World*, edited by Thomas Hansen and Finn Stepputat. Princeton: Princeton University Press.

———. 2006. "On Politics as a Form of Expenditure." In *Law and Disorder in the Postcolony*, edited by Jean Comaroff and John Comaroff. Chicago: University of Chicago Press.

Meillassoux, Claude. 1981. *Maidens, Meal and Money: Capitalism and the Domestic Community*. Cambridge: Cambridge University Press.

Meyer, Birgit. 1998. "'Make a Complete Break with the Past': Memory and Post-Colonial Modernity in Ghanaian Pentecostalist Discourse." *Journal of Religion in Africa* 27 (3): 316–49.

———. 1999a. *Translating the Devil: Religion and Modernity among the Ewe of Ghana*. Edinburgh: Edinburgh University Press.

———. 1999b. "Popular Ghanaian Cinema and 'African Heritage.'" *Africa Today* 46 (2): 93–117.

———. 2002. "Occult Forces on Screen: Representation and the Danger of Mimesis in Popular Ghanaian Films." *Etnofoor* 15 (1/2): 212–21.

———. 2003. "Ghanaian Popular Cinema and the Magic in and of Film." In *Magic and Modernity: Interfaces of Revelation and Concealment*, edited by Birgit Meyer and Peter Pels. Stanford: Stanford University Press.

———. 2004a. "'Praise the Lord. . . .': Popular Cinema and Pentecostalite Style in Ghana's New Public Sphere." *American Ethnologist* 31 (1): 92–110.

———. 2004b. "Christianity in Africa: From African Independent to Pentecostal-Charismatic Churches." *Annual Review of Anthropology* 33:447–74. Palo Alto, Calif.: Annual Reviews, Inc.

Middleton, John, and David Tait, eds. 1958. *Tribes Without Rulers: Studies in African Segmentary Systems*. London: Routledge.

Miles, Donna. 2006. "U.S. Increasing Operations in Gulf of Guinea." *American Forces Press Service*. July 5. http://www.defenselink.mil/news/newsarticle.aspx?id=65.

Mitchell, Timothy. 1988. *Colonising Egypt*. Cambridge: Cambridge University Press.

Moore, Donald. 2005. *Suffering for Territory: Race, Place and Power in Zimbabwe*. Durham, N.C.: Duke University Press.

Moore, Henrietta L., and Todd Sanders, eds. 2001. *Magical Interpretations, Material Realities: Modernity, Witchcraft and the Occult in Postcolonial Africa*. New York: Routledge.

Morris, Rosalind. 2006. "The Mute and the Unspeakable: Political Subjectivity, Violent Crime, and 'the Sexual Thing' in a South African Mining Community." In *Law and Disorder in the Postcolony*, edited by Jean Comaroff and John Comaroff. Chicago: University of Chicago Press.

Ndjio, Basile. nd. Feymania: Magic Money, Social Mobility and Power in Contemporary Cameroon. Ph.D. diss., University of Leiden.

Nora, Pierre. 1972. "Mémoire collective." In *La nouvelle histoire*, edited by Jacques LeGoff, Roger Chartier, and Jacaues Revel. Paris: Les Encyclopédies du Savoir Moderne.

———. 1989. "Between Memory and History: Les Lieux de Mémoire." *Representations* 26:7–24.

Nyamnjoh, Francis. 2006. *A Nose for Money*. Nairobi: East African Educational Publishers.

Ong, Aiwa. 1999. *Flexible Citizenship: The Cultural Logics of Transnationality*. Durham, N.C.: Duke University Press.

———. 2006. *Neoliberalism as Exception: Mutations in Citizenship and Sovereignty*. Durham, N.C.: Duke University Press.

O'Reilly, Brian. 2000. "Death of a Continent." *Fortune* 142 (11): 258–70.

Ortner, Sherry. 1996. "Resistance and the Problem of Ethnographic Refusal." In *The Historic Turn in the Human Sciences*, edited by T. McDonald. Ann Arbor: University of Michigan Press.

Oyekani, Felicia, ed. 2000. *Men, Women and Violence*. Dakar, Senegal: CODESRIA.

Piot, Charles. 1999. *Remotely Global: Village Modernity in West Africa*. Chicago: University of Chicago Press.

———. 2001. "Atlantic Aporias: Africa and Gilroy's Black Atlantic." *South Atlantic Quarterly* 100 (1): 155–70.

———. 2002. "Des cosmopolites dans la brousse." *Les Temps Modernes* 620–21:240–60.

———. 2003. "Heat on the Street: Video Violence in American Teen Culture." *Journal of Postcolonial Studies* 6 (3): 351–66.

Prakash, Gyan. 1990. "Writing Post-Orientalist Histories of the Third World: Perspectives from Indian Historiography." *Comparative Studies in Society and History* 32 (2): 383–408.

———. 1994. "Subaltern Studies as Postcolonial Criticism." *American Historical Review* 99 (5): 1475–90.

Ranger, Terence. 1996. "Colonial and Postcolonial Identities." In *Postcolonial Identities in Africa*, eds. Richard Werbner and Terence Ranger. London: Zed Books.

Rasch, William, ed. 2005. *World Orders: Confronting Carl Schmitt's "The Nomos of the Earth,"* special issue *The South Atlantic Quarterly* 104 (2).

Redfield, Peter. 2005. "Doctors, Borders and Life in Crisis." *Cultural Anthropology* 20 (3): 328–61.

———. 2009. "Sacrifice, Triage, and Global Humanitarianism." In *Humanitarianism in Question: Politics, Power, Ethics*, edited by T. Weiss and M Barnett. Ithaca: Cornell University Press.

Robbins, Joel. 2004a. *Becoming Sinners: Christianity and Moral Torment in a Papua New Guinea Society*. Berkeley and Los Angeles: University of California Press.

———. 2004b. "The Globalization of Pentecostal and Charismatic Christianity." *Annual Review of Anthropology* 33:117–43. Palo Alto, Calif.: Annual Reviews, Inc.

———. 2007. "Continuity Thinking and the Problem of Christian Culture: Belief, Time, and the Anthropology of Christianity." *Current Anthropology* 48:5–38.

Rodney, Walter. 1981. *How Europe Underdeveloped Africa*. Washington, D.C.: Howard University Press.

Roitman, Janet. 1998. "The Garrison-Entrepôt." *Cahiers d'Études Africaines* 150–52: 297–329.

———. 2005. *Fiscal Disobedience: An Anthropology of Economic Regulation in Central Africa*. Princeton: Princeton University Press.

———. 2006. "The Ethics of Illegality in the Chad Basin." In *Law and Disorder in the Postcolony*, edited by Jean Comaroff and John Comaroff. Chicago: University of Chicago Press.

———. 2009. "The Anti-Crisis." Paper presented at Duke University, April 2009.

Rose, Nikolas. 2001. "The Politics of Life Itself." *Theory, Culture & Society* 18 (6): 1–30.

———. 2007. *The Politics of Life Itself: Biomedicine, Power and Subjectivity in the Twenty-First Century*. Princeton: Princeton University Press.

Said, Edward. 1978. *Orientalism*. New York: Pantheon.

Sassen, Saskia. 1996. *Losing Control? Sovereignty in An Age of Globalization*. New York: Columbia University Press.

Schatzberg, Michael. 1988. *The Dialectics of Oppression in Zaire*. Bloomington: Indiana University Press.

———. 2001. *Political Legitimacy in Middle Africa: Father, Family, Food*. Bloomington: Indiana University Press.

Schmitt, Carl. [1922] 2007. *The Concept of the Political*. Chicago: University of Chicago Press.

———. [1927] 2006. *Political Theology: Four Chapters on the Concept of Sovereignty*. Chicago: University of Chicago Press.

Shaw, Rosalind. 2002. *Memories of the Slave Trade: Ritual and Historical Imagination in Sierra Leone*. Chicago: University of Chicago Press.

———. 2007. "Displacing Violence: Making Pentecostal Memory in Postwar Sierra Leone." *Cultural Anthropology* 22 (1): 66–93.

Smith, Craig. 2004. "U.S. Training African Forces to Uproot Terrorists." *New York Times* May 11: A1. http://query.nytimes.com/gst/fullpage.html?res=9901E7DA133CF932A25756C0A9629C8B63

Smith, Daniel Jordan. 2007. *A Culture of Corruption: Everyday Deception and Popular Discontent in Nigeria*. Princeton: Princeton University Press.

Smith, James Howard. 2008. *Bewitching Development: Witchcraft and the Reinvention of Development in Neoliberal Kenya*. Chicago: University of Chicago Press.

Smith, Stephen. 2003. *Négrologie: Pourquoi l'Afrique meurt*. Paris: Calmann-Lévy.

Soussou, Innocent. 2002. "Les différentes formes de tortures au Camp Landja de Kara." *La Tribune du Peuple* (Togo), June 26.

Stoler, Ann Laura. 1995. *Race and the Education of Desire: Foucault's "History of Sexuality" and the Colonial Order of Things*. Durham, N.C.: Duke University Press.

Stoller, Paul. 1987. *In Sorcery's Shadow: A Memoir of Apprenticeship among the Songhay of Niger*. Chicago: University of Chicago Press.

———. 1989. *A Taste of Ethnographic Things: The Senses in Anthropology*. Philadelphia: University of Pennsylvania Press.

———. 1995. *Embodying Colonial Memories: Spirit Possession, Power and the Hauka in West Africa*. New York: Routledge.

———. 1997. *Sensuous Scholarship*. Philadelphia: University of Pennsylvania Press.

Strathern, Marilyn. 1988. *The Gender of the Gift: Problems with Women and Problems with Society in Melanesia*. Berkeley and Los Angeles: University of California Press.

Thompson, E. P. 1966. *The Making of the English Working Class*. New York: Vintage Books.

Thompson, Grahame. 2000. "The Limits to 'Globalization': Taking Economic Borders Seriously." http://cgirs.ucsc.edu/conferences/plg/.

Toulabour, Comi. 1986. *Le Togo sous Eyadéma*. Paris: Karthala.

———. 2005. "Togo: Les forces armées Togolaises et le dispositif sécuritaire de contrôle." http://www.letogolais.com/article.html?nid=2370.

Trouillot, Michel-Rolph. 2003. *Global Transformations: Anthropology and the Modern World*. New York: Palgrave Macmillan.

Tsing, Anna Lowenhaupt. 2004. *Friction: An Ethnography of Global Connection*. Princeton: Princeton University Press.

van Dijk, Rijk. 1997. "From Camp to Encompassment: Discourses of Transubjectivity in the Ghanaian Pentecostal Diaspora." *Journal of Religion in Africa* 27 (2): 135–60.

———. 1998. "Pentecostalism, Cultural Memory and the State: Contested Representations of Time in Postcolonial Malawi." In *Memory and the Postcolony: African Anthropology and the Critique of Power*, edited by Richard Werbner. London: ZED Books.

———. 2001a. "Contesting Silence: The Ban on Drumming and the Musical Politics of Pentecostalism in Ghana." *Ghana Studies* 4:31–64.

———. 2001b, "Time and Transcultural Technologies of the Self in the Ghanaian Pentecostal Diaspora." In *Between Babel and Pentecost: Transnational Pentecostalism in Africa and Latin America,* edited by Andre Corten and Ruth Marshall-Fratini. Bloomington: Indiana University Press.

van Geirt, Jean-Pierre. 2006. *Togo: Autopsie d'un coup d'état permanent.* Paris: Atelier de Presse.

Vergès, Françoise. 2007. *Figures d'une humanité superflue.* Paris: Flammarion/Musée du Quai Branly.

Wagner, Roy. 1977. "Analogic Kinship: A Daribi Example." *American Ethnologist* 4:623–42.

Weiss, Brad, ed. 2004a. *Producing African Futures: Ritual and Reproduction in a Neoliberal Age.* Leiden: Brill Publishers.

———. 2004b. "Introduction: Contentious Futures: Past and Present." In *Producing African Futures: Ritual and Reproduction in a Neoliberal Age,* edited by Brad Weiss. Leiden: Brill Publishers.

———. 2009. *Street Dreams and Hip Hop Barbershops: Global Fantasy in Urban Tanzania.* Bloomington: Indiana University Press.

Werbner, Richard. 1996. "Introduction: Multiple Identities, Plural Arenas." In *Postcolonial Identities in Africa,* edited by Richard Werbner and Terence Ranger. London: Zed Books.

Werbner, Richard, and Terence Ranger, eds. 1996. *Postcolonial Identities in Africa.* London: Zed Books.

West, Harry. 2007. *Ethnographic Sorcery.* Chicago: University of Chicago Press.

White, Luise. 2000. *Speaking with Vampires: Rumor and History in Colonial Africa.* Berkeley and Los Angeles: University of California Press.

Williams, Patrick, and Laura Chrisman. 1994. *Colonial Discourse/Postcolonial Theory.* New York: Columbia University Press.

World Bank/UNDP Report. 2004. "Republic of Togo: Country Re-Engagement Note." http://www.tg.undp.org/docs/Togo%20CRN.pdf, p.13.

World Christian Database. 2008. http://pewforum.org/surveys/pentecostal/africa/.

Young, Robert. 1990. *White Mythologies: Writing History and the West.* London: Routledge.

———. 1995. *Colonial Desire: Hybridity in Theory, Culture and Race.* London: Routledge.

———. 2001. *Postcolonialism: An Historical Introduction.* Malden, Mass.: Wiley-Blackwell.

Yunus, Muhammad. 2003. *Banker to the Poor: Micro-Lending and the Battle Against World Poverty.* New York: PublicAffairs (Perseus Books).

INDEX

35007604R00127

Made in the USA
Lexington, KY
27 August 2014